Bad Humor

Bad Humor

Race and Religious Essentialism
in Early Modern England

Kimberly Anne Coles

PENN

UNIVERSITY OF PENNSYLVANIA PRESS

PHILADELPHIA

Copyright © 2022 University of Pennsylvania Press

All rights reserved. Except for brief quotations used for purposes of review or scholarly citation, none of this book may be reproduced in any form by any means without written permission from the publisher; except, song lyrics courtesy of Amythyst Kiah, "Black Myself," track 1 on *Songs of Our Native Daughters*, Smithsonian Folkways, 2019, compact disc.

Published by
University of Pennsylvania Press
Philadelphia, Pennsylvania 19104-4112
www.upenn.edu/pennpress

Printed in the United States of America on acid-free paper
10 9 8 7 6 5 4 3 2 1

A Cataloging-in-Publication record is available from the Library of Congress
Hardcover ISBN 9780812253733
eBook ISBN 9780812298352

For Graham

i carry your heart with me(i carry it in my heart)

CONTENTS

Preface — ix

Introduction — 1

Chapter 1. "Soules drown'd in flesh and blood":
The Fluid Poetics of John Donne and Christopher Brooke — 21

Chapter 2. Bad Faith: The Color of Wrong Religion
in Ben Jonson's *The Masque of Blackness* and Mary Wroth's
Pamphilia to Amphilanthus — 48

Chapter 3. Moral Constitution: The Color of Blood
in Elizabeth Cary's *Tragedy of Mariam* and the New English Tracts — 69

Chapter 4. "Soule is Forme": The (Re)formation of the Body
in Edmund Spenser's *The Faerie Queene* — 88

Chapter 5. Moral Husbandry: Cultivating Right Religion
in New Worlds — 117

Coda. The One-Drop Rule — 140

Notes — 143

Bibliography — 181

Index — 195

Acknowledgments — 201

PREFACE

Racial Profiling

Even before my son was born, I became acutely aware of how differently his body, as a Black boy and man, would navigate the world from mine. But I was not prepared for the fact that I would watch my son grow with a pride that mixed with increasing alarm. Every inch, I worry: his self-confidence, his mouth, the accruing strength of his body—all of these things are requisite for the life in front of him, and all place him in further jeopardy. I live in a country that makes me afraid of his body, as if it were a growing threat. This fear acknowledges the moral encoding that attaches to his body. Not to him: to his skin. The meanings that his skin conveys in public space have a history, but it is not his history. It is not the history of his life, his character, his behavior—it has no attachment to what he has lived or what he has accomplished. The moral meanings that attach to his skin have a history of ideology to which he has, as yet, hardly contributed but from which he will nonetheless derive his identity.

The history will become his history. His identity will emerge, has emerged, as mine has, from how his body is read in political space. But while the materials of its making are the same as mine, his body signifies differently in the society it inhabits. The outer form will shape the interior: the social signification of his body will impress his psychic life, and facts about his relationship to juridical and social power will cause him to believe fictions about himself. When we inquire into the processes and histories of embodiment, the inquiry is never without self-interest. The bodies that we have create us. The representation of the body in political space—how the social and political ambient enacts upon and interacts with it—informs its modes of survival and the means by which it is clothed, fed, and protected. If identity is never privately engaged, because publicly derived, these issues of survival and security are the terms that animate it and structure its social and political imbrication.

One of the chief problems of attempting to historicize race is that the consequences of racial strategies are borne into the present, even if their conduct is not without revision. So too, embodied identity is particular to its time and place, but our point of entry into understanding it is always now. We are circumscribed by the histories that create us. But understanding those histories also allows us to evaluate the terms and relations that rendered them possible in the first place. If our bodies appeal to a history that is cultural, not personal, then the burdens of our cultural history need to be unpacked. The meanings that attach to my son's skin were "stamped from the beginning" of English colonial settlement. "Black skin [was] an ugly stamp," Ibram X. Kendi explains of his use of this phrase from a speech by Jefferson Davis for the title of his book on the history of racist ideas in America, "a signifier of the Negro's everlasting inferiority."[1] Davis rationalizes an unequal share of social and political power in terms of proprietorship: White Europeans built America because White Europeans owned the labor of slaves and built it by proxy.[2] The guarantee of ownership is secured by surface markings that assure the servile status of Black people. But the story that Davis tells of Black servitude stamped on the skin is not far wrong. The institution of chattel slavery is the catalyst that galvanizes a long history that articulates a relationship between black melancholy and wrong religion. It is the unique convergence of a theory of bad humors with the historically contingent institution of slavery that accounts for the reading of black skin as pagan. Marked for damnation, the obdurate bad faith of dark people became the premise for their permanent servitude.

Bad Humor: Race and Religious Essentialism in Early Modern England charts the process whereby religious error, first resident in the body, becomes marked on the skin. Early modern medical theory bound together *psyche* and *soma* in mutual influence. By the end of the sixteenth century, there is a general acceptance that the soul's condition, as a consequence of religious belief or its absence, could be manifest in the humoral composition of the physical body. Certain strategies of color, I argue, were premised upon religious identity and identification in a system that assumed the corporal manifestation of belief and that read the body for its moral codes. The concept of race as it is understood in the modern Anglophone world is certainly not transhistorical, but it also does not have a discrete point of origin. Its history is composed of various strands, braiding together classically informed scientific theories of the human body with late medieval conceptions of hereditary blood.[3] But the specific agendas of settler colonialism compel the weaving together of these ideas.[4] The racial logic of hereditary blood in the early modern period guaranteed the stable transfer of power and wealth through the assurance of superior physiological and moral traits as a family inheritance. The same logic, adapted as a narrative of moral decline and degeneracy in Old English families, and the corruption of the Gaelic Irish, authorized English troops to slaughter the Irish people and seize their land for the use of New English planters. A similar logic of inherent degeneracy and inherited depravity secured a workforce of Black Africans in perpetuity in the New World. I have argued elsewhere that "race in the early modern period is a concept at the crossroads of a set of overlapping concerns of lineage, religion, and nation."[5] This book is about how these concerns converge around a pseudoscientific system that confirmed the absolute difference between Protestants and Catholics, guaranteed the noble quality of English blood, and justified English colonial domination.[6]

This research is in concert and conversation with the work of critics such as Janet Adelman, Dennis Austin Britton, Urvashi Chakravarty, Jane Hwang Degenhardt, Ania Loomba, and M. Lindsay Kaplan.[7] But medievalists have shown that the genealogy of this thinking is long-standing.[8] It was common in the texts of medieval and early modern Europe to describe religious outsiders, minorities, and foreigners in terms of color. The sources for Robert Burton's final section on "Religious Melancholy" in his 1621 *Anatomy* of the disease shows that for a century prior, doctors and divines had discussed the physiological foundations of atheism, irreligion, and religious despair.[9] But the specific history that this book unfolds describes developments in natural philosophy in the early part of the sixteenth century that force a reconsideration of the interactions of body and soul and that bring medical theory and theological discourse—or, science and religion—into close, even inextricable, contact. This cultural crisis produces a discursive concerning psychosomatic relations that is particularly pliable to economic and political agendas. What I hope to show is that the absolute correspondence of black skin and paganism could not have happened with either one of the forces operating on its own terms. In the racial narratives described here, science and religion meet nascent capitalism and colonial endeavor to create a taxonomy of Christians in Black and White.[10]

Bad Humor specifically appraises how early modern science, or natural philosophy, is applied to the racialization of people who are expelled from the faith as religious outsiders. English colonial activities were largely directed against other Christians. But the violence of the colonial project could not be effected against members of the same faith. These members—Irish Catholics, Spanish Catholics, converted Africans, and Indigenous peoples—had to be forcibly evicted. Of course, this is problematic as the doctrine of Christianity, in particular Pauline Christianity, insisted that all who were baptized in the spirit were incorporated in the faith. In *Becoming Christian*,

Dennis Britton has brilliantly exfoliated how in arguing against the necessity of baptism, John Calvin, and subsequently Calvinists, created a race of Christians—of those born into faith. A Protestant sect that denied the value of sacraments offered permanent election to parents anxious about the fate of their unbaptized children.[11] The account that Britton provides is of a rhetorical remedy, where heredity is based upon assurance and secured by sacramental theory. The racial narratives outlined here argue for religion, or irreligion, as a somatic condition that descends through bloodlines as a bodily concern.

Both Patricia Akhimie and Urvashi Chakravarty have examined lineage and rank, as well as constructions of service and servitude, as sources for structures of race and early modern racialized slavery. Both have understood the indelible marks of servitude as part of a system that promoted "stigmatized somatic difference" in the production of "the racialization of class difference."[12] In understanding hereditary blood and rank as a necessary component in the racialization of religion, my work sees a prior system of moral difference and moral constitution applied to assessments of religious affiliation and religious essentialism. The humors—the four bodily fluids of yellow bile, black bile, phlegm, and blood—were thought to be in equilibrium in noble subjects. This condition supplied them with better physical, intellectual, and moral capacities and conferred their right to rule.[13] If an earlier racial ideology licensed particular people to rule through their presumed moral authority, later developments of racial logic condemned other people to serve premised upon similar ideas of the internal manifestation of moral capacity. Dark bodies were inserted into, and subsequently read through, the prior system of encoding that marked moral differences.

Theologians, moralists, and physicians from the mid-sixteenth century to the early seventeenth century resorted to Galen as a model for understanding the body as a contact point between the immaterial soul and the physical world. But the soul's transactions with the body created the possibility that it might take corruption from the body. Melancholy, as a bodily humor that affected the mind—and therefore infected the rational soul—captured the danger that this contact presented to the soul. Marsilio Ficino writes in *Platonic Theology* that "festering" in those who are atheist "is . . . a disease of the soul and a . . . doubting that stems from their body's depraved complexion."[14] The "disease of the soul" that Ficino invokes is atheism or irreligion, which he attributes to an excess of black bile in the "complexion," or balance, of humors. Love of God, it was maintained, was natural to man—an inclination toward the pinnacle of beauty and the highest good. The corruption of this disposition was considered a form of madness. This was Burton's rationale in classifying "Religious Melancholy" as a species of love melancholy.[15] Black melancholy was responsible for the lunacy of atheism or irreligion: "so from the corruption of the complexion is born not religion, but ... impiety."[16] The humoral imbalance of melancholy resulted in the redirection of the soul's itinerary.

This book outlines the physical mechanics of a process that put dark people beyond the reach of baptism. Lineage assumed the descent of humoral superiority. The pseudoscientific system that secured the permanent depravity of certain colonial subjects relied upon similar ideas of humoral inheritance. The differentiation of groups of people as manifestly and materially holding right or wrong belief—and as capable of conversion or not—exploited the interchange between body and soul.[17] But it also traded upon older systems of racial logic that relied upon hereditary blood. The colonial project demanded subjects that were not Christian—slaughter and enforced servitude could not be enacted against other members of the faith. As Holly Brewer notes, Charles II admitted the possibility of justifying the freedom of slaves through conversion by being willing to bring converted slaves into the commonwealth as low-status subjects. And both theological and legal arguments from the sixteenth century onward throughout Europe in general, and in England in particular, held that Christians could only enslave heathens.[18] (This was never actually written into English law, but as Matthias Fischer has shown, many colonists of the Anglo-Americas thought that it was and acted accordingly.)[19] Since many of the casualties of English colonial policy actually *were* Christian, they had to be *proven* non-Christians. This proof took the form of a permanent, heritable condition of irreligion—the mark of which was black melancholy—that passed from parent to child and that made baptism or conversion to Christianity impossible for certain groups. Thus a 1682 Virginia statute defined "as slaves all those without Christian ancestry or 'parentage.'"[20] But the statute exploited a long history of aligning black melancholy with wrong religion; what is new is the legal and absolute alignment of dark skin and permanent bad faith. Prior to 1682, Africans who arrived converted, or Indigenous people who were converts, could be impressed "for noe longer time then the English or other christians are to serve."[21] After 1682, there were no conditions under which they would be legally accounted Christian. In a system that assumed the heritability of belief—and of heathenism—surface markings eventually became both evidence and justification for holding groups of people outside of Christian communion.

No medical discourse—and certainly no theological one—is ever monolithic. The status of the soul, and the corruption that the body offered to it, was an active debate throughout the sixteenth and seventeenth centuries. This book traces its passage through a number of cultural materials. But literature in particular is used as an index of how pervasive it was. Race is a strategy. Each time that we examine such strategies of naturalization, we better understand the strategies themselves—how these polemics serve specific interests (political, economic, social). In a powerful presentation titled "Race After the Reformation" at the September 2019 "Race and Periodization" symposium, Britton insisted that "if race and religion are mutually constitutive in the medieval and early modern periods . . . studying race alongside Christianity also begs for [both a] transhistorical . . . *and* historically specific analysis."[22] These appear to be mutually exclusive scholarly approaches. But Britton rightly asks, "What might the transhistorical . . . analysis of race and Christianity tell us about any historically specific manifestation?"[23]

The moral encoding of raced subjects informs later incarnations of racial logic, although the particulars of each occasion inform precisely how. As Atiya Husain cogently puts it:

> The ongoing urgency of understanding race and religion as two key features of American life that shape the distribution of resources, life chances, and domination and oppression suggests a need for advancing scholarship on their interrelation. . . . [S]ince the moment that "race" was born in early modern Europe, religion was racialized. After that moment, religion is embedded in the racialized social system. As a result . . . the question scholars should be asking is not *if* religious groups are racialized [and vice versa] but *how* and *to what end*.[24]

In early modern England, the underlying assumptions of the system of lineage—that the inheritance of humoral constitution secured social position—become the argument for the rationalization of permanent and perpetual enslavement. But in the revised racial logic of the early English slave codes, the black melancholy that identifies the pagan, and the enforced labor that attends this surface marking, was the heritage that was assured. One's relationship to God was marked on the skin. The negotiations of New World labor betray the soul's condition as the argument for whether a body could be pressed into service; and they reveal the complexion of belief as the premise for what bodies—and what lives—matter.

Bad Humor

INTRODUCTION

> Your precious God ain't gonna bless me
> 'Cause I'm Black myself.
> —Amythyst Kiah, "Black Myself"

This is a history of black and white. Historically—if episodically—throughout Europe, religious others are marked somatically and biopolitically.[1] Geraldine Heng has shown England as "the first racial state in the West" in its targeted and organized campaign of violence against Jewish bodies before their expulsion in 1290.[2] But in early modern Protestant England, other Christians are marked in these terms. The brutality of the English colonial project was largely enacted against others of the same faith. This was enabled by the radical breach in Christian communion caused by Reformation; but it was compelled by commercial and colonial impulses. Fellow Christians, either born into the faith or converted to it, were the objects of English economic agendas to seize land and impress people. But precisely because of this fact, these Christians had to be reinscribed. The principal project of this book is to describe a process of color-coding, whereby certain Christians—Irish Catholics, Spanish Catholics, converted Africans, and Indigenous peoples—are marked as pagan for colonial purposes.

Bad Humor: Race and Religious Essentialism in Early Modern England traces how English colonial activities are justified through the racialization of imagined others—but these strategies are complicated by the very fact that they are directed against actual members of the same religion. Proximity creates problems: rationalizing the brutal regime requisite to genocide, land seizure, or perpetual enslavement is impossible if the subjects of the violence are perceived as equally human. The system of racialization that underwrote early modern English colonial activity, then, established physiological differences, secured by lines of descent, that assured that certain people could neither be Christian nor convert to Christianity. Their paganism was guaranteed by their essential nature. When members of the same faith are encoded in this way, these differences are rendered in color.[3] This is not to say that there is anything inevitable about dark skin as a final repository of religious error. Both White and non-White subjects are blackened by the same racial logic explored in this book.[4] The history that this book pursues, then, is precisely *how* black and brown skin eventually became an index of the religious melancholy residing within. This story has to include the objectives of land and labor in the New World and how such objectives shaped the racial narratives deployed against a target of dark-skinned people. But it finally reveals religion as the principal idea, in coordination with concepts of nation and lineage, which permits the dark bodies of others to be imagined as permanently pagan and past reform.

This is a moment in English cultural history when science and religion come into unprecedented contact precisely because others of the same faith are the focus of these strategies. The bar to their inclusion in Christian communion must be imagined as a permanent obstruction. The blackness with which they are marked is therefore underwritten by a medical theory that makes the mark indelible, somatic, and heritable. This exposes race as a strategy in response to economic or political agendas. But it also lays bare the extent to which the form that the tactic takes is dependent upon its targets. The black melancholy of wrong belief is initially used to mark any colonial subject, but it settles, by the end of the history that this book traces, upon the bodies of Black and brown people.

It is precisely at such moments that we are able to perceive the production of a race concept: the medical theory that allows for belief to posit bodily consequences is innocuous enough in the hands of writers like John Donne—who might potentially be scored by it—but can be weaponized when it makes contact with colonial programs or pogroms. If race is an opportunistic fiction, responsive to particular policies or agendas, then it is composed of the cultural materials that are available. What is available to the construction of race in the sixteenth century is specific to an early modern debate concerning the very nature of the soul.

While both physicians and metaphysicians had debated the relationship of soul to body, and the precise habitation of the soul within the body, since antiquity, the theories of Pietro Pomponazzi in the early part of the sixteenth century forced a reinterrogation of the definition of soul. Pomponazzi argued that since the soul "acted materially in sense-perception and immaterially in intellection, it must partake of both ontological realms." He therefore assigned the soul to the material realm, positing the soul as "the highest material form" of human being.[5] Of course he was correct: it had proved beyond the means of natural philosophy to show how sense-perception and imagination could be part of intellection—an activity emanating from the higher, rational soul— and to not implicate the soul as material form.

As Angus Gowland has observed, melancholy assumed a prominent role in the controversies concerning body-soul transactions precisely because melancholy was understood to affect both.[6] As such, it had the potential to cast a cold light on both sides of human being. Melancholy, as both an excess of black bile in the body and an instrument of delusion and despair, became the chief term by which the transactions of body and soul were negotiated. Medical theory concerning melancholy and other diseases of the mind had seemed to set the higher faculties of the rational soul within the range of "the phisicians hand."[7] Such developments threw the status of the soul as immaterial and immortal into doubt. But the disorder had also long signaled, from Ficino to Burton, moral corruption and the madness of irreligion and atheism. In his 1586 *Treatise of melancholie*, Timothy Bright, the chief physician to the Royal Hospital of St. Bartholomew, asserts that by the time of his writing many "esteemed the vertues themselves, yea religion, no other thing but as the body hath ben tempered . . . & neglect of religion and honestie, to [be] nought else but a fault of humour."[8]

Belief about the nature and relationship between the body and soul played a role in the characterization, categorization, alienation, and exploitation of the non-White body. Surface markings became an index of an internal humoral complexion that determined the moral faculty of the human. Bright's utterance, attributing a lack of both virtue and religion as emanating from the same source, describes a cultural attitude—even if he does not himself ascribe to it. Any "fault of humour" that corrupted the soul's capacity to receive Christianity also contaminated the will to virtue. A system of moral classification based on blood already underwrote ideas of heredity. While reading the exterior body for a set of interior moral characteristics is recognizable as a modern construction of race, in its early modern context, surface markings eventually account for moral differences that have corresponding features in the blood. In the sixteenth century, and throughout much of the seventeenth, Irish and Spanish Catholics are also negrified in these constructions—as humoral imbalances, with attendant moral and religious defects, are ascribed to bodies of all hues. *Bad Humor* tracks a racial history—over an arc that is neither linear nor evolutionary but episodic and opportunistic—that encodes bodies as White or Black.

This is, in fact, the period when the moral encoding of skin color is under construction. It is not simply the time that the term "complexion" shifts from an interior reality to an external expression of that state but when "having shifted from the invisible internal blend of fluids in one's body to something identifiable on the skin, it became a congenital and immutable category."[9] This is certainly not to claim that skin color did not previously hold moral meanings or that medieval and early modern physiognomies did not read the body for the moral messages it contained. For the last twenty years, research in pre- and early modern studies has explored contact points between race, religion, and color.[10] M. Lindsay Kaplan, Lisa Lampert-Weissig, and Cord Whitaker have examined how race-thinking in the medieval period grounds the constructions of modern racism.[11] Kim F. Hall's 1995 study of the early modern marking of cultural others and politically marginalized people is still the best work on the subject.[12] The story of race is not about invention but reinvention: race reinvents itself for occasion. What distinguishes the race concept at this early modern moment is stability.[13] Blackness becomes the stain of a nature that is obdurate to Christian faith—which is to say that what is imagined as immutable is the religious disposition that black skin signifies.

Medievalists have exposed the instabilities of this model under a Catholic orientation. In her influential analysis of the Middle English *King of Tars*, Heng has shown that the romance, "as a medieval artifact, supposes *the normativity of whiteness*, and of *the white racial body*, as the guarantor of normalcy, aesthetic and moral virtue, European Christian identity, and full membership in the human community."[14] But Heng's assertion that the romance is an index of the "theory that an essence resides within Christianity that has the power to trump ordinary human biology" demonstrates the fundamental distinction that I am making between medieval and early modern readings of the body in relation to religious identity: in Heng's analysis, Christianity has the power to trans*form*.[15] Whitaker has provided a different assessment of this literary episode, noticing the fact that the "sultan ... is already white at the moment of conversion," having become white when the priest bestows his name in preparation for baptism.[16] Whitaker suggests that this underscores the association of black skin with sin and white with salvation, with the capacity of Christianity to convert "the most foreign and the most sinful" of men (indicated by blackness), as an index of its power.[17] But in both of these readings, salvation—signaled by conversion to whiteness—nonetheless reveals that conversion was possible.

The need to make conversion to Christianity *impossible* for certain groups is what distinguishes early modern racial strategies. It is also what makes the consequences of these strategies so durable and enduring. Science is the discourse through which theological difference is defined and essentialized. The manner and method of this rationalization of human difference render faith a feature of the blood and not of belief or conversion. The fact that there are early apparitions of pseudoscientific racial logic, and that science (however construed) grounds claims of human difference, does not undercut the point that race and racialization are fundamentally cultural in their terms. Because racial logic often resorts to available science in order to naturalize discriminations that are social, economic, or religious also does not mean that natural philosophy and medical theory are necessary components in racial construction.[18] Bodies are here, as always in racial scripts, essentialized in terms of their relationship to power. But drawing attention to these scripts also attends to the fact that "the distinction between the politico-cultural and pseudoscientific vocabularies of racial discrimination" that Ania Loomba and Jonathan Burton recommend we track in earlier histories is sometimes simply not there—precisely because moral and religious differences that are cultural and contingent in our terms are embodied and essential in theirs.[19]

Dennis Britton has also observed and reconstructed a fantasy of lineage that conveys through Protestant theology. The baptismal theology of the Church of England, Britton avers, conveys Christianity as a function of inheritance, not baptism. John Jewel writes that "the issue which cometh of faithful parents is born holy, and is a holy progeny, and that the children of such, being yet inclosed in the womb, before they draw breath of life, be nevertheless chosen into the convent of life everlasting."[20] But whether doctrinal or medical in its terms, either one of these fictions is equally irrational. It seems important, however, to underscore how cultural scripts complement each other in the construction of difference. Treatises of natural philosophy and medical theory do not work in cooperation with what we define as cultural texts but are themselves cultural texts that write fantasies of the body. In this case, theological and scriptural treatises provide a rationale for "a holy progeny" to the exclusion of other groups—and books of medical theory, or tracts on natural or political philosophy, supply the physical technologies that make such ideas of descent work. Race does not tell one story.

The story that I am telling here is one of faith in the blood.[21] Christianity becomes White as a function of inheritance; Blackness becomes the guarantee of the absence of Christian faith. As I detail at length in the final chapter, Rebecca Anne Goetz shows how ideas of "hereditary heathenism" reimagined what it meant to be Christian and "White" in the early English Americas—and how these ideas informed early English slave codes. But Goetz fails to account for how these ideas reached the other side of the Anglo-Atlantic world or for the wide circulation of these ideas in prior English colonial activities. It was, in fact, this wide dissemination that allowed for the legal codification of Christianity in Black and White in the early British American colonies. Literature is the mechanism through which the circulation of this discourse is explored in this book because literary culture is the best index of how these discourses are produced and secured. This is not least because it operates on the same imaginative plane as fictions of race. I have argued, with others, elsewhere that "the colonial project is stitched in and through the language and literatures of the pre- and early modern periods; the politics and economics that ultimately produced settler colonialism, chattel slavery, the forced migration of peoples, and the development of the British empire animate these early English texts."[22] The colonial project that *Bad Humor* discovers is the underlying eviction of Christians from the faith—one that ultimately permits its violent endeavors.

The Inside Story

The effect of the body's humoral disposition on the mind is a well-plowed field.[23] At present, however, few studies have explored the consequences for the state of the soul in early modern psychosomatic relations.[24] The assumption that "the body and soul are knit together by a certain Sympathy or Consent, and derive virtue and vice from one another," is neither uniformly held in early modern England nor uncontested in its terms.[25] But it is widely available: it populates medical treatises, theological tracts, political theories, and personal correspondence. The debate concerning the nature of the soul, the extent of "Sympathy or Consent" between body and soul, and the consequences of this commerce for human being permeates the culture through the latter part of the sixteenth century and throughout the seventeenth century.[26] Part of the purpose of this book is to demonstrate how pervasive these notions of close contact were through the rehearsal of these ideas in a wide range of early modern English texts—legal, medical, theological, political, polemical, aesthetic, and personal.

Advancements in medical treatment for melancholy and other diseases of the mind had situated the higher faculties of the rational soul within the scope of natural philosophy, and Galenic medical theory itself (from which these treatments were derived) insinuated the soul's corporal nature. While no medical writer of the period unequivocally asserted that the soul was matter—as Galen himself was ambiguous on the point—the accretion of these arguments provided the strong suggestion of a material aspect of the soul.[27]

But this was made possible by the failure of natural philosophy to prove the immortality of the soul—a failure thrown into sharp relief by Pomponazzi.[28] While Pomponazzi opposed the Averroist position of a single and unified intellect animating the form of man,[29] he also opposed the Thomist view: in Aquinas, sensations and sense desires, possessed in common with other animals, have their seat in the organism. In the case of abstract and universal concepts such as reason, will, and moral judgment, the soul is still held to the organism, as a disease of the body can impede the exercise of any of these faculties. But the condition of the body is only an external condition: it is not responsible for the existence of thought or of will in its very essence. Pomponazzi countered that this was an untenable position philosophically since it was premised "on the assumption of the divine creation of the human soul, which was opposed to the principles of nature." He further argued that both Aquinas and Averroes, in "supposing the soul to be an immaterial and incorruptible form acting in a material subject," had not resolved the issue of how different parts of the body, motivated by one soul, behaved differently.[30] In the end, Pomponazzi declared, after Duns Scotus, that the question of the immortality of the soul was beyond the scope and practice of natural reason.

In his influential *Liber de anima*, Philip Melanchthon simply cedes the field to Pomponazzi: he declares the soul is immortal but admits that his assertion cannot be proven by philosophy; it is instead affirmed by scripture.[31] Melanchthon goes on to further argue that a full description of the whole human body is required in order to know the powers of the soul, since the soul can only be known through its actions.[32] Because the manner of cooperation of the material and the immaterial in the human soul was precisely the point of rupture between natural and Christian philosophy, Melanchthon asserts his definition of the soul in conscious opposition to natural philosophy.[33] But the removal of natural philosophy as an explanatory model makes the operations of the soul entirely opaque. And so, Melanchthon declares that insofar as the soul is intelligible, its powers can only be discerned through the motions that it supplies to the body—a definition offered by Galen.[34] Subsequent to Melanchthon's formulation, it became commonplace to contend that Pomponazzi was wrong in saying "that the soul [was] mortal according to [natural] philosophy" but that perhaps "he was not wrong to say that the immortality of the soul cannot be proved by natural reason."[35] And Duns Scotus is cited, against Aquinas, as the patristic authority for the position. By these lights, what could be known about the soul was manifest in the body.

Since the powers of the soul can only be known through its actions, a full description of the whole human body is requisite to such knowledge. Melanchthon therefore begins his section titled "What thing is the soul?" ("Quae res sit anima?") with Galen's tripartite division, in which the three functions of the human soul are seated in bodily organs: the rational soul in the head, the sensitive soul in the heart, and the nutritive soul in the liver.[36] As Garrett Sullivan puts it, from this time forward in both "theology and natural philosophy, the relationship between the tripartite soul and the immortal soul was both widely assumed and, in its details, continually renegotiated."[37] The rift between natural and Christian philosophy at the start of the sixteenth century had meant that philosophy was no longer "identical with Aristotle, nor Aristotle with St. Thomas and the teaching of the church."[38] The tradition by which Aristotle was adapted to Christian doctrine had been diverted. Rather, "a philosopher could be a Thomist, an Aristotelian, a Platonist or anything else," and philosophers and churches staked different positions.[39] But by the mid- to late sixteenth century, psychology, or the philosophical study of the soul, became, in many ways, the legitimate concern of Christian physicians.

In his turn to Galenic anatomy as a model of the soul's operations, Melanchthon revised the entire apprehension and understanding of the soul in both medical texts and theological discourse. It is difficult to describe the influence of Melanchthon's *Liber de anima* to both areas of knowledge: more than seventy editions of the work were printed in the six decades between its first appearance in 1540 and the end of the century. It was an important textbook in universities throughout Europe for the second half of the sixteenth century. But it was, in fact, rarely published free-standing. Melanchthon's work was reproduced in numerous medical commentaries, and this was largely the mode through which the treatise was transmitted throughout the sixteenth century. Two dozen different printers in more than ten different European cities produced some version (part or whole), mostly with commentary, in the sixteenth century—implying a wide dissemination of the work.[40]

In an early modern world where the soul's condition was made legible through the body, what we would term "culture"—religious belief—was read as nature. Intellectual historians such as Gowland and James Hankins have argued that belief itself—the excess, defect, or lack of religion—was apprehended and understood largely in terms of temperament in the latter part of the sixteenth century.[41] The reason why this matters is that the discourse of natural philosophy composed numerous arguments against religious others throughout the sixteenth century. Luther, Melanchthon, Zwingli, and Calvin had all offered arguments depicting religious opponents as humorally distempered and deluded, subject to the madness that an excess of melancholy produces.[42] As Hankins has observed, there was at the time a "virtuous mean of 'true religion,'" depending, of course, upon which religion was reckoned to be "true."[43]

Faith in the Blood

Theories of psychosomatic relations merged with notions of hereditary blood around the particular humoral imbalance of black melancholy. Fifteenth-century notions of hereditary blood, derived from books on animal husbandry, supplied the narrative of a natural ruling class.[44] But an ideology that assumes a superior humoral inheritance that secures a license to rule is easily turned—as Patricia Akhimie, Urvashi Chakravarty, and Jean Feerick have shown—to the purposes of justifying other social hierarchies.[45] The differentiation of groups of peoples as manifestly and materially holding right or wrong belief, as capable of conversion or not, exploited the interchange between body and soul. But it also traded upon prior systems of racial logic. Charles de Miramon writes that "the revival of hereditary blood early in the fourteenth century" and its transfer from discourses about races of dogs, pedigrees, and selection methods to human subjects "is ... [an] example of the cultural and political evolutions that explain the birth of race."[46] Of course, there is no "birth of race" but a process by which existing discourses get pressed into different service—and the discourse concerning the governing social hierarchy was particularly well-developed in the early modern period. Anxieties anatomized in texts such as Thomas Elyot's *Boke named the governour* (1531) about the corruption of noble blood also describe the operations by which virtue—both physical and moral—was understood to convey through bloodlines. Older modes of thinking concerning the virtue of the ruling class are reworked rather than abandoned; materials of manufacture get recycled, and echoes of a former racial logic can be heard in later discourse. The pliant nature of humoral theory allowed it to underwrite a host of political arrangements and discriminations.

The race concept arrogates what is already at large in the culture. As Jonathan Burton notes: "Race . . . scavenges and improvises, calibrating to the moment whatever ideas are available."[47] Indeed, it is this very continuity of cultural materials that lends it political force. The ideology of hereditary blood, and the numerous cultural materials that underwrote it, passed along two crucial components to the racialization of religion in the early modern period: moral constitution and lines of descent. For power to transfer seamlessly, the guaranteed transmission of traits to wield it was requisite. The privilege to own land and control people was premised on the idea of an inherited moral and intellectual authority. As Levine Lemnie explains, the soul's "concretion" with the body occurs at conception when it mixes with "the Parentes Seed, which is . . . of the purest and best concocted bloude."[48] Lemnie delivers a fairly straightforward Aristotelian brief in which the soul is united and spread throughout the body as its substantial form, endowing the "rest of the members of the bodye" with its powers and giving "such shape and proportion to the thinges animated, as daily we see represented and set before our eyes."[49] The soul directs and governs "the mynd and vnderstanding," but these faculties, insofar as they inhabit the body, are subject to its corruption.[50] Lemnie's whole treatise concerns the complexion, or humoral disposition, of the body in order to maintain both mind and body in health.[51] In his description of a soul taking a body, Lemnie makes clear that it is the mixture of parents' blood from which humoral complexion is initially composed. But while superior humoral disposition was thought to descend to nobles through bloodlines, it was left to the individual to maintain the quality of his or her constitution. This moral-psychological obligation compelled the analysis of the vices and virtues attached to various complexions that filled folios of contemporary medical tracts.[52] Lemnie proceeds to deliver such a moral exposition of bodily temperament in subsequent pages. So that "euery man may perfectlye know the nature and condicion of this complexion and constitution," as well as the potential hazards of its degeneration, Lemnie provides the "marks and tokens" of humoral disposition in color-coding: which constitutions make "the colour of the face and bodye fayre or foule, good or badde."[53]

Patricia Akhimie has done more than any other scholar to re-create the racial logic and social demarcation enforced by the many conduct books and medical tracts written for "a privileged group . . . characterized by its capacity and desire to improve."⁵⁴ Akhimie argues that in spite of the implied flexibility of the model, "rigidity [was] a constant counterpoint to fluid concepts of identity" in early modern constructions of racial and social difference.⁵⁵ If early modern society assumed that nobles could, and would, cultivate their environment in order to preserve their superior nature, they also assumed that those of *inferior* nature "were marked by a devastating lack: an inability to be better and even know better—that is, to know that they *should* be better."⁵⁶ Lemnie betrays this thinking when he observes that "we see the common sorte and multitude, in behauiour and maners grosse and vunnurtured whereas the Nobles and Gentlemen (altering theyr order and diet, and digressing from the common fashion of their pezantly countreymen) frame themselues & theirs, to a verye commendable order, and ciuill behauiour."⁵⁷ Of course, such declarations reiterate the racial fantasy of physiological superiority that supports the governing structure. But it also speaks to the extent to which moral and "ciuill" virtue was the understood effect of humoral disposition.

In their introduction to a special edition of *Shakespeare Quarterly* dedicated to the appraisal of current critical race studies of the early modern period, Peter Erickson and Kim Hall caution against an emphasis upon "fluidity" in early modern racial constructions. Such an emphasis, they argue, serves to isolate early modern developments of racial discourse from modern ones, reifying a distinction between cultural and scientific racism—and the past from the present.⁵⁸ Burton counters this formulation, arguing that "Race is a powerful fiction because it is relentlessly adaptive, innovating, and recycling."⁵⁹ The apparent contradiction here does not really reveal a conflict at all. The race concept is fluid, opportunistic, and mutable in its terms. It adapts to the agenda for which it supplies a rationale—to maintain a social hierarchy, exploit a particular labor population, or annihilate a people in order to secure their land. But the story that it supplies, the particular tale that confirms the validity of a racial logic at a particular time, is almost always one of continuity, stability, and inheritance.

Ficino claims that "it is not only the unbalanced complexion contracted from one's parents ... but a quality resulting from constant use ... that draws mankind away from religion."⁶⁰ Embedded in his formulation are the assumptions that ground the work of Lemnie: that while humoral complexion might be pliant to outside forces, its particular concoction originates with parents and is maintained—*if* it is maintained—through persistent attention. This would seem to make conversion possible. But as

Akhimie notes, the countervailing impulse to the instability of identity is to calcify its terms. This is particularly the case where shared Christian faith impedes colonial objectives. In the racial productions of colonial programs, black melancholy as an index of wrong religion, or atheism, was also guaranteed in lines of descent. But the "indelible . . . difference" that this marking signified, in subjects marked for the purpose of English colonial enterprise, was irremediable bad faith.[61]

Color Codes

This is when Black and White is in formation. This development is often linked to chattel slavery.[62] But while the social and legal process of attempting to classify people as property was what finally fully invested pagan identity in black and brown skin, the rationalization of human difference that underwrote early English slave codes had a long trajectory. The still too common assertion that the discriminations of premodern and early modern peoples were based solely upon cultural, as opposed to physiological, difference is grounded in the fact that these discriminations were so often directed against religious others. Of course, racial discriminations are always grounded on cultural difference. But science tells its own story. Heng observes that

> In encounters between human populations and communities productive of race, it's of utmost importance to note that *religion*—the magisterial discourse of the European Middle Ages, as science is the magisterial discourse of the modern era—can function socioculturally *and* biopolitically to racialize a human group: subjecting peoples of a detested faith to a political hermeneutics of theology that can biologize, define, and essentialize an entire community as fundamentally and absolutely different in an inter-knotted cluster of ways.[63]

I have been arguing that in the *early* modern era, the discourses of science and religion combine and cooperate in the construction of race. The psychosomatic relationship that I have been describing produces a context in which bodies are perceived as moral machines. These pseudoscientific ideas are applied to set certain people permanently outside of faith.

In "Dogma-Line Racism," Leerom Medovoi argues that rather than the common suggestion that religion only *informs* constructions of race, religion is, in fact, a "second axis of race": "religion," he writes, "is not merely one more semiotic coordinate, alongside the codes of descent, phenotype, cultural identity, through which bodies become racially ascribed as white or nonwhite"; rather, he maintains, "religion ... has historically generated a supplemental racial dynamic that cannot be reduced to the assignation of color, although it interacts with it."[64] While I fundamentally agree with Medovoi's formulation, I would modify his claim for early modern England: at this time the assignation of color is the index of religion—or its absence. White Europeans do not simply become White against the production of racialized Black people at this time: Whiteness becomes the value by which Christianity is bestowed.[65]

The cultural history that attends the violent colonial history that drives the production of these designations is the subject of this book. In exfoliating the story that attends this process, I have relied upon the literature of the period to tell it. Since my objective is partly to appraise how commonly available the discourse concerning the transaction of body and soul—and the material manifestation of atheism and wrong religion—actually was, I have analyzed works that different populations of English audiences and readers would have encountered. Consequently, I read sonnets, masques, closet drama, epic poems, and stage plays. I have tried to bring the same analysis to the fiction of race that we apply to English literature: evaluating the materials of its making in order to see how it was composed. Each of the first three chapters is divided in two: the first section takes a discourse sufficiently in the mainstream so as to be introduced to swim in the waters of cultural signs and symbols with the expectation that a learned audience can fish them out. I then appraise the extent to which the mainstream attitude is polluted by political agenda in the second half of the chapter. Since I am examining a discourse, both theological and medical, that can be politically exploited—deployed when the threat from religious others is most acutely felt—each chapter will juxtapose the discourse against its exploitation.

It is for this reason that the opening texts of the first three chapters are authored by Catholic converts in England proper: as potential targets of this discourse, these authors are less likely to deploy its terms in the service of a racial episteme. This will make the production of the race concept more visible, as their handling is juxtaposed against those who put it toward a racial construction. The first three chapters show the accretion of this discourse of racialization: Chapter 1 demonstrates the traffic of body and soul that permits a trade in the corruption of both; Chapter 2 reveals how the corrupt soul shows its true colors on the skin; and Chapter 3 exhibits exactly how bodily disorder and a degenerate soul can be passed on to offspring. The "fault of humour" of melancholy disposition marks the bodies of religious others: melancholy becomes the index of a mind deluded by atheism and a rational soul turned from God. But in the fantasies about the body that constitute the race concept, medical theory can only provide an explanation. The racial epistemology itself relies upon anxieties about difference—or, more often, likeness—to activate its terms. It also requires social or political objectives.

The final two chapters appraise how these notions of religious essentialism underwrite the way that bodies in colonial contexts are treated in both poetics and policy. Catholics in England represent a separate case: although not entirely accepted, their exposure to English climate, diet, and other nonnaturals made their bodies more prepared for reform. But this very logic exposes, in its exception, English colonial domination as the actual objective of the racialization of religion. It is in colonial activity that a production of difference that thrusts certain people outside of human community becomes requisite. The first three chapters tease apart the principal anxieties that animate the early modern race concept; the final two show how these anxieties knit together to compose fictions of race in colonial contexts. All of these chapters collectively show that the material consequences of wrong belief manifest culturally in color codes that over time (in Medovoi's terms) racially ascribe people as White or non-White.

The first chapter looks at how the transaction between body and soul was understood to take place at this early modern moment by exploring the construction of residual Catholic identity in John Donne's Holy Sonnets. In a letter to Sir Henry Goodyer, Donne argues against a change in religion by claiming that: "You shall seldome see a Coyne, upon which the stampe were [altered] ... but it looks awry and squint."[66] Given the fluid transactions of faith in early modern England—in spite of the hard lines of the English Church—the complete demonization of English Catholics was untenable. But the distinction between English and Irish Catholics lies in the potential for the reformation of Catholics on English soil. Donne's conversion provided him with an unusual perspective: not many people were positioned to hold as nuanced a view of religious ideology. It is surprising, then, that when Donne considers his conversion—which he does in little and in large in the Holy Sonnets—he casts a change in religion in somatic terms. Precisely because he reveals an understanding of the material presence of religious disposition, Donne's humoral constitution of faith in the Holy Sonnets anatomizes the uneasy transactions of body and soul in the organization of the human subject.

The second half of the chapter considers how notions of religious temperament inform a poem written by Christopher Brooke, which, Kasey Evans declares, "surely ranks among the most shockingly racist texts of the Renaissance."[67] Donne's lifelong friend and near neighbor utilizes the same terms as Donne in representing the 1622 Powhatan attack on Jamestown. Brooke's *Poem on the Late Massacre in Virginia* writes the Christian settlers and their godless assailants "in Characters of blood" (A3v).[68] The English are "Images of Christ" who "propagate *Religion*" (A4r) whereas the Indigenous people are entirely devoid of humanity: "For . . . consider what those Creatures are, / (I cannot call them men) no Character / Of God in them: Soules drown'd in flesh and blood" (C1r). What is striking about Brooke's partition of Christian and pagan is that the distinctions are drawn in humoral terms. Mary Floyd-Wilson has shown how the humors underwrite geopolitical affiliation in the early modern period.[69] Brooke's poem, one of a number of early modern texts, shows us how religion, region, and humoral disposition align. Such considerations matter when the English are cultivating Christian faith in New World contexts: Brooke accuses the English of being poor planters, casting their seeds upon earth where they will not grow.

Chapter 2 will discover how widespread the discourse of religious materiality was by examining another representation of Catholic conversion, Ben Jonson's *The Masque of Blacknesse* (1605). Molly Murray has argued that the masque is a performance of devotion by Queen Anne: Anne's rumored Catholicism had caused her husband considerable political problems, and the masque stages her supplication and suggests that the queen will be converted by the king.[70] But the masque should also be placed at the convergence of religion and the body that this book describes: since external complexion is the mark of internal traits, the promised change in complexion for the Ethiopian ladies at the end of the masque should be understood as a material conversion. Anne, who is the likely author of the conceit, exploits a trope of blackness for the masque performance that had attached to her as a foreign and religious outsider since pageants first celebrated her entry into Edinburgh. But the number of European pageants from which she is able to draw inspiration for the idea—where black figures represent expelled Catholics—point to prevailing notions of religion as a product of humoral disposition and blackness as a mark of religious melancholy.

In Robert Burton's *Anatomy of Melancholy*, religious melancholy (a term he coins) is classified as a variety of love melancholy. Burton inherits the idea, if not the actual expression, from a long tradition, reaching as far back as Augustine, that understands the misdirection of love from God as a form of madness. But it is Ficino's *Platonic Theology* in particular that promotes religious excess or defect as both a deviation of proper love and the product of the bodily disorder of melancholy.[71] The second section of the chapter looks at the contemporary polemical significance of this idea of excessive or defective religious love and how it gets applied to foreign bodies. In *Pamphilia to Amphilanthus*, Mary Wroth uses themes of blackness and paganism—themes she may have borrowed from Jonson's masque—in order to situate her body and its desires outside of the legitimating structures of community, religion, and race. The fact that she adores the wrong god and, "Like ... the Indians, scorched with the sun," is scored by its effects, is exactly the point: if her desire is illegitimate, then so too is the body that produced it.[72] But her purposeful misdirection of the Neoplatonic ideal indicates that notions of religious others as deviant lovers, sick with excessive melancholy, were widely available. It also indicates, as Sharon Patricia Holland claims, that "Blackness ... not only produces 'erotic value' for whiteness, but it holds the very impossibility of its own pleasure through becoming the sexualized surrogate of another."[73] In the representation of the love quest of both Ethiopians and Indigenous people, Jonson's masque and Wroth's sonnet sequence show the melancholy bodies of religious others denied access to divine love and its adjunct, Christian charity.

The third chapter analyzes how Catholic identity is passed through the bloodstream. I begin with the logic that grounds notions of hereditary blood as exemplified in Elizabeth Cary's *The Tragedy of Mariam*. If Cary's *Mariam* is "about" anything, it is about rank—and the privileges of moral courage and supremacy that rank bestows. Mariam's whiteness against the colored background of Salome and Herod constitutes the moral encoding of raced subjects—but the race in question is a difference in rank. Cary posits a moral constitution in her play: moral differences that are literally a feature of the blood—or humoral disposition—and that are revealed in the external complexion of her characters. The play represents subjectivity from the inside out, and interior moral and physiological characteristics are marked on the skin. But how this gets applied to the race of ruling families exposes assumptions, grounded in early modern medical theory, of moral composition and constitution as an inherited trait.

The relevance of this mode of thinking for a polemical text such as John Temple's *Irish Rebellion* might not be immediately apparent. But the idea of moral superiority as a feature of the blood, and of humoral disposition as an inherited trait, is precisely the mechanism by which the New English tracts characterize the Irish—of both English and Gaelic descent—as a corrupt and unrecoverable people. A series of tracts in manuscript and print, produced in reaction to growing insurrection in Ireland, sketch the outline of a theory of religious difference grounded in a discourse on the humors. The construction of Irish Catholics as physically degraded is not only a strategy of nationalist ideology by the latter part of the century but also indicates an understanding of the material presence of religious disposition. By the time that Temple writes his 1646 *Irish Rebellion*, "the malignant impressions of irreligion . . . [are] transmitted down"[74] through the bloodstream.

In Chapter 4, Edmund Spenser sets the Castle Alma episode at the end of Book II of his *Faerie Queene* squarely within the late sixteenth-century debate concerning melancholy and the status of the soul. Spenser's peculiar treatment of Maleger in the Castle Alma episode of his book "Of Temperaunce" implies that the rational soul is subject to the corruption of the body. Cold and dry, the melancholic figure of Maleger is the chief enemy of Alma's Castle of Health. His attack on the rational soul seems entirely physical, through the instrument of melancholy. But Maleger is not killed by sword or suffocation; he is thrown into a lake, defeated in a ritual that resembles baptism. Spenser's conflation of physical disease (melancholy) and spiritual affliction reveals that he understood religious affliction as requiring both a physical and spiritual remedy. This suggests that Spenser saw the operations of body and soul as mutually constituted.

Of course, Spenser's understanding of the body and its operations in relation to the soul matters precisely because he is implicated in the English colonial project in Ireland. The image of the hermaphrodite that concludes the 1590 *Faerie Queene* is an emblem not of ideal marriage but of our own incorporation as "members of [Christ's] bodie" (Eph. 5:30).[75] At the end of Book III of *The Faerie Queene*, he imagines bodies reformed in a unification that represents the ideal church. But by Book IV, the hermaphrodite has turned monster, and androgynous figures such as Lust, who, with an excess of flesh, lacks the predisposition to love God, populate the terrain. Spenser also sees atheism and irreligion as a species of love melancholy—but in Books III and IV, the *corpus Christianum* is opposed by fleshy figures such as Lust, whose carnal impulses attempt to devour Love itself (in the figure of

Amoret). If the image of Spenser's ideal church is one of incorporation, where charity fuses the "members of [the] bodie," then the figures of Error and Lust, whose love is misdirected and whose commitments to their own flesh obstruct Christian communion, stand in opposition to the life of the soul. Spenser's religious allegory fashions religious others in *The Faerie Queene* as bodies that are deformed, constitutions that are diseased, and "Soules [that are] drown'd in flesh and blood."

The final chapter considers hereditary blood and inherited heathenism. In previous chapters I argue that moral rectitude is understood in essentialist terms in the early modern period and that one of these registers is through noble blood. In Chapter 5, I trace how religious essentialism attaches to chromatic difference in a way that is sustained, codified, and legally affirmed. If inherited moral authority supplies the nobility with the license to rule, and guarantees the transfer of power and property through generations, ideas about hereditary blood and inherited religion, or rather irreligion, give sanction to the permanent enslavement of particular people. Two works primarily serve to discover this shift in racial logic over time: William Shakespeare's *Othello* (1601/2) and Thomas Southerne's *Oroonoko: A Tragedy* (1695).[76] In *Othello* we perceive a racial ideology different from that which kept the social hierarchy of rank in place: *in spite of* superior lineage, Othello lacks the virtue of religion. This defect of the soul colors his entire disposition: the humoral equilibrium that is his noble heritage is dismantled along with his mind. The end of the play exposes Othello as an unbeliever by nature—as one who is possessed with the madness of melancholy and unable to perceive love.

If *Othello* forecasts a new social arrangement in which religion, not rank, is the primary determinant of virtue, Southerne's *Oroonoko*, like the novella from which it borrows, challenges this New World order. Oroonoko, whose reason and virtue are guaranteed by bloodline, is not the natural governor of this New World and instead government is given over to men of "such . . . complexion" as "to countenance all [they are] prone to do, / [and] Will know no bounds, no law" (III.ii.218–21).[77] But because the Imoinda of Southerne's play is White, not Black, and her enslavement, as well as that of her unborn child, requires explanation, Southerne's play also reveals different legacies of laboring bodies in the New World.[78] Imoinda is a permanent slave because she is pagan; her child will be born a slave for the same reason. While presumptions of inherited heathenism eventually break down along color lines, written into the slave codes of different colonial sites at different times but finally adopted everywhere, Imoinda's figure assumes other possibilities that are foreclosed. But the alteration of Imoinda's racial identity to "Indian" in the epilogue (written by Southerne's friend William Congreve after the play's original composition) discovers assumptions about the alignment of "pagan" and "Black" already legally codified in the New World.

The color-coding of moral degeneracy and wrong belief in the early modern period lays bare fantasies of human embodiment that map onto modern ones.[79] This is not an evolutionary tale. But the history of embodiment that this book describes finds fictions of race trading upon ideas of moral difference carried in the blood and marked on the skin.[80] These notions of religious essentialism get written into slave codes and become the rationale for the capture of dark bodies as permanent property. While there is nothing inevitable about how material bodies are understood in political space, the texts surveyed here reveal how bodies are written to accommodate political and economic interests. This is certainly not the only time that religion is racialized in Europe, but it is the episode in English history when Christianity becomes Black and White.

CHAPTER 1

"Soules drown'd in flesh and blood"
The Fluid Poetics of John Donne and Christopher Brooke

> Inconstancy unnaturally hath begot
> A constant habit, that when I would not
> I change in vows and in devotion.
> —John Donne, "Oh, to vex me"

I have promised to unfold a story of race—one of marking the flesh with the stigma of irreligion. This process of race-making has a long trajectory over the early modern period, and a number of component parts. But it begins with a debate over the corporality of the soul, one in which John Donne participates as both prelate and layman. In Donne's consideration, however, we see the materials that manufacture race without the effect: Donne delineates the anxieties concerning the material residue of religion—its impressions upon the body—but as a former Catholic, it is his body that is marked. Christopher Brooke, Donne's lifelong friend, has no residual effect of religious change, and he demonstrates in the second half of this chapter how these materials could be pressed into the service of a racial fiction. If Donne's terms are not innocent—insofar as he imagines the body marred by religious difference—he lacks the agenda that activates the production of race.

In an exchange of letters with Henry Goodyer, written sometime between the fall of 1607 and early spring of 1608, Donne engages in an exposition of the status of the soul: "So many doctrines have grown to be the ordinary diet and food of our spirits, and have place in the pap of Catechismes, which were . . .

accepted in a lazie weariness, when men, so they might have something to relie upon, and to excuse themselves from more painfull inquisition, never examined what that was. . . . I think it falls out thus also in the matter of the soul."[1] Donne's inquiry into the nature of the soul, and the nature of the soul within the body, was not an investigation peculiar to himself: it was peculiar to the period to which Donne belonged. Arguments in natural philosophy and theology had set the matter of souls at the foreground of religious debate. The "lazie weariness" that Donne invokes was earned by "long disputations and controversies" within "all sects of Christians" concerning the soul's essence.[2] The theoretical success of arguments (such as those of Pomponazzi) that affirmed the soul as "the highest material form" of human being had forced a re-litigation of what, precisely, the soul was.[3]

The proliferation of treatments and treatises prescribing for mental disorders had further rendered the category to which the soul belonged subject to question. In his treatise, Timothy Bright writes that the success of medical remedies in the treatment of melancholy had ostensibly put the rational soul itself under the care of physicians. While Bright spends much of the tract prescribing for the physical problem of melancholy, the stress of his argument falls upon the distinction between the malady of the body and "that heauy hande of God vpon the afflicted [soul], tormented with remorse of sinne, & feare of his iudgement."[4] The purpose of his treatise is to draw the distinction between physical and spiritual disease, and between material and spiritual causation, and thus avoid the implication, in accordance with Galenic materialism, that bodily disorder could effect the decay of the soul. Such an apprehension of the Galenic system offered a challenge to Calvinism's assertion that God would act irresistibly and directly upon the soul.[5] Bright's treatise is an index of a debate that only becomes more strident in its wake. Many persons, Bright complains, have "accompted all maner affection [of the soul] to be subiect to the phisicians hand, not considering herein anything diuine, and aboue the ordinarie euents, and naturall course of thinges."[6]

No early modern poet was more concerned with "That subtle knot which makes us man," with the matter of the mind, the status of the spirit, or the nature of the soul than Donne ("The Ecstasy," 64).[7] In a verse letter to the Countess of Bedford, "At New Year's Tide," Donne wittily plays upon present controversy and declares himself "of stuff and form perplexed, / Whose what, and where, in disputation is" (3–4).[8] Donne's complaint is that "there is yet [due to recent controversies] no opinion in Philosophy, nor Divinity, so well established as constrains us to beleeve, both that the soul is immortall, and that every particular man hath such a soul."⁹ In the realm of opinion, it was every man for himself. Donne argues against the "soul result[ing] out of matter" on the grounds that such a position "can never [prove] necessarily and certainly a naturall immortality in the soul."¹⁰ But he also rejects the idea that the soul is an "infusion from God" because of the radical immateriality of the terms of the proposition—that the soul exists essentially and intrinsically independent of the purely corporal organism.¹¹ In refuting the doctrines of traducianism and creationism, respectively ("in both which opinions there appear . . . infirmities"),¹² Donne also undermines both the Galenic and Platonic positions in contemporary debates.¹³ The soul cannot be matter because, in that case, proof of the immortality of the soul cannot be derived from its nature. But it also cannot be decoupled from the body; rather, the soul, by its nature, must be joined with a body.¹⁴ "All that the soul does," he claims, "it does in, and with, and by the body."¹⁵

The Holy Sonnets, in particular, register the perplexity "of stuff and form"—of the material and immaterial. Donne arbitrates experience through the body; its humoral temperament is the arrangement that determines his fate. "My physicians by their love are grown / Cosmographers, and I their map," he writes, but it is he who tries to discover the progress of his soul through the disposition of his body: "this is my south-west discovery / *Per fretum febris*, by these straits to die" ("Hymn to God My God in My Sickness," 6–7, 9–10).¹⁶ The southwesterly turn in the poem indicates the excess of heat that will cause his decline, or sunset. It is through the raging heat (since *fretum* can mean either "strait" or "heat") of choler that Donne will steer his passage. But the question, repeated whenever Donne attends to his death, is the terminus of his journey. The speaker does not know where his destination lies, as all straits lead somewhere, whether north or south (17–18). His map is unclear, and he tries to read it in his own body: "As the first Adam's sweat surrounds my face, / May the last Adam's blood my soul embrace" (24–25). The waters that Donne tries to navigate to his final home are the fluids that his body and Christ's body share.¹⁷ But the liquid economy that structures his conceit is the most recurrent subject—and persistent anxiety—of the Holy Sonnets. The gross substance of his body, the "sweat [that] surrounds [his] face," may well be what guarantees that God's grace is withheld. Temperament itself, the disposition of humors in the body, potentially inhibits or even obstructs God's activity within the soul. Donne is not sure that the very nature of his body does not prevent God's intercession. Hence his special pleading: "May the last Adam's blood my soul embrace." The implacable question of the Holy Sonnets is whether or not God will intervene on his behalf. The humoral language that frames the central concerns of body and soul is no accident. The Holy Sonnets are shot through with Galenic terminology in order to underscore the instability of the soul's condition.

Donne's sonnets have often been read as records of religious despair, anxiety, or melancholy; frequently, these readings focus upon Donne's conversion as the source of his angst.[18] But while the pressures of religious conversion have been seen to leave their mark upon the form of the poems, no critic has taken seriously Donne's claims concerning the imprint of faith upon the physical subject.[19] "You shall seldome see a Coyne, upon which the stampe were removed . . . but it looks awry and squint," Donne declares about the orientation of a person who changes religion.[20] For Donne, belief posits bodily consequences. The operation of the rational soul—reason—is subject to the body's influence but the body conversely responds to the conditions of mind and soul. "Mysteries" of the mind and its affections "in souls do grow, / But yet the body is [the] book" ("The Ecstasy," 71–72) in which they are expressed. The impact of this conviction upon Donne's confessional attitudes has yet to be assessed, or how it might have energized the drama of the Holy Sonnets, which lies in the anxious situation of the soul amid a collaboration of flesh and fluid that stood to frustrate its passage.

Donne outlines his own opinion of how soul and body produce cognition in another letter: "we consist of three parts, a Soul, and Body, and Minde: which I call those thoughts and affections and passions, which neither soul nor body hath alone, but have been begotten by their communication, as Musique results out of our breath and a Cornet."[21] Cognition is produced by the concert of body and soul. But such cooperation makes reason—a power of the rational, or intellective, soul—susceptible to the body's organic temper. This is a thought to which Donne immediately turns: the substance of his letter to Goodyer concerns the vulnerability of the mind to the disease of the body.[22] For Donne, in common with many medical theorists of the period, cognition could not be abstracted from somatic operations. "Though our souls would goe to one end, Heaven," Donne writes, "and all our bodies must go to one end, the earth: yet our third part, the minde, which is our naturall guide here, chooses to every man a severall way."[23] In stitching together what Montaigne refers to as "the narrow suture" of the soul and body, Donne makes reason a product of both.[24] Tying cognition to embodiment in this way introduces the corruption of the body to the "naturall guide" of reason—and if the guide is impaired, the soul could be lost. While Galen refused to render an opinion on the somatic character of the soul, the two-way causal relationship between the humoral temper of the body and the soul's capacities is central to Galen's interpretation of how body and soul interact.[25] Christian physicians insisted on the immortality of the soul, but most accepted that the soul's capacity for reason could be compromised through bodily corruption.

Donne's construction of cognition is telling in that his own psyche was beset by melancholy. In the assessment of his own affliction Donne binds the psychic life to the human organism, so that material and immaterial work together in close relation. The perils of such proximity lie in the ability of the body to harm the soul. Melancholy, in Galenic terms, was attributable to the humoral excess of black bile in the body. If Donne was not a Galenist in an absolute sense, he saw the humoral system of Galen as the best descriptive model of the body's technologies. The stepson of a prominent physician, Donne had been exposed to medical theories, quite possibly Galen's, early; he came to espouse Galen, and to defend his theories against Paracelsus, who, Donne claimed, "would have undertaken to have made [man] in a limbeck."[26] But humoral theory did not present a comfortable (or comforting) model for Donne. To the contrary, the extent to which his "Minde" was subject to the vagaries of humoral fluctuation—and the implications for the state of his soul—produced in him an acute anxiety. That the soul could be misdirected by the diminished reason of a (humorally) imbalanced mind is a recurrent torment for Donne.

The frustration evident in Donne's epistolary exchange with Goodyer is expressive of the confused state of psychology (or, the study of the soul) at the time of his writing and of the consequences for an individual in search of his soul. There was no longer, as Donne complained, a template: "no *Criterium*, no Canon, no rule."[27] Philip Melanchthon's revision of natural philosophy created a baedeker for the Protestant community and made the body a map through which to read the soul.[28] In trying to provide a clearer conception of what the soul might be, Melanchthon returns it to the purview of natural philosophy and follows Galen's definition of the human soul, grounded in the body.[29] But this provided very uncertain directions for navigation, and for explorers like Donne it made the path forward unclear. If physicians had indeed become "Cosmographers," or geographers of both celestial and terrestrial worlds,[30] then the state of the soul was described in relation to flesh and fluid. For English Calvinists in particular, the physiological terms by which the soul's condition was charted posed a serious soteriological problem.

Donne's theology is difficult to label with confidence. In its most public expression, his sermons, it maps the coordinates of Calvinist thinking.[31] Most

Protestant divines in England by the time of Donne's ordination, regardless of their affiliations within church politics, considered themselves Calvinists.[32] For most English Reformers of the late sixteenth century, both in the church and at university, the central Calvinist tenet of salvation given to the elect through predestination was orthodoxy.[33] While many critics set the composition of the bulk of the sonnets to an earlier date than Donne's entry into the church (1609–10),[34] even at this time Donne was asserting the superiority of the "Reformed" church, or of "our Church," in private letters to Goodyer.[35] There is abundant evidence that Donne believed in election. But whether or not election was unconditional was an uncertain and anxious question for him. Calvinist doctrine held that man is resistant to God (due to sin) but that God will draw his elect to him. Donne, however, is not always convinced that the offer of salvation through grace will act irresistibly upon him. He was not supplied with the comfortable separation of body and soul that the Platonic position might have allowed.[36] Since he perceived the rational soul to be susceptible to the body's organic character, there was no guarantee that God could act upon the soul unobstructed by bodily disorder. Donne does not so much doubt the doctrine of irresistible grace as struggle to uphold it.

"A Fault of Humour"

As a practicing Catholic for the first half of his life, Donne was uncertain of the "stampe" this practice had left upon his psyche. Protestant polemics had represented religious others as subject to melancholic delusion for some time: Luther, Melanchthon, and Zwingli had particularly targeted Catholics in these terms.[37] Even Calvin himself attributed Catholicism and superstition to humoral temperament.[38] While written in 1621, and enlarged in 1628, Robert Burton's taxonomy for religious melancholy in his *Anatomy of Melancholy* has a long history and draws heavily from these polemics. He sums up the position in this way: "Religion is twofold, True or False; False is that vaine superstition . . . when false gods, or that God is falsely worshipped . . . 'tis a miserable plague, a torture of the soule, a meere madnesse . . . or *insanus error*, as *Seneca* [calls it], a franticke error, or as *Austin, Insanus animi morbus*, a furious disease of the soule."[39] Donne shows us the position of a former Catholic—one supplied with medical knowledge—and exhibits the consequences of this thinking for his salvific imagination.

Calvin's attribution of Catholicism to humoral distemper is ironic because, as John Stachniewski has rightly observed, "medical and [Calvinist] spiritual discourses are in ideological opposition" at the time of Bright's composition of his treatise.[40] This conflict only increases in subsequent decades.[41] Bright's treatise, in fact, indicates that Calvinists were not secure in the belief that God would arrange the disposition of the elect so that they would be saved; rather, he seeks to arrange the operations of the body so as to make it impossible to frustrate God's purpose.[42] Bright defines the faculties of "the spirite and body to be wholly organicall," while the faculty of the soul is immortal. The spirit, which is susceptible to the same forces of region and diet as the body, mediates between it and the soul. While the soul is itself not corrupted by the substance of the body, "the spirit being disordered, either in temper . . . or entermixed with straunge vapours . . . worketh annoyance, and disgraceth the worke, and crosseth the soules absolute intention."[43] The spirit is both organic and perishable; it is an instrument of the soul and embraces its faculty "so farre as bodely vses require."[44] Anyone familiar with Aristotle or Aquinas will be unsurprised by Bright's separation of an organic and an inorganic soul. But Bright's orientation of the spirit as a mediating figure keeps the immortal soul apart from the organic operations of the body. The spirit is informed by the soul's intentions but does not emanate from a divine origin. "The whole nature of man," according to Bright, is "compounded of two extremities, the soule, and the bodie," and because of the arbitration of the spirit, "the soule receaueth no other annoyance by the bodie; then the craftes man by his instrument: with no impeach, or impaire . . . but [as a] hinderance of exercising the excellent partes of his skill."[45]

Donne's acquaintance with Bright's treatise is fairly assured.[46] But Donne is unable to draw the separation between body and soul that Bright insists upon: "in the constitution and making of a natural man, the body is not the man, nor the soul is not the man, but the union of these two makes up the man."[47] It is not that Donne's terms are different—he too sees the vital spirits as performing the "office to unite and apply the faculties of the soul to the organs of the body"—but the habitation of the soul within the body is different.[48] Bright's formulation understands the soul existing independently, so that the body is an extremity—an instrument that effects the soul's will but not an entity that informs it. Bright takes the Platonic position that "the soul is untouchable by physical causes."[49] Donne, by contrast, insists that the soul, by its nature, requires a body for its expression: "the perfect natural state of the soul . . . is . . . to be united to the body," and when body and soul are separated, the soul is rendered "unperfect."[50] Donne understands the vital spirits as a binding force that ties the soul as tightly to the body as possible: "the body and soul do not make a perfect man except they be united . . . our spirits (which are the active part of the blood) do fit this body and soul for one another's working."[51]

It was certainly possible to see the spirit(s) as something other than a bulwark against the corruption of the body.[52] In his exposition of the various contemporary arguments concerning the nature of the soul, Pierre Charron, a close friend and associate of Montaigne's, cites the "absurdities" of the (Calvinist) Platonists who "not knowing . . . how to ioyne and vnite the *Soule* with the bodie, make it to abide and reside therein, as . . . a Pilot in his ship, a Coach-man in his coach: but this were to destroy all, for so the *Soule* should not be the forme, nor inward and essentiall part of a creature, or of a man, it should haue no need of the members of the bod[i]e to abide there, nor any feeling at all of the contagion of the bodie, but it should be a substance wholly distinct from the bodie."[53] Charron asserts an Aristotelian theory of causation and situates his arrangement of the human subject according to Aristotelian arguments. The soul unites substantially with matter. It is *forma informans*, not *forma assistens*, which is to say that it moves through the body, infusing the parts of the body with its powers: "The *Soule* is in the bodie as the forme in the matter, extended and spred throrowout the body, giuing life, motion, sense to all parts thereof . . . and there is no mean or middle that doth vnite and knit them together."[54]

Bright satisfies the problem of the inevitable collision of Galenic materialism and Calvinist theology by driving a wedge between body and soul by means of the spirit. The spirit animates the organic body, and the soul directs the spirit, but the two are not intermixed: "the spirite of man . . . [was] raised from the earth, together with the body." But though "it may seeme more likely, to be infused, and inspired, into the bodie, with that breath of life, which was the soule of man, at what time, god had first made his corps," Bright refuses this possibility.[55] Rather, "although it be an excellent creature, and farre excedeth the grosse substance of our bodie; yet it is baser, then to be attributed to so diuine a beginning, as from God immediately; especially considering it hath not only beginning; but perisheth also."[56] It is not, or not only, the ability of the material organism to hinder the operation of the soul that Bright seeks to prevent. If the disposition of the material body can unsettle and even unseat the divine image, the ability of God to work through man is ultimately disrupted.

This strong line of separation is held by Calvinists such as William Perkins. Perkins argues for a qualitative difference between the disease of the body and that of the soul, between melancholy and what he terms a "holy desperation: which is when a man is ... out of all hope euer to attaine saluation by any strength or goodnes of his own." "Many," he writes, "are of the opinion that this sorrow for sinne is nothing else but a Melancholike passion."[57] Crucially, the desperation that Perkins describes is central to Calvinist spiritual existence and one of the chief instruments by which a congregant can determine the state of his or her election. Spiritual crisis cannot be a medical problem precisely because it is the means by which God works through the conscience of the elect. Such affliction therefore cannot be thought to have a basis in the natural operations of the body. Perkins spends a good deal of ink in making the distinction: "Sorow that comes by melancholy ariseth onely of that humour annoying the body, but this other sorrow ariseth of a mans sinnes for which his concience accuseth him. Melancholly may be cured by phisicke[,] this sorow can not be cured by any thing but by the blood of Christ."[58] The recuperation of spiritual crisis—as opposed to physical melancholy—was clearly an urgent theological problem for Calvinists. An abundance of Calvinist spiritual manuals press the terms of Galenic materialism into the service of the prescribed treatment for spiritual depression. The use of medical language as metaphor in the instruction of spiritual health underscores the absence of a physical remedy for spiritual crisis. As John Abernethy writes, the remedies of his text "are not gathered from amongst animals, vegetables, or minerals, (a whole world of those are not able to ease the soule for one moment) but out of the cleere streames of reason, and most pure and perfect Fountaine of Diuine Scripture. The body and soule haue their fittest physicke out of their owne proper elements: that from beneath, this from aboue."[59] Galenic terminology is turned into an empty—and emptied—device instead of an applied medical therapy. Which is to say that the terms are evacuated by the very displacement of their use.[60] But this anxious effort to decouple soul from body, far from conveying that committed Calvinists succeed in releasing the soul from the degrading effects of the humors, rather suggests the failure of the project.

Bright also insists that religious passion is unresponsive to medical remedies. In claiming the soul's condition to be outside the scope of natural philosophy, Bright's strategy might at first appear to replicate that of Melanchthon. But while Melanchthon insists that proof of the soul's transcendent nature lies in scripture, the operations of its faculties are detected through, and dependent upon, the body's technologies. Indeed, because the "whole man" was Fallen, Lutheran conception made reason an impaired instrument.[61] There is an obvious argument against the idea that the body could disrupt the reception of grace: that God tempers his elect to receive it. That Calvinists do not employ this argument is telling. One of the things it demonstrates is that the dispute had to be engaged on its own terms: the accretion of philosophy from antiquity forward could not be answered by doctrine alone; rather, natural philosophy had to be pressed into the service of doctrine.

However much Bright wants to insist upon the "vnmoueable, and vnchaungeable facultie of the soule," the soul is still vulnerable to the assault of the humors in his construction.[62] His attempt to recuperate natural philosophy for a Calvinist ethos logically fails. Like the Calvinist divines, he wants to insist that the soul "cannot beare any mixture" with the body but that it is a simple and uniform faculty, "and as the soule is one, and indued with one only facultie, so the spirit is also one."[63] The soul is affected by body and spirit "as the instrument hindreth the worke of the artificer; which is not by altering his skill, or diminishing his cunning, but by deprauing the action through vntowardnesse of toole, and fault of instrument."[64] But these divisions are rhetorical. If the spirit, as an organic faculty, is susceptible to humoral fluctuations and is able to pervert the intentions of the soul, the effect upon the human subject is the same. Bright admits that if the mind, "the soueraigne [part] of our nature," were buffeted by "diuersitie of complexion" or an "excesse of the foure humours," this would necessarily call into question the impervious nature of the soul.[65] If reason, moral judgment, and the apprehension of faith can be fatally disturbed by the "temper of the bodie" then the fate of the soul is tenuously poised.

While Bright fashions reason as the machinist in the operation of body and spirit, Donne sees cognition—notably, reason—as a product of the interaction of body and soul. In Donne's conception, the mind does not manage the body in purely instrumental terms. His definition of the mind as "those thoughts and affections and passions, which . . . soul [and] body . . . [produce] by their communication," makes clear that while the musician motivates the instrument, it is the instrument itself that makes music. This is simply to say that the instrument is requisite in the production of sound and that the body is needed to produce reason. Donne may wish the body's operations to be subject to reason, but elsewhere it is evident that he cannot reasonably sustain the idea. "Every distemper of the body," he writes to Goodyer, "is complicated with the spleen. . . . Every accident is accompanied with heavy clouds of melancholy. . . .

It is the spleen of the mind."⁶⁶ The odd phrase, "the spleen of the mind," underscores the proximity of body and rational mind in Donne's perception.

The impressions of the mind have their inflection in the body as well: melancholy of mind affects the spleen—every "accident" produces black vapors. The relationship is sympathetic. The two-way traffic of soul-body transactions (as opposed to the one-way street attributed to Plato) is abundant in the medical literature of the time, as it is central to Galen's theoretical model. Indeed, Bright's formulations are quite unusual in contemporary medical theory (although clearly not within Calvinist spiritual manuals). Even among medical theorists who perceive a utilitarian purpose for the body in relation to the soul, such as Levine Lemnie, care of the body represents care of the soul: "it [is] right needfull . . . to haue a diligent eye and respect to the body, leaste (otherwise) it should be a burthen to the Soule, and hinder it from matters of . . . wayght and worthines."⁶⁷ In the next sentence, Lemnie treats mind and immortal soul as overlapping in their offices and situates a "healthy" mind within a body of the same quality. For most early modern medical theorists, the health of the body and the mind was mutually constituted. The humoral complexion of the body affected the behavior of the mind, with consequences for the higher faculties of the rational soul. Conversely, the impressions of the mind were also understood to leave traces of their passage in the body's temper.

"Humorous is my contrition"

Change in devotion, infidelity, and idolatry are the persistent themes of the Holy Sonnets. The exposition of the anxieties that attend them issues forth in a humoral language that represents the fluctuations of the soul and the fluctuations of the body as sympathetic and reinforcing. In the context of a medical system that allows the attainted body to impair the activity of the soul—or, the spirit under such subjection to frustrate the soul's intentions—the source of belief is inevitably suspect, the material corruption of wrong belief is potentially long-standing, and the faith in God's ability to act irresistibly is challenged.

> Oh, to vex me, contraries meet in one:
> Inconstancy unnaturally hath begot
> A constant habit, that when I would not

> I change in vows and in devotion.
> As humorous is my contrition
> As my profane love, and as soon forgot;
> As riddlingly distempered, cold and hot;
> As pray'ng, as mute; as infinite, as none.
> I durst not view Heav'n yesterday, and today
> In prayers and flattering speeches I court God.
> Tomorrow I quake with true fear of his rod.
> So my devout fits come and go away
> Like a fantastic ague, save that here
> Those are my best days when I shake with fear.[68]

When Donne depicts his conversion in little and in large, it is through the fluctuations of his body; his inconstancy is described as a bodily disorder. Indeed, the only constant in the poem is his changeable nature. The distemper of the poem is not a metaphor. Change of faith is read in and through the body because that is how Donne understands it. His "change ... in devotion" not only causes him to doubt his own election but also forces him to regard with suspicion the very instabilities of the nature that produced it. The anxiety that Donne felt concerning his conversion has long been recognized. But Donne's convictions concerning the agency of the body recognized the possibility that the body's constitution could contribute to delusion and misapprehension.

The potential for bodily disorder or distemper to impair the soul undermines God's agency and his ability to act upon the elect. This is what produces the frequent, and frequently abrupt, reversal of many of the Holy Sonnets. The love of the speaking subject is profane because it is human and therefore polluted by the substance of the organism. His crisis of faith is expressed through the changeable body that is the source of his devout convulsions. He therefore turns to the stabilizing force that can secure his salvation. But whether God will intercede, and indeed whether God *can* intercede, is a point on which Donne is desperately uncertain. He is not at all sure that his sickness is the sign of spiritual affliction and not a "Melancholike passion." The sudden insertion of God at the conclusion of the poem is a remedial fantasy: a frantic attempt to convince himself that God's hand is upon him.

Critics of Donne's work, from Carey to Cummings, Stachniewski to Strier, Targoff to Trevor, have struggled with how to identify the voice that emerges from the Holy Sonnets.[69] The personal, and at times inartful, address of these works has provoked the question "of to whom such unreasonable poems might reasonably be addressed." As Brian Cummings writes, "Sometimes their only satisfactory audience is God or Donne himself."[70] Certainly the artifice of form demands an acceptance of them as highly wrought pieces. Moreover, while some of the sonnets appear in only one manuscript, others are reproduced in as many as fifteen. Packages of poems that Donne sent to patrons additionally make clear that some of these sonnets were addressed to outside readers. In the analysis of Donne's lyrics most critics have settled on a "biographically inflected interpretation" or upon the speaker of the sonnets as a fashioned projection of the historical author.[71] Since at least some of the sonnets may have been intended to convince Lady Bedford of his "Christian resolution,"[72] they should not be read as "literary incarnation[s] of . . . mental states."[73] But they must be read as representations of Donne's religious conviction—a convergence of identity, faith, and performance. Donne is an actor in his sonnets just as he is an actor of his sermons: both are performance pieces. This is not to suggest that Donne's belief was insincere; it does not reject the possibility that his passion sometimes (even often) overtook the poems. The sonnets are intended to anatomize a faith. It is the faith of a convert.

In defending Goodyer against the indictment of a "various," or changeable, religious nature, Donne writes that he is "angry, that any should think, you had in your Religion peccant humors, defective, or abundant."[74] Transfer of affection to the Catholic faith is an index of a corrupt humoral disposition. Donne is not, in his appraisal of this "fault of humour," claiming that the Church of Rome provides no spiritual sustenance—for both churches, the Catholic and Reformed, are "sister teats of [God's] graces."[75] But he is saying that each church appeals to a particular constitution: "As some bodies are as wholesomly nourished as ours, with Akornes . . . which would be dangerous to us, if we for them should leave our former habits . . . so are many souls well fed with such formes, and dressings of Religion, as would distemper and misbecome us, and make us corrupt towards God."[76] Douglas Trevor has observed that Donne describes his faith in humoral terms.[77] But he reads this rhetorical arrangement as a set of image clusters, a collection of terms descriptive of how Donne's melancholy mind informs his religious inquiry. Donne's terms are far more embodied than critics have previously been prepared to admit.[78] Part of the reason for this resistance, no doubt, is that Donne is notably irenical in his attitude to Christian religion. The habitation of religious identity in the human, humoral body seems peculiarly essential in one whose posture is so flexible. The other reason, of course, is that Donne's religious identity itself, as his vexed sonnet makes clear, is not stable.

"Much of Donne's poetry," Molly Murray writes, "registers his own changeability with regret or even disgust."[79] Donne is anxious about his changeable nature precisely because his membership in both churches, at different points in his life, renders the status of his constitution uncertain. His declaration concerning the imprint of conversion is not a metaphor but a material description. Donne is claiming that once religion is dented in the mind, its dint remains in the body as well. He tells Goodyer: "You shall seldome see a Coyne, upon which the stamp were removed, though to imprint it better, but it looks awry and squint. . . . And so, for the most part, do mindes which have received divers impressions."[80] Given the transactions of the "three parts [of] Soul, and Body and Minde" that Donne outlines, it would be impossible for the "divers impressions" of the mind to fail to impress the body. And while the rational soul is held in close relation to the body in Donne's construction, he is appealing to current physiological assumptions. Thomas Wright claims that it is the work of "naturall Philosophers, to explicate the maner how an operation that lodgeth in the soule can alter the body, and mooue the humors from one place to another."[81] Donne's description of conversion in his letter to Goodyer suggests that belief itself had a temper and that religious identity could be stamped on the body. He reads the body as a humoral text and sees religion inscribed there. The problem for Donne is that his body is a palimpsest.

The sonnets record the anxieties of a person of uncertain constitution. The persistent question for the poet-speaker of the sonnets is whether his humoral disposition makes him fit for God or "corrupt towards [him]." Holy Sonnet 1, "As due by many titles," begins in the attitude of complete confidence. The speaker affirms himself God's creature ("I am thy son," 5). He enumerates the reasons for ownership: God's creation of him; God's defense of him through Christ. But the poem soon assumes the position of uncertainty that, in spite of his resignation, God will accept him:

> Why doth the devil then usurp in me?
> Why doth he steal—nay ravish—that's thy right?
> Except thou rise and for thine own work fight,
> Oh, I shall soon despair, when I do see
> That thou lov'st mankind well, yet wilt not choose me,
> And Satan hates me, yet is loath to lose me.
> (9–14)

Stachniewski observes that "the lines are haunted by the fear that God will disdain to intervene in [his] behalf."[82] But the cause of God's disdain—or, perhaps, his incapacity—is the direct object of the final couplet: "That thou lov'st mankind well, yet wilt not choose me, / And Satan hates me, yet is loath to lose me." The lines are hendecasyllabic and, more significantly, make logical sense absent the concluding word. The addition of "me" to the end of each line breaks the meter and spoils the rhyme.[83] But it nicely underscores the problem. The two enjambments of the poem, at its beginning and middle, are also completed by the same word: "I resign / Myself"; "I betrayed / Myself" (1–2; 7–8). The structural revelations of the poem are that the speaking subject cannot resign himself to God; he is not God's creature. Instead, the obliteration of God's image in him at the Fall assures that not only can he not act for himself but God might not be able to act for him. The poem is frequently read in terms of God's revulsion. But another interpretation is available: one might read Donne's awkward imposition of himself on the poem as the formal enactment of his predicament: "I betrayed / Myself." Just as the inclusion of his subjectivity impairs the poetry at the end, so the fact of it ruins the harmony that he could have with God. Instead of God's rejection, the focus of the poem falls on the speaker's (involuntary) resistance to God. This is consistent with the hesitation of the opening line: "I resign / Myself."

His melancholy and his own physical frailty left Donne with an anxious concentration upon the operations of the body. He frequently fashions his body as a site of struggle: "God ... when he could not get into me, by standing, and knocking ... hath shaked the house, this body, with agues and palsies, and set the house on fire with fevers ... and frighted the master of the house, my soul ... and so made an entrance into me."[84] But as often happens in Donne, such certain declarations of God's care are inevitably followed by despondency that "god should lose and frustrate ... his own purposes ... and leave me, and cast me away."[85] The fevers that he suffers are suddenly the receipt of hell. Calvinist devotional practice demands the experience of dejection. But for Donne, repeatedly, the source of his hopelessness is his physical self:

> I am a little world made cunningly
> Of elements and an angelic sprite,
> But black sin hath betrayed to endless night
> My world's both parts, and, oh, both parts must die.[86]
>
> (ll. 1–4)

Donne quibbles on the term "sprite."[87] While the whole nature of human being is body and soul (or "angelic sprite"), those "parts" that inhabit the world—the earthbound "elements"—are composed of body and spirit. The "spirits in man," Donne claims, "are of a kind of middle nature between soul and body."[88] Because of this intermediate status, Donne uses the term "spirit" to signify "either the soul itself, or the vital spirits . . . or the superior faculties of the soul in a regenerate man."[89] The "manifold acceptations"[90] of the term allow Donne to suggest that the perishable components, body and spirit, whose death is assured by original sin, can condemn the other part of the constellation of the human, the "angelic sprite," to death as well.

Galenic materialism held a correspondence between microcosm and macrocosm, between the four humors and the elements of earth, air, fire, and water. The body's materials morph into the elements of the cosmos, but the poem still unmistakably inhabits the human organism. The conceit of the poem is that his worldly concerns encompass the fate of all men. But if it looks to the horizon of new discovery, it returns to the sphere of the body. If it peers over the edge of Apocalypse, into the fire of final judgment, the "vngodly [man]" (2 Pet. 3:7) incinerated is the speaker of the poem.

> But oh [the body] must be burnt! Alas, the fire
> Of lust and envy have burnt it heretofore,
> And made it fouler: let their flames retire,
> And burn me, O God, with a fiery zeal
> Of thee and thy house, which doth in eating heal.
> (ll. 10–14)

In the end, the reader is returned to the dwelling of his burning body. Donne makes good use of Psalm 69 in his conclusion: "I am become a stranger vnto my brethren. . . . For the zeale of thine house hathe eaten me, and the rebukes of them that rebuked thee, are fallen vpon me" (Ps. 69:8–9). But rather than follow the scriptural verse and be consumed by a holy passion, the speaker instead consumes the bread of sacred remembrance, the body of Christ.[91] Donne's shift in syntax, so that eating the sign of the Passion heals the zealous Christian, reveals a radical underpinning idea. The Host, the foundational sign for both Protestant and Catholic churches, and the most contested symbol between them, is restorative to all Christians. It is unclear which house is meant: the institutional church or the individual. But Donne's use of a biblical narrative in which the speaker's religious zeal alienates him from his "brethren" is transformed into a poetic moment that superimposes Protestant, Catholic, and Christian.

In his global application of humoralism, Donne can conceive of a Christian fellowship; but in most of the Holy Sonnets, what he imagines is the fatal error of wrong belief. When he pleads with Christ to "Show me . . . thy spouse, so bright and clear" ("Show me, dear Christ," 1), he seems to need, as Murray observes, to believe his adjectives more than to receive an answer.[92] "For such as haue receiued the gift of true faith," Perkins writes, "haue also another gift of discerning whereby they see and know their own faith."[93] Donne receives no such comfortable assurance. That Donne does not feel assured of the status of his salvation leaves him to question if he is constitutionally prepared to receive God. Since he has been a member of both churches, he is uncertain which religion "distemper[s] and misbecome[s]" him. Further, he cannot be sure that conversion eradicates the "peccant humours" of a former faith.[94]

The polluted creature that repels God is standard Christian typology. The fleshy orientation of the sonnets has long been understood to signal the corruption of original sin. This reading is undeniably available in the poems. But beneath the surface of the sonnets, a network of humors flows through the lines, betraying underlying anxieties about the fluids beneath the flesh. Holy Sonnet 2 ("O my black soul!"), with its exclusive address to the soul, seems entirely separate from any operation of the body:

> O make thyself with holy mourning black,
> And red with blushing, as thou art with sin;
> Or wash thee in Christ's blood, which hath this might:
> That, being red, it dyes red souls to white.
> (11–14)

And yet Donne is reading a complexion of the soul here. On the subject of the soul that is most acceptable to God, Donne says:

> There are complexions that cannot blush; there growes a blacknesse, a sootinesse upon the soule, by custome in sin, which overcomes all blushing, all tendernesse. White alone is palenesse, and God loves not a pale soule, a soule possest with a horror, affrighted with a diffidence, and distrusting his mercy. Rednesse alone is anger, and vehemency, and distemper, and God loves not such a red soule, a soule that sweats in sin, that quarrels for sin, that revenges in sin. But that whitenesse

that preserves it selfe, not only from being died all over in any foule colour, from contracting the name of any habituall sin, and so to be called such or such a sinner, but from taking any spot, from coming within distance of a tentation, or of a suspition, is that whiteness, which God meanes, when he sayes, *Thou art all faire my Love, and there is no spot in thee*. ... To avoid these spots, is that whitenesse that God loves in the soule. But there is a rednesses that God loves too; which is the Erubescence that we speak of; an aptnesse in the soule to blush, when any of these spots doe fall upon it.[95]

Expressions that describe a "soule that sweats" in its "distemper" might suggest that Donne's humoral language is altogether metaphoric. But this language is affected by the affinity that Donne perceives between body and soul. "Never say," Donne charges, that "God asks the heart, that is, the soul, and therefore rewards the soul, and hath no respect to the body.... Never go about to separate the thoughts of the heart, from the college, from the fellowship of the body."[96] Soul and body mimic each other because they are mutually dependent and informing: "[God] made us all of earth, and all of red earth. Our earth was red, even when it was in Gods hands: a rednesse that amounts to a shame-fastnesse, to a blushing at our own infirmities, is imprinted in us, by Gods hand. For this rednesse, is but a conscience, a guiltinesse of needing a continuall supply, and succession of more, and more grace.... And another rednesse from His hand too, the bloud of his Sonne, for that bloud was effused by Christ, in the value of the ransome for All ... and this rednesse is, in the nature thereof, as extensive, as the redness derived from *Adam* is; Both reach to all."[97] The blood of conscience is also the blood in the face. This mimetic relationship is promoted by the medical philosophy of numerous treatises of the period. Wright maintains that "there is no passion" of the mind "but that it altereth extreamly some of the four humors of the body."[98] While Donne is disturbed by this changeability, he is also fascinated by the mutable possibilities of the flesh.

Of the four extant sermons on the conversion of Paul (preached between 1624 and 1629), only one focuses on the moment of conversion itself—and the body is the site of the conversion.[99] Donne chooses the episode of Saul's mortification ("*he fell to the ground*, And *he fell blind*")[100] to expound on earth. "Earth" is the clay of human invention, the source of bodily weakness, and the inconstant substance that draws the congregant toward hell: "You heap earth upon your soules, and encumber them with more and more flesh, by a superfluous and luxuriant diet." But this signature of the flesh is also the means of transformation: "There are natures, (there are scarce any other) that dispose not themselves to God, but by affliction."[101] The trials of the flesh—weakness, infirmity, old age, and death—are the means by which the clay of the body is remolded.

> Thou hast made me: and shall thy work decay?
> Repair me now, for now mine end doth haste:
> I run to death, and death meets me as fast,
> And all my pleasures are like yesterday.
> I dare not move my dim eyes any way,
> Despair behind, and death before, doth cast
> Such terror; and my feebled flesh doth waste
> By sin in it, which towards hell doth weigh.
> (ll. 1–8)

The sonnet pulls the themes and language of Psalm 38 into its poetic ambit: "There is nothing sounde in my flesh, because of thine angere; neither *is* there rest in my bones because of my sinne.... I am weakened" (Ps. 38:3–8).[102] But the penitential Psalm from which the poem draws is foul with bodily corruption: "My wounds putrified, and corrupt because of my foolishnes.... My reines are ful of burning, and there *is* nothing sounde in my flesh" (Ps. 38:5–7). The sonnet invokes chastising the flesh as a means of "repair[ing]" the state of the soul; the psalmic images to which it alludes, however, are gruesome depictions of an oozing body. The speaker of the Psalm is left alienated due to his repellent physical state ("my louers and my friends stand aside from my plague" [38:11]). His "heart panteth," and "the light of [his] eyes, euen thei [is] not [his] owne" (Ps. 38:10) just as the speaker of the sonnet "dare not move [his] dim eyes any way" due to "such terror." These parallels matter in that the conclusion of the poem departs significantly from that of the Psalm. The sonnet insists upon a loving God who rescues the subject: the gross substance of his earthly body is reformed to a metal that cannot refuse God's magnetic powers. This confident portrayal of irresistible grace is undercut by the allusive presence of the Psalm: "Forsake me not, O Lord: be not far from me, my God" (Ps. 38:21). The Psalm permits a different end—one in which the subject is left pleading for relief. Doubt is introduced through an intertextual strategy: the Psalm does not end in transformation but rather concludes where the poem began.

The humors are a recurrent theme of Donne's imagination because of the problem they pose to his election. In many of the Holy Sonnets, the instabilities of his faith imitate the fluctuations of his body. In those sonnets, where no such fluid transactions occur, the source of his "thoughts and affections and passions," and their effect upon the status of his soul, still seems to touch the speaking subject of the poems:

> If faithful souls be alike glorified
> As angels, then my father's soul doth see,
> And adds this, ev'n to full felicity,
> That valiantly I Hell's wide mouth o'erstride.
> ("If faithful souls," 1–4)

"If" all faithful souls are beautified in the afterlife, regardless of religious affiliation, "then" his father's soul can bear witness to his efforts.[103] There is a double meaning here: Donne plays upon the debate of whether or not angels knew the thoughts of men to also raise the doubt that his father's soul has achieved heaven.[104] He then converts questions of how we are known, and can be known, to the researches of the soul. The "mind's white truth" (8) that he hopes will be visible quickly becomes the dark and inward contemplation of sin. Once again, the speaker searches for relief and reassurance: "Then turn, / O pensive soul, to God, for he knows best / Thy true grief, for he put it in my breast" (ll. 12–14).[105] But the origin of the thought is complicated. The grief that concludes the poem might be melancholy ("that humour annoying the body") or the "sorrow [that] ariseth of a mans sinnes for which his concience accuseth him." Of course the speaker is insisting on the latter, as this would be an index of God's affection. But he cannot be sure: "if . . . then." If God cultivates the care of his soul, then his grief is spiritual crisis. Doubt creeps into the final sentence through a shift in possessive pronouns: the address to the soul ("Thy") seems to convert to a corporeal self ("my").

Donne's portrait of religious identity in the Holy Sonnets exhibits a conviction of the material presence of religious disposition. Medical philosophy had mapped the physiological implications of thoughts, affections, and passions. Donne's apprehension of the substance of thought caused him to question the status of his own salvation. The humors are uncertain waters upon which to navigate the passage of the soul, and for Donne the ripple effects of prior passions and beliefs within the fluid transactions of the body were a source of acute anxiety. If Donne did not understand religion, as itself, as a material category, he at least apprehended religious identity in terms of its material consequences.

But there is no reason to think that Donne was alone in his appreciation of the material effects of belief. Bright writes his treatise to correct those who "haue esteemed the vertues themselves, yea religion, no other thing but as the body hath ben tempered"; the extent of Calvinist efforts to separate soul from body in the cultural imagination indicates that this estimation, which Bright deplores, was common to no small number of people. The distinction that modern scholarship makes between physiology and culture, between matter and belief, is not evident in this early modern moment. Donne's sonnets and sermons had an audience to whom their terms appealed. This alone should force a reconsideration of the matter of belief in early modern religious identity.

"Soules drown'd in flesh and blood"

While Donne exhibits anxieties concerning the physiological causes and consequences of wrong belief, this does not prompt him to write a racial script— not least because in this context, he would have been implicated in it. But *A Poem on the Late Massacre in Virginia*, written by Christopher Brooke on the occasion of the attack of the Powhatan tribes upon Jamestown, demonstrates how the ideas exhibited in Donne's writing can be turned to notions of religious essentialism and projects of racial polemic. Brooke was a lawyer who shared chambers with Donne while the two were at Lincoln's Inn, but it is also clear that the pair were close: Brooke was a witness to Donne's marriage to Ann More in 1601, and his brother Samuel conducted the ceremony. In the last eleven years of his life, Brooke lived in the house across from Donne on Drury Lane in London, and he left a number of paintings to his "deere ancient and worthie freind D[o]c[t]or Dunn," upon his passing.[106] While the two men were evidently friends, the nature of their intimacy late in life is not clear—there are no surviving letters, such as Donne's correspondence with Goodyer (but, living across the street from each other, there would also be no need). While both answered the March 1622 attack on the settlement, and, as Kasey Evans has observed, both used humoral terms in their address, their responses were radically different.[107]

I have argued that the production of race is a strategy, the formulation of which depends upon both objectives and targets. It is moments such as this— where a set of shared cultural beliefs are applied differently—that we are best able to perceive this production. If race is constructed out of available cultural materials, it also true that those materials are not themselves, by their nature, inherent to its construction. I have relied heavily upon the work of intellectual historians—Gowland, Hankins, Des Chene—none of whom perceive the racializing potential of the work that they have done.[108] Justin E. H. Smith, however, has recently argued that a "historical examination of the emergence of our current racial categories is necessary in order to gain a clearer picture of what is recent and contingent in racial thinking, and what, by contrast, is deep-seated."[109] In actually turning his attention to race, Smith traces these "current racial categories" back to the seventeenth century and to much of the medical theory concerning melancholy and temperament that I have been outlining here. But Smith fails to consider the underlying religious polemic that animates the humoral terms of a cleric such as Burton. (Indeed, one of the striking features of early modern English medical treatises is the number composed by clerics, precisely because of the entanglements of psychosomatic relations at the time.)[110] Instead, he argues for a number of "false positives"— narratives that *look like* race but are instead of another character—prior to the eighteenth-century emergence of a scientific race concept in which "a person's nature came to be associated with his or her external physical features."[111] But this is not the race concept of sixteenth- and seventeenth-century England, nor was phenotype initially its premise. And if we are to understand the "deep-seated" effects of this early modern construction of race, we need to explore the process by which phenotype became a marker for a prior racial construction premised on religious difference.

While Brooke sets out in his *A Poem on the Late Massacre in Virginia* to "Shew [the] natures" of peoples in terms of the regions they inhabit and their humoral effects, what he actually produces is a regional map of religious identity. Brooke's narrative is a rehearsal of pagan regions and religions that are ultimately supplanted by the blessed plot of England where climate and conditions encourage Christian faith. England, of course, had the ideal conditions in which to foster faith. (This is the principal reason that Catholics within England proper are regarded differently from their counterparts in other nations.) Christian and European are not coterminous categories in England at the turn of the seventeenth century, but the perceived potential for reformation, of both body and soul, figured largely in how the human subject was classified—or, as Brooke exhibits in his characterization of Indigenous peoples as "creatures," in whether the subject is regarded as human at all.

But it is important to bear in mind that when we read Brooke's poem, we are reading the construction of a racial script. The confederated Indigenous tribes killed 347 people in a matter of hours in an attempt to eradicate the English foothold in the early colony of Virginia. But prior to this moment, the tribes were regarded as potential, if suspect, partners in the English New World. "From the 1500s into the early 1600s," Joyce E. Chaplin writes, "when the English thought and wrote about technology, they saw forms of equivalence between their culture and those of natives, and they exchanged information (for instance, about food) and tools (such as iron implements) with Indians."[112] Indigenous peoples were frequently imagined as a form of Adam, or as early Britons.[113] Of course, Chaplin argues that "the English saw nothing but separation and differentiation" when it came to the comparison of their bodies and those of the Indigenous peoples.[114] But I would argue that this occurred after the attack of the Virginia Algonquins on Jamestown. This was when the meaning of Indigenous peoples changed: when, instead of partners, they were perceived as colonial subjects, and when their bodies became exploitable property. From 1622, it becomes possible to hold an Indigenous person in slavery.[115]

An early investor and legal advisor to the Virginia Company, Brooke seems to have penned the "company's official lament" for the colonists.[116] He begins (once he recovers his speech) with a prayer:

> O thou *Eternall Beeing*,
> All sublunary Creatures ouerseeing,
> Vile (in respect of Man) to whom th'hast giuen
> An Arme of sceptered Powre, and vnder *Heauen*
> Made him they Substitute, to take command,
> Predominating all Works of thy hand:
> Why do'st thou not thy Care to him extend?
> No difference betweene a hellish Fiend
> And natures Angell? O shall brutish rage
> Act Scænes so bloody (sparing Sex nor Age)
> On this worlds Theater? shall men-monsters, fell,
> (Confin'd in vnbeliefe, and damn'd to Hell)
> So many Images of *Christ* deface,
> Sign'd with his Crosse, regenerate by his Grace?
>   (A4r)[117]

Brooke represents a contest between demons from Hell and "natures Angell[s]." Significantly, heaven does not take part in the contest—but in the poem's conceit, heaven fails to take the part of "Man," who has been extended control over all things under it. This construction of power relations is one to which we are accustomed in colonial contexts: the Indigenous people of North America are inhuman "Fiend[s] and "monster[s]" because they refuse to be ruled by "The true Inhabitants" of the land who have only recently arrived to "propagate *Religion*, and [God's] Glorie" (A4r). The implication is that (English) Christian faith will be cultivated in the New World only by strong tillage: rooting out the pagan forces that are planted there.

In *The Tempest*, Miranda gives voice to a colonial idiom:

> Abhorred slave,
> Which any print of goodness wilt not take,
> Being capable of all ill! I pitied thee,
> Took pains to make thee speak, taught thee each hour
> One thing or other: when thou didst not, savage,
> Know thine own meaning, but wouldst gabble like
> A thing most brutish, I endow'd thy purposes
> With words that made them known. But thy vile race,
> Though thou didst learn, had that in't which good natures
> Could not abide to be with.
> (I.ii.353–62)[118]

Caliban is "earth" (I.ii.316) who will not take the imprint of religion or language (even though his "gabbl[ing]" suggests he has his own). His subjection is guaranteed by their religious and cultural superiority. Such a construction is visible in Brooke's description of George Thorpe's failed ministration:

> Thou that wert vsed to negotiate
> In matters of Religion, as of State;
> Who didst attempt to make those *Indians* know
> Th'Eternall GOD; their sinewie necks to bow
> To his obedience; and on that ground
> To make them apt to what thou didst propound
> For our Commerce with them; their good, our peace,
> And both to helpe with mutuall increase.
> (B4r)

But being "earth" still implies clay that might be molded. Like Donne's image of the imprint of the mind that has its reproduction in the impression upon the material body, "earth" still holds the potential to respond to certain pressures. And Thorpe's failed mission points to a different colonial project that conquers through proselytization "and by propagation of [the] *Gospell*, to recouer out of the armes of the Diuell, a number of poore and miserable soules . . . [and] to endeauour the fulfilling, and accomplishment of the number of the elect."[119] Such a project presumes the recuperation of pagan subjects in the New World. But Brooke renders such recovery impossible.

"For . . . consider what those Creatures are," he writes, "(I cannot call them men) no Character / Of God in them: Soules drown'd in flesh and blood" (C1r). Rather than being "Confin'd in vnbeliefe," but capable of redemption, Indigenous people are put beyond reach. They are all earth: indeed, "The very dregs, garbage, and spawne of Earth" (C1r). Here, the rational soul is not vulnerable to the body's temperament but entirely consumed by it: the spark of God remaining after the Fall is extinguished in a flood of humoral disorder. Brooke's reading of human diversity in the New World is through the optic of natural philosophy, but the lens is distorted by a racial ideology. If Melanchthon's revision of natural philosophy made the body a humoral map through which to read the soul, Brooke's mapping of New World "creatures" discovers them without one.

Brooke also maps human natures ordered according to the disposition of divine will, and each "Region, Contrey, Clyme" is accounted in terms of its humoral effects. On the African continent, the "Sunne [is] so firie hot, it scorches men; / Singes their hayre, and (from their heads to soales) / Makes them in nature seeme like breathing coals" (B1r). While blood and temper run hot at the equator, the sun "thinns his heate" in the North until it "Freezeth [the] Bloo[d]" in the veins. This "passionate weather of inconstancie" (B1r) is mimicked in the temperament of the human tenants of foreign lands, but Christians (presumably English Christians) are enjoined to "grow / Where yee are plac't, that ye may plant, and sow / To multiply your store" (B2r). Of course, Mary Floyd-Wilson has considered early modern constructions of the humor of nations, what she has termed "geohumoralism," and their relationship to constructions of race.[120] But Brooke depicts not merely the nature, but the nature of the soul: Indigenous people are constitutionally deprived of souls; but the English are prime subjects for the cultivation of right religion. If there is any doubt of how their disposition will thrive in a New World, it is refused in Brooke's poem. While the Powhatans assume the "vgly formes" of "Hell-hounds" (B3r), the English colonists are the "Images of *Christ*" cut down.[121]

Of course, Brooke's depiction is intended to draw more colonists across the Atlantic. The English are encouraged to plant religion in this "Field of *Golgotha*" (B2v) that is left in the wake of the attack. But the challenge is also to wrest the land from "Errors of Nature," who were not even among "those creatures / Adam gaue names to" (C1r). Certainly, the Indigenous peoples of North America are not meant to inherit the earth. In *Purchas his Pilgrimes* published in 1625, Samuel Purchas first lays out arguments for why it is *not* "lawfull for Christians . . . to usurpe the goods and lands of Heathens": "they are," he writes, "villains not to us; but to our and their Lord," and they also participate in the "one bloud [of] all Nations of men."[122] But the land deal is rescinded on the grounds of inhumanity of Indigenous people specifically: "if they bee not worthy of the name of a Nation, being wilde and Savage: yet as Slaves, bordering rebells, ecommunicates and out-lawes are lyable to the punishments of Law, and not to the priviledges; So is it with these Barbarians, Borderers and Out-lawes of Humanity." By this logic, "England may both by Law of Nature and Nations challenge Virginia for her owne peculiar property."[123] Purchas's argument is far more legalistic in its terms, but it concludes in a similar place: you can only negotiate contracts and laws with other human beings. The rights to Virginia are not due to "the naturall Inheritance of the English" but rather "the unnaturall outcries of so many unnaturally murthered" that commands vengeance and the "rooting out [of] the authors and actors" of the attack.[124]

As Ania Loomba and Jonathan Burton have observed, "both culture and nature are organically interconnected . . . concepts that . . . [are] central to the ideologies of human difference."[125] The dark and demonic other can be written many ways—but written in the blood achieves permanent obduracy to faith. Cultural and natural philosophical scripts are collaborative and mutually reinforcing in the construction of race and racism, but they can perform different work. However much Purchas portrays Indigenous people as "Slaves . . . ecommunicates and out-lawes" to humanity, he still allows for their recuperation. In numbering the reasons that the English should take possession of Virginia, the first is the propagation of religion and the second is "Humanity" that recognizes a "common Nature" and "forbids [us] to turne our eyes from our owne flesh; yea commands us to love our neighbors as our selves, and to play the good Samaritan with these our neighbours . . . to recover them if it be possible, as by Religion, from the power of Sathan to God."[126] In the project to "plant Christianity [and] to produce and multiply Christians," the natives to the land are not beyond recovery.[127] But in the Galenic language that flows through Brooke's poem, the disposition of the humors in indigenous bodies obstructs God's activity within the soul until there is "no Character / Of God in them."

It is only possible to enslave an Indigenous person after 1622.[128] The legal rationale is their inherent, and inherited, paganism.[129] Enslaved Indigenous people and Africans could negate, or at least challenge, English claims to their labor through conversion to Christianity—as they did in increasing numbers in the mid-seventeenth century.[130] This made religion an unstable justification for slavery. Ideas of lineage, blood, and religion converge to produce legal statutes of inherited servitude premised upon a permanent pagan status.[131] A 1667 decree of the Virginia Assembly was the first to assure that "the conferring of baptisme doth not alter the condition of the person as to his bondage or ffreedome."[132] But these ideas of faith transmitted in the blood trade upon the religious essentialism that we see in evidence in Brooke's poem: as "Soules drown'd in flesh and blood," the Indigenous people are only bodies, and the waters of baptism will still not allow faith to grow there.

CHAPTER 2

Bad Faith

The Color of Wrong Religion in Ben Jonson's *The Masque of Blackness* and Mary Wroth's *Pamphilia to Amphilanthus*

> I am blacke, ô daughters of Ierusalém, but comlie, as the frutes of a Kedár, and as the curtines of Salomón.
>
> Regarde me not because I am blacke: for the sunne hathe loked vpon me. The sonnes of my mother were angrie against me: thei made me the keper of the vines: but I kept not mine owne vine.
> —Song of Salomon 1:4-5, Geneva Bible

Melancholy is the principal cause of wrong religion. Excess of melancholy produced the delusion of atheism. In a tradition that spans from Ficino to Burton, we are naturally inclined to love of God and the religious belief that is an index of this is sustained by a tempering of humors in the body. It was precisely the effect of melancholy upon the instrument of the mind that called into question the extent to which the faculties of the rational soul were susceptible to organic properties. But if the soul's condition was vulnerable to the effects of the body, the state of the soul was also legible in the expression of the body's effects. Literary texts supply evidence of how widely disseminated a particular racial discourse was, and to whom, and of how the racial logic was reproduced and redistributed at a specific cultural site. Ben Jonson's *The Masque of Blackness* (1605) shows how the madness of religious error becomes marked on the skin. In its own participation in race-making, the masque rehearses a discourse of religious difference and delusion inhabiting the body and demonstrates the physical mechanics of a process that makes darkness visible.

Molly Murray has argued that *The Masque of Blackness* is a narrative of conversion centered on England's queen, who played a leading role in the masque.[1] Anne was a rumored Catholic convert, and the masque was played at court before her presumed coreligionist, the Spanish ambassador. Murray suggests that the miraculous whitening of the Ethiopian ladies at the end of the masque, through the agency of King James I, was Jonson's message that the queen would be dyed in the colors of the king's devotion. I would instead suggest that the alteration in outward complexion of the queen and her ladies is a demonstration of a change in inward disposition—since skin color is read as the external expression of an internal humoral balance. Jonson graphically portrays the complexion of conversion in his masque—the constitution of the "Catholics" onstage is restored through the virtuous Protestant example of the king of England. Of course, this reading is complicated by the fact that Jonson was a convert to Catholicism at the time of his composition of the masque. We should not, however, regard his hyperbole as a position; we should instead pay attention to the humoral terms of the compliment: "This sun [James] is temperate, and refines / All things on which his radiance shines" (234–35).[2] Just as Dudley Carleton, in his infamous remarks regarding the masque performance, perceived significance in the Spanish ambassador's willingness to blacken his hands and lips in his dance with the queen,[3] I expect the king and court to have read a code of color in terms of religious conversion—and, apparently, so too did Jonson.

Melancholy was not an interior disposition alone—it was both inward and outward, personal and social. In *The Melancholy Assemblage*, Drew Daniel argues that far from being understood simply as an internal terrain of feeling, "melancholy also abides ... in and as a plural social and material assemblage": "In both its intrasubjective and intersubjective dimensions, then, melancholy is an assemblage, and this plurality modulates how we understand the term *melancholy*, taking away its connotations of solitude and interior essence in favor of a model based on social extension. Put crudely, melancholy goes from being something that shows up first and foremost 'in here' to being something that is always also 'out there.'"[4] With six nonnaturals that are both internal and ambient (air, diet, intake and evacuation, sleeping and waking, passions, and exercise), the humors that constitute the body as a moral engine draw from within and without. And the particular affective tremor of melancholy was more than a pressure on the mind; it was an impression upon the soul. As Burton explains: "as the Body workes vpon the mind, by his bad humours, troubling the Spirits, sending grosse fumes into the Braine; and so *per consequens* disturbing the Soule, and all the faculties of it... so on the other side, the minde most effectually workes vpon the Body, producing by his passions and perturbations, miraculous alterations."[5] Any humoral imbalance had social implications. But the special status of melancholy in the network of social meaning lay not just with melancholy as a species of madness; it also posed special challenges to the relationship of the subject to both human and divine. It differed from other species of delirium (mania and frenzy) because it was chronic and produced paranoia, delusion, hallucination, fear, sorrow, solitude, and suicide.[6] The problems such manifestations pose for social interaction are clear enough. But in delusion, sorrow, and suicide, the expressions of melancholy were also frequently offenses against God.

Using black melancholy as an index of religious error indicates an audience that Jonson assumed could read these codes. Indeed, Jonson was probably not the author of the conceit at all: he writes that "it was her majesty's will to have [the women performing the masque] blackamores at first" (18–19). In performing compliance, Anne literally paints herself in the color of bad faith. But the strategy that she pursues also shows the instrumental role that White Christian womanhood plays in legitimating social structures and how the category negotiates the relationships of privilege and power. As Dennis Britton points out: "Not only were Ethiopians known to be Christians, but they were also viewed as a potential ally... [in] Europe's fight against Muslim Turks and Moors. Consequently, the Ethiopians' skin color could not always be viewed as an outward sign of infidel identity."[7] But Jonson's masque depicts the migration of *failed* Christians—Christians in error (or, Catholics)—who seek the right faith and correct course to love.[8] Using Ethiopian women, whose correction is assured once their "blanch[ing]" (225) is promised, produces White Christian womanhood as a figure of compliance and submission. In her appeal to the king, Anne exposes both the strategic value and strategic uses of the category—and the social, cultural, and political value that attaches to it.

Of course, in his claim that the queen was the source of the strategy, Jonson might have been distancing himself from the controversy surrounding the masque in the aftermath of its performance, as Clare McManus notes.[9] But McManus proceeds to make a persuasive case in favor of the queen as the source of the idea.¹⁰ "Blackness," she observes, "is a marker of difference closely connected to Anna's performance career."¹¹ Anne's liminal position as a foreign consort was marked by an escort of "Black" performers who led her into the city of Edinburgh in her first coronation. A similar image had previously been used "to express the problematic relationship of the Scots to their English queen Margaret Tudor."¹² But while the motif of blackness in Scottish court culture was resurrected in Anne's coronation in order to underscore the feminine and foreign as markers of difference, it was increasingly used as an emblem of exclusion in her case. This shift in meaning becomes obvious in the festivities that celebrate the baptism of her first son, Henry, in 1594.

While Anne was present at the banquet in celebration of Henry's baptism at Sterling, she was absent from the ceremony itself and the Countess of Mar supplied her place. (Nor was this an isolated incident, as Anne also did not attend the baptism of Prince Charles in 1600.) McManus suggests the possibility that, given her later conversion to Catholicism, Anne had wanted to be churched and was prevented due to the Catholic resonances of the act. Refusal to enter the church would then be consonant with Catholic practice.¹³ The entertainments surrounding the occasion of the christening set blackness, religious difference, and femininity in close thematic proximity.¹⁴ From the tableau of goddesses drawn in by a Moor at the banquet to the nobles outfitted as Turks, Moors, and Amazons in the tournament performance,¹⁵ these entertainments enact exoticism, religious diversity, and femininity as elements to be suppressed or expelled.

Anne had another example of the conceit of blackness as an emblem of Catholic expulsion available to her from the Danish court. As Mara Wade explains, "The themes of the coronation pageants [of northern European courts] focused on the revival of Classical Rome, its heroes, and its virtues with strongly anti-Catholic tones."¹⁶ In the coronation of Anne's brother, Christian IV, the revival of ancient Roman heroes is preceded in a mumming procession by twelve noblemen dressed as Moors who "wore over their bare bodies black bombazine, so that it appeared as if they were naked" to the waist, and twelve trumpeters "dressed in long Persian coats . . . and on their heads Persian hats."¹⁷ The forces driven out by the Roman heroes—and therefore the ones associated with Catholics in King Christian's mumming pageant—are the Moors and the Persians (or Turks).¹⁸ Since, no doubt, a detailed description of the entire festivity had been transmitted to Anne (and to James) through her brother, Ulrik, Anne had multiple examples of the performance of blackness as an explicit anti-Catholic message.¹⁹

By the time of her second coronation, "the images of otherness so prominent in her Edinburgh entry were subsumed into those of religious difference"—but this time she controlled the message.[20] Anne had converted sometime before (likely influenced by her friendships within an aristocratic Catholic faction at court),[21] and she was installed during her coronation on her throne to watch silently as James received communion.[22] If Jonson can be taken at his word, *The Masque of Blackness* was another attempt on the part of the queen to stage-manage her own performance of religious difference. Given the stage history outlined, blackness was an obvious marker through which to convey religious difference. But in the performances surrounding Anne these emblems of difference, and how they are deployed, appear to fit within constructions that Kim Hall has already described: blackness is a trope "applied not only to dark-skinned Africans but to Native Americans, Indians, Spanish, and even Irish and Welsh as groups that needed to be marked as 'other.'"[23] The performance history does little to explain the humoral terms of the conceit of blackness in Jonson's masque. Each of these groups, however, shares the common situation of being excluded from, and written outside of, the Book.[24] The way that they are represented in association with Catholics, particularly in Protestant propaganda of northern Europe in the sixteenth and early seventeenth centuries, is often in the service of a campaign to render Catholicism no longer Christian but pagan.[25]

Melancholy and the Matter of the Soul

In John Florio's 1598 *A World of Wordes*, an entry for the word "Marano" reads: "A Jew, an Infidell . . . a nickname for a Spaniard."[26] This cluster of meanings throws suspicion of Spanish religious identity into sharp relief. The "Spaniard" is either "Jew" or pagan—but certainly not Christian in either case. Eric Griffin has argued that cultural attacks that targeted Moors, Jews, and Black Africans[27] were coded in assaults on Spanish Catholics and the "Roman Catholic system that generates the spiritual error of the 'pagans' who live according to its . . . logic."[28] Which is to say that these systems of classification are grounded in religious difference.[29] Further (and more crucially for my purposes), the terms and relations of these systems were situated in humoral theory, and thereby essentialized. But while "the essentializing humors of the Black Legend . . . contributed motivating energies to England's drama no less than to the nation's religio-political polemic,"[30] these Spanish associations with blackness are still often read, in critical terms, as allusions to Spain's Moorish past.[31] The extent to which both Irish and Spanish Catholics are negrified, however, raises the prospect that these instances are not, or not only, slighting references to cultural corruption. Rather than treating this discourse of color purely as recreation within a semiotic field, I want to propose that it represents an actually perceived somatic difference based upon religious identity.

The way that the conceit of blackness is deployed in *The Masque of Blackness* shows the humors underwriting the religious difference, and the possibilities of religious transformation, explored in its performance. Jonson's concern with the relationship of body to soul—and with the fluid transactions that negotiate this relationship—pervades the masque and is in evidence from the first time that Niger speaks:

> since the immortal souls of creatures mortal
> Mix with their bodies, yet reserve forever
> A power of separation, I should sever
> My fresh streams from thy brackish, like things fixed,
> Though with thy powerful saltness thus far mixed.
> *Virtue, though chained to earth, will still live free,*
> *And hell itself must yield to industry.*
>   (101–7)

The expressed confidence in the separation of soul and body is misplaced. The extent to which soul and body were separate and inviolate, or involved and mutually corrupting, was the subject of considerable interrogation and debate at this time. Jonson's confident tone is both deliberate and strategic: by maintaining the "power of separation" of soul from body (and Jonson follows Aquinas here),[32] he tacitly asserts that whatever delusions or errors that the mind might hold in the realm of belief, virtue itself, or the fundamental condition of the soul, will be unaffected. He is able, in other words, to make the claim that the soul's condition is uncorrupted by the body's influence (since delusions can be prompted or influenced by humoral imbalances). The soul cannot be misdirected by the body's corrupting influence because "*hell itself* [will] *yield to* [the] *industry*" of untainted virtue.

But in humoral theory, the boundaries of the body, like the waters of Niger himself, are almost themselves liquid. If melancholy appeared subject to physical rules, and physical remedy, the close contact between the worldly and otherworldly through the body seemed contiguous. The liminal position that melancholy occupies has to do with its transformations of the mind and implications of this for the rational soul. Indeed, numerous contemporary arguments make body and soul seem almost fungible in their terms. Philip Melanchthon could himself be accused of such depictions when, for example, he charges Christian physicians with the custody of men's natures in the same section that he describes the transforming and monstrous effects of the melancholy humor.[33] In ascribing virtues and vices to humoral disposition, commentaries in which Melanchthon's treatise was contained go even further in conveying the sense that the soul was circumscribed by the body's effects.[34] Angus Gowland has criticized both Gail Kern Paster and Michael Schoenfeldt as having moved "from a largely accurate account of the relationship between body and soul—in which each influences the other reciprocally—to an inaccurate one in which the physical qualities of the body are more or less determinative of the functions of the soul."[35] But while Gowland is right to insist upon the scrupulous parsing of the offices of soul, body, and spirit in the encounter with each argument—as these vexed and vexing questions produced a surfeit of arguments and argumentative arrangements—it is probably not right to insist that many did not, in fact, produce the effect that "esteemed the vertues themselves, yea religion, no other thing but as the body hath ben tempered."[36]

Because of its associations with madness, and particularly the acute madness of atheism and irreligion, melancholy, more than any other humor, provoked serious questions of whether "the physical qualities of the body [were] . . . determinative of the functions of the soul." Melanchthon is, in many ways, responsible for the misconception. By turning to Galen's definition of the human soul, declaring that its nature could be discerned by its actions, Melanchthon made the soul, if not manifest in the body, legible through it. "By addressing the nature of the soul through the operations of the body," Gowland writes, Melanchthon "was able to demonstrate that the manifestations of psychic dysfunction were physically pathological and spiritually sinful, and that the manifestations of sinfulness could themselves be physical."[37]

Burton declares that Melanchthon calls the "grand sinne of Atheisme or impiety . . . monstrosam melancholiam, monstrous melancholy."[38] But he would have culled this opinion not simply from Melanchthon's *De Anima* but from the Galenic commentary that framed the 1603 edition from which he drew.[39] This is worth mentioning because of the numerous medical commentaries through which Melanchthon's work was read throughout the sixteenth century.[40] But the situation of Melanchthon's *De Anima* within the frameworks of medical theory also starts to make sense of Bright's assertion that by the latter part of the sixteenth century, many had "accopted all maner affection [of the soul] to be subiect to the phisicians hand."[41]

The attempts to mark Catholics as not merely errant or misdirected but pagan can be placed within this widely circulated—and, to educated early moderns, widely known—discourse. Catholics represented on stage, and in the pageants, masques, and dances described, are aligned with Moors and Turks not only to render them pagan by association. Rather, these groups are read as similarly constituted—all subject to the "monstrous melancholy" of unbelief.[42] Since external complexion was understood at the time as the outward demonstration of an inward humoral disposition, the association of Catholics with blackness underscores the excess of black bile that is the source of their religious error.

This does much to explain the humoral terms that govern the representation of religious difference in Jonson's *Masque of Blackness*. In fact, the masque demonstrates the currency of the idea. While he was not the author of the conceit of blackness for the masque performance, Jonson's deployment of the conceit shows the availability of the humors as an explanatory model for religious difference. After Niger assures the "fixed" quality of his "fresh streams," however mixed with "brackish" waters—just as the immortal souls of "creatures mortal" remain uncorrupted by the fluids of the bodies that they inhabit—the masque engages in an extended consideration of black complexion (both interior and exterior). Jonson emphasizes the sun as the source of Ethiopian blackness in order to retain the flattery of James as the more "temperate" sun that "refines / All things." The story that Niger tells of the "intemperate fires" of the sun that "scorch[es]" (150) the cheeks and limbs of the Ethiopian nymphs was not the common account of the source of blackness (except by those with little or imperfect medical knowledge).[43] Rather, the common source was understood as an excess of black bile. But there was a second kind of black bile that always produced toxic effects: "adust melancholy" was produced by scorched or combusted humors. In Avicenna's classification of "good" and "bad" humors, "unnatural" black bile emanates from burnt yellow bile, blood, phlegm, or natural black bile.[44] The daughters of Niger, burnt by the sun, seem maddened by a sun "that heat[s] / Their bloods" (165–66) and they seek the "comfort of a greater light" (169). Before "Phaëton . . . fired the world" (136) we are told, "the Ethiops were as fair / As other dames" (138–39) but "now black with black despair . . . their complexions [have] changed" (139–40).

The humoral complexion that accounts for the surface markings of their bodies is "black despair," or melancholy. According to Hippocratic-Galenic convention, the primary organ affected by an excess of melancholy was the brain. For medical theorists of the period, cognition could not be separated from somatic operations—though theories concerning the mechanics of the operation varied. Medical theorists such as Alberto Bottoni, Ercole Sassonia, and later Burton specified the apprehensive powers of the internal senses of the brain—of which the imagination was one—as those directly affected by humoral disposition and, crucially, humoral imbalance.[45] This preserved the *essence* of the immortal, rational soul from corruption. But the effect was the same in practical terms: reason, misinformed by a corrupted imagination, could fall into error.[46] And the most madding mixture was adust melancholy, the implied source of the dis-ease to which the Ethiopian women are subject.[47]

As Ian Smith has noted, the origin myth of Phæton's accident as the source of black skin is derived from Ovid: "the sun coming too close to the earth scorched the skin of the inhabitants of the nearby land called Ethiopia, the name meaning, literally, 'sunburned.'"[48] He then quotes from Golding's translation of *Metamorphoses*: "(The bloud by force of that same heate drawn to the outer part / And there adust from that time forth) became so blacke and swart."[49] The daughters of Niger are full of "error" (152; 204) and seek the "sun [that] is temperate" so that "their beauties shall be scorched no more" (233). Of course, the error to which they are most afflicted is that they do not know "how near divinity they [are]" (128). Instead, the slanders of the time have caused them to despise their "faithful hue" (125) and to be jealous of the "complexions" (140) of other women—believing them to be subject to the love that their own "scorched cheeks" forfeit (150). Jonson is careful in the terms of his conceit: the "power of separation" upon which he insists leaves the virtue of the nymphs untainted, but it is nonetheless clearly imperiled in the masque. The women are not aware of any essence of the soul that remains unaffected by bodily corruption (they cannot perceive "how near divinity they be"). Instead, they seek superior complexions that are worthy of (divine) love. The more common usage of the term "complexion" in the early modern period was the mixture and proportion of humors that were the basis of physical, mental, and moral health. The evidence of humoral complexion in the skin, its tincture, was another meaning—but one produced by assumptions about how physiological (mental, moral) constitution could be read on the surface of the body. Jonson, of course, leans heavily upon the double meaning in his masque. But his emphasis falls upon the temperament that is prepared for grace.

However "faithful" the temperament of the nymphs, and however free "from [the] passion[s] or decay" (129) of the body they are, they are still subject to delusion. They are prone to excited imaginations that compromise their sight: while we are assured that "Ethiops never dream" (160), the vision that they follow is an image reflected in a pool. The journey of the "zealous daughters" (199) toward "a greater light" is led by the false goddess of the moon. The misdirection of their journey is revealed at the masque's conclusion, when Niger ask for "particular grace" (198) to shine upon his daughters and Aethiopia demurs: "Thy daughters' labors have their period here, / And so thy errors" (203–4). The moon goddess defers to the superior sun (son) of Britain. But there is no mistaking her crypto-Catholic terms: the daughters (and Niger) should cease in the "error" that their own "labors" can achieve salvation and sue for grace from a greater power.

But James's light is not saving, it is merely refining. If the whole man, body and soul, is subject to grace, James's "sun" prepares the faithful daughters for receipt of it.

> [England is] ruled by a sun that to this height doth grace it,
> Whose beams shine day and night, and are of force
> To blanch an Ethiop, and revive a corse.
> His light sciential is, and, past mere nature,
> Can salve the rude defects of every creature.
>
> (223–27)

God's appointed on earth has limited powers of grace. But James's "light *sciential*" (not celestial) is able to purify the body to the requisite condition for grace. The "corse" of the Ethiopian ladies is then "revive[d]" to the light of God. As many critics have observed, this is a promise forestalled at the end of the masque. But the fact that the promise is deferred is consistent with the complement: Anne will be subject to the king's refining influence, which, over time, will enliven her to the "true" religion and abolish her errors. The promise of White Protestant Christian identity produces Whiteness as the index of the properly Christian.

Jonson claims, in his preface to the published work, that the masque performance itself is preoccupied with the "carcas[e]," which will be defaced over time, but his role in it, and his principal concern, is to prevent the "spiri[t]" from "perish[ing]" (7–8). (Of course, he is alluding to the fact that the masque scenery would be destroyed by spectators and to the need to preserve the text of the performance in print.) In the end, the religion that enlivens is not made explicit in *The Masque of Blackness*; it is, instead, implied that it is whatever religion James supports. What is clear in the complement is the queen's willingness to be subject to the transformative potential of her husband. James's "sciential" beams, the light of reason, will warm the queen to reform. Her imagination, excited by an excess of black bile, will be exposed to the calming influence of "temperate," or rational, discourse. Since the alterations of body and mind are sympathetic and reinforcing, a change of mind will cause a change in melancholic disposition. Neither Anne nor Jonson seeks to defend their present religious affiliation (except in oblique terms at the start of the masque). The conceit of blackness, deployed by the queen and subject to Jonson's "invention" (preface), serves the purpose of promising that she will be alive to her husband's influence and consequently, and quite literally, re-formed. Anne appropriates a crucial symbol of the performance history surrounding her—blackness—and Jonson's humoral terms put it to ironic use: instead of a sign of religious difference, it becomes the device that signals her conversion.

Scorched w[ith] the sunne"

It has been suggested that the image of the "Indians, scorched wth the sunne," in Mary Wroth's Sonnet 19 (Folger V.a.104, F75) of *Pamphilia to Amphilanthus*, is derived from her participation in the controversial masque performance.[50] Wroth also uses the theme of blackness in her sonnet sequence in order to press complaint into the service of a gendered political statement. Hall has previously examined the racialized terms of *Pamphilia to Amphilanthus*, but I want to explore how race and religious difference become the signatures not just of outside status but also of female empowerment.[51] If "our erotic selves have been compelled not just by state intervention but also by such terms as 'community,' 'home,' and 'race,'" as Sharon Holland suggests, Wroth's sonnet sequence works to wrest desire from any of these claimants and to set it out of reach of state or social control.[52] Wroth deploys the themes of paganism and blackness explored in Jonson's masque precisely in order to place herself, her body, and its desires outside of these social structures.

Lurking behind Wroth's poetic strategy is the assumption of the approved status of White European Christian womanhood within heteronormative structures and the ability of the category not just to confirm but also to create "'community,' 'home,' and 'race.'" Hall reminds us that the "racial formation" of Whiteness, particularly "the ideology" that surrounds White female beauty, "helps construct a visual regime that uses human bodies and their signification to determine access to political, social, and economic power."[53] As Mary Wroth uses the themes of Jonson's masque for her own rescue, she creates White Christian womanhood against the illegitimate (and delegitimated) form of the Black female body. Pamphilia's love for Amphilanthus is commonly described in pagan terms ("the sunn wch they doe as theyr God adore" [F75]); these terms are used to signal the release of the female subject from cultural and political norms. Wroth, like Anne, uses the signature of blackness in order to exploit the opportunities of an outside status—opportunities that can only be claimed by White women already in power.

One cannot read *Pamphilia to Amphilanthus* as autobiographical, yet Wroth was surely aware (as her uncle before her) that her circumstance would be read through her poetic work. With an eye toward this social performance, modeled after the strategies of Jonson's court masque for which she blackened her own body, I want to read Wroth's sonnet sequence as both a savvy political statement and yet another instance where White Christian womanhood is produced against the stigmatized Black female body. Though *Pamphilia to Amphilanthus* was not performed on stage, Wroth uses the female body in the sonnet sequence as a represented and flexible term. Her purpose is to place her body outside of juridical control. In the first sonnet of the sequence, her body is literally re-formed in order to be removed from the social structures that restrain her:

> When nights black mantle could most darknes proue,
>   and sleepe deaths Image did my sencesses hiere
>   from knowledg of my self, then thoughts did moue
>   swifter than those most swiftnes need require:
>
> In sleepe, a Chariot drawne by wing'd desire
>   I sawe: wher sate bright Venus, Queene of loue,
>   and att her feete her sonne, still adding fire
>   to burning hearts wch she did hold aboue.
>
> Butt one hart flaming more than all the rest
>   the goddeis held, and putt itt to my brest.
>   dear sonne, now shute, sayd she: thus must wee win

> Hee her obay'd, and martir'd my poore hart,
>   I, waking hop'd as dreames itt would depart
>   yett since: O mee: a louer haue I bin.
>   (*PA* F1)

When the speaker's self-awareness ("knowledg of my self") and self-control are temporarily suspended, her body is possessed, and transformed, by the Goddess of Love. Her religious affiliation changes, and rather than turning, she burns as a martyr to an idolatrous god. The metamorphosis seems total in both body and soul.

> Like to the Indians, scorched wth the sunne,
>   the sunn wch they doe as theyr God adore
>   soe ame I vs'd by loue, for euer more
>   I worship him, less fauor haue I wunn,
>
> Better are they who thus to blacknes runn,
>   and soe can only whitenes want deplore
>   then I who pale, and white ame w^t griefs store,
>   (*PA* F75, 1–7)

But if fleshy transformations become religious and moral ones in Wroth's sonnet sequence, I want to call attention to the play of Black and White in the representation of the body's meaning. The scorched body is blackened here, and in her association with sunburnt "Indians," the speaker is again turned heretic through bodily alteration. But in re-creating herself as a racialized and pagan subject—setting herself outside of any orthodox religious system—the speaker sets her body and its desires beyond the reach of social and political control.

David M. Halperin begins his seminal article "Is There a History of Sexuality?" with the claim: "Sex has no history. It is a natural fact, grounded in the functioning of the body, and, as such, it lies outside of history and culture."[54] Desire, he claims, *has* a history, made legible through the representation of systems of power, but not the body. But, as I have argued (with Eve Keller) elsewhere, "the body too, with its vulnerabilities and transformations, is malleable, unfixed, not a priori in its terms in relation to political formations."[55] This particularly matters in terms of the raced body. If, as Holland observes, "how the body *appears* to another and how [this appearance] is *historicized* makes it legible," then the raced body is evaluated within "a historical interface where blackness is denied access to a white social contract."[56] Which is to say that the desires of a Black body are subordinated, even nonexistent, in a political context where that body is subordinate and not reckoned to have value at all. But this is precisely the role that the speaker of the sonnet sequence assumes. Melissa Sanchez has pointed out that the premise of *Pamphilia to Amphilanthus* is one of political and personal abjection, through which right forms of service are explored.[57] But in its repeated images of idol worship, colonization, and enslavement, the sonnet sequence consistently situates its speaker outside of the "white social contract."

Holland reminds us that the sex of body, as well as its erotic desires and operations, does not lie outside of how it is socially represented. As Keller and I have written, "We are created as subjects, not just political subjects, through representation."[58] Representation creates a corporeal subject upon which social power can be exercised: the body is created as a political subject and our interactions with state and social power are premised upon these creations.[59] When we imagine a person rather than flesh, a sex rather than a body, a race rather than a human without alliance, allegiance, or nation, we create meaning from matter and affix identity. If we can say that material things—bodies in political space—occupy real dimensions, we cannot say that there is anything inevitable about how those bodies are accessed and understood in the space they occupy. What I am putting in relief here is the extent to which racial and religious transformation is achieved in *Pamphilia to Amphilanthus* through similar strategies by which the body acquires meaning within political arrangements in the first instance. Both the appearance and historical situation of the speaker's body—as well as its social and political relations and obligations—are altered through a system of representation. The political imaginary of the sequence, then, is to become, through another process of signification, a different subject.

Blackened, burned, scorched, and consumed, Pamphilia's body can be neither legitimated by nor excluded from the political order precisely because she withdraws from it. Her subjection, religious and political, is to Amphilanthus. Serving a false god severs all social relations. This outside status seems a more comfortable political position:

> Better are they who thus to blacknes runn,
>   and soe can only whitenes want deplore
>   then I who pale, and white ame w^t griefs store,
>   nor can haue hope, butt to see hopes vndunn;

> Beefids theyr sacrifies receaud's in sight
> of theyr chose sainte: Mine hid as worthles rite;
> grant mee to see wher I my offrings giue,
>
> Then lett mee weare the marke of Cupids might,
> in hart as they in skin doe Phœbus light
> Nott ceasing offrings to loue while I Liue.
> (PA F75, 5–14)

It is not, however, one that the speaker can maintain. The racialized others, "thus to blacknes runn," are in a better situation than Pamphilia, "who pale, and white . . . w^t griefs store," cannot worship her "chose[n] sainte ." But marked on the skin by their God, they are scored as a people outside of the faith. Early debates concerning faith of works and of the body against the faith of the spirit put emphasis upon the Pauline distinction between the flesh and the spirit. The flesh that is scored by circumcision marks the body as within the Law but outside of the spirit:

> 28 For he is not a Iewe, which is one outward: nether is that circumcision, which is outwarde in the flesh:
>
> 29 But he is a Iewe which is one within, and the (*) circumcision is of the heart, in the (o) spirit, not in thy letter, whose praise is not of men, but of God.[60]
> (*) Colossians 2:11. (o) In the inwarde man & heart.

Marked by Judaic Law, Jews (and Catholics), according to Luther, are committed to the flesh but without the spirit of Christian faith that is inclusive of all men.[61] In wearing the interior mark of her God "In heart as they in skin" the speaker colors this debate: the spirit gets racialized as white, the flesh as black by the marked skin.

If "our erotic selves have been compelled . . . by such terms as 'community,' 'home,' and 'race,'" Wroth attempts to alter the political gravity that attaches to her body and its desires through transmogrify. Breaching the prohibitions of family and community, her transgressive, adulterous desires are given scope and expression when situated outside of her religious and racial context. "The erotic thus recalls the impossibility of community with *an*other, mocking our ability to connect," Holland observes, "and also highlights the reciprocal nature of subjectivity, or what it means to be a subject."⁶² Subjectivity is experienced as a belief in the discrete self and its actions, but it is derived from the experience and understanding of the self in relation to others. Community and family prove persistent forces here. "Pale . . . and white," the speaker of her sonnet sequence is constant only in her grief. She is constantly recovered by her former alliances, her former identity, her former self—and her switchback course admits her desire only temporarily. When the speaker returns to her context and community, she is denied her "chose[n] sainte." In order to love, she must cease to be all that is counted good.

> Good now bee still, and doe nott mee torment
>   w^t multituds of questions, bee att rest,
>   and only lett mee quarrell w^t my brest
>   wch still letts in new stormes my soule to rent;
>
> Fy, will you still my mischiefs more augment?
>   you say I answere cross, I that confest
>   long since, yett must I euer bee oprest
>   wth yor toungue torture wch will ne're bee spent?
>
> Well then I see noe way butt this will fright
>   that Diuell speach; Alas I ame poísest,
>   and mad folks senceles ar of wisdomes right,
>
> The hellish spiritt absence doth arrest
>   all my poore sences to his cruell might
>   spare mee then till I ame my self, and blest.
>   (*PA*, F52)

When she is herself, she cannot have human love; she can be "blest," but not touched. In her attempts to place her desire outside of social constraints, outside of herself, the speaker of *Pamphilia to Amphilanthus* shifts shape: she changes in color, religion, nation, and even (at times) sex. In so doing, the sonnets reveal the extent to which not just gender and identity but the materiality of the body itself is contingent, created, interpreted. The sonnet sequence shows how apprehension of the body—in social and political terms—gives it shape.

"The materials of early modern humoral theory," Gail Paster writes, "encode a complexly articulated hierarchy of physiological differences paralleling and reproducing structures of social differences."⁶³ "Burton's innovation," in his *Anatomy of Melancholy*, Gowland observes, "was to integrate a basically polemical position within a medical-scientific framework."⁶⁴ This is another way of saying that Burton writes, among other things, a racial script: a rationalization of human difference written in pseudoscientific mode in order to "prove" its claims. While one can argue about the innovation of the strategy, what makes Burton's *Anatomy* so valuable is its range of sources: from Aristotle to Augustine, from Avicenna to Aquinas, from Cicero to Seneca, from Ficino to Ebreo, from Luther to Melanchthon to Calvin, Burton brings together the cultural materials from which the logic of religious essentialism is composed. While not contemporary to the works of either Jonson or Wroth, *The Anatomy* shows a particular strategy by which religious affiliation and moral constitution (the framework within which religion is understood) are made physiological, heritable features of the blood. I will address hereditary blood in Chapter 3; this chapter explores how religious others become both alienated and marked. There is certainly more than one strategy—but Jonson, Wroth, and Burton all show scientific and cultural materials closely bound together in the fabrication of stories about foreign bodies and alien religions. If both Jonson and Wroth demonstrate—in different ways—how the materiality of the body in political space is itself contingent and created, Burton gathers the cultural materials that explain its creation.

In cataloging his "new" species of bodily disorder, religious melancholy, Burton sets it among various kinds of love melancholy, since Augustine calls the *"splendor of the diuine God"* the "quintessence of beauty":

> All . . . other beauties faile, varie, are subiect to corruption, to loathing, *But this is an immortall vison, a divine beauty, an immortall loue, an indefatigable loue and beauty,* with sight of which wee shall neuer be tired, nor wearied, but still the more we see the more we shal couet him. For . . . *where this vision is, there is absolute beauty, and where is that beauty, from the same fountaine comes all pleasure and happinesse, neither can beauty, pleasure, happinesse, be separated from his vision or sight, or his vision from beauty pleasure, happinesse.* In this life we haue but a glimse of this beauty and happinesse, wee shall hereafter . . . *see him as hee is, thine eyes . . . Shall behold the King in his glory,* then shall we be perfectly inamored, haue a full fruition of it, desire, behold and loue him alone, as the most amiable and fairest obiect, our *summum bonum,* or chiefest good.⁶⁵

While Burton cites Leone Ebreo as the source for this Neoplatonic conceit, he might as well invoke Ficino: in *Platonic Theology*, contemplation of the divine is the one credit to the human rational instrument that has no parallel among other animals. Although human beings "excel over all . . . animals in our genius for art and government . . . we share this industriousness with the beasts nonetheless." But humans alone are capable of "contemplation of the divine": "the lifting of our mind to God . . . is as properly ours as the raising upright of our body towards heaven."[66] "Religion is true"; and in loving true beauty, the human is made a creature of moral rectitude.[67] But Ficino is important to Burton not simply in providing the Neoplatonic conception of human desire properly directed toward divine beauty; he matters because he describes the perversion of this love in terms of melancholy and the monstrous distortion of human nature.[68]

In Burton's formulation, Augustine's conception of *amor Dei* is conflated with Neoplatonic ideas of all beauty proceeding from divine beauty and God as the ultimate object of human love. While his construction finds a close parallel in Ficino, he largely resorts to religious authority (Augustine and Melanchthon) rather than ancient philosophers (Aristotle and Plato) to add credit to his claims. Melanchthon is used to describe how diversion from love of God is a perversion of nature: "*And him our will would haue loued and sought alone as our summum bonum, or principall good, & all other good things for Gods sake: and nature as she proceeded from it would haue sought his fountain, but in this infirmity of humane nature this order is disturbed, our loue is corrupt*: & a man is like to [a] monster."[69] While Burton embellishes his Latin here, the point is that it is Melanchthon—not Hippocrates, Plato, Aristotle, or Galen—who can, and who frequently does, license Burton's assertions of the physiological defect of religious others. This underscores the importance of a Protestant revision of *De Anima*, but it also calls attention to the role of Protestant cultural scripts in writing religious others outside of the Christian communion.[70]

Jonson's *Masque of Blackness* and Wroth's *Pamphilia to Amphilanthus* both demonstrate the availability of this cultural script: both works write their subjects as lacking (and looking for) love. The daughters of Niger are in the progress of a love quest, seeking the complexions that made "other dames queens of all desires" (151) and in search of the "sun" that will "blanch an Ethiop" and cool the blood that runs hot under the "intemperate fires" of their own climate. Jonson enacts a Neoplatonic fantasy in which the daughters of Niger leave "that climate of the sky / To comfort of a greater light, / Who forms all beauty with his sight" (168–70). While they are "faithful," and "zealous" in their faith, they were not born under the right sky and therefore cannot fully receive the light of

God. If the surface markings of Ethiopians "could not always be viewed as an outward sign of infidel identity," as Britton tells us, they nonetheless rendered the nature of their religion suspect. They are not the *right kind* of Christians: denied access to divine love and its adjunct, Christian charity, they are written outside of the Christian communion. As Jonson's masque and the European pageants from which the conceit of blackness was derived indicate, Catholics are negrified in Protestant performances—an exterior sign of their internal "error" (152; 204) in religion that does not permit them to perceive the true light of God. But Jonson's fantasy allows (as it would need to) for recuperation: Catholics, at least in England, have the promise of a "light *sciential*" that will clear their complexion. By contrast, the scorched and brown bodies of *Pamphilia to Amphilanthus* remain permanently cast out and consigned to error.

If it is necessary for us to see desire as historically produced, the particular history of religious essentialism that I am tracing forces us to reevaluate the expression of desire in early modern Neoplatonic conceits and to reconsider the racialized bodies that they contain. Both Jonson and Wroth exploit a cultural discourse that understands all those outside of the Protestant faith as suffering from love melancholy, driven mad by black bile, and excluded from true religion. But they exploit this discourse to different ends: while all of these bodies are marked by bad faith, some can be re-formed. Jonson trades upon this idea in order to proffer a message of concession. But Wroth uses blackness to situate her speaker outside of a Christian community (*Spare me . . . till I am myself, and blest*). She both exhibits and exploits a cultural belief that some bodies cannot be reformed, are beyond religious recovery, and are permanently pagan by nature. For Wroth, the body that cannot be recuperated is crucial to the composition of an erotic self that must be set beyond the reach of the communal, social, or familial. The racial logic(s) of the period, then, are written into the erotic landscape of her sonnet sequence.

In *Pamphilia to Amphilanthus*, Wroth develops a conceit that runs directly counter to Neoplatonic ideals:

> Loue, thou hast all, for now thou hast mee made
>   soe thine, as if for thee I were ordain'd;
>   then take thy conquest, nor lett mee bee pain'd
> more in thy Sunn, when I doe seeke thy shade,
>
> Noe place for help haue I left to inuade,
>   (*PA* F53, 1–5)

"Scorched wth the sunne" herself, the speaker is "ordain'd" for the wrong faith. Wroth's conceit(s) throughout the sonnet sequence rely upon arguments marshalled in Ficino: irreligion is the result of "a melancholic bent, one sick and contrary... to life... that both perverts the human temperament and brings with it a weakness with regard not only to our confidence in life but also to the governance of human affairs."[71] The "madness" of those who do not believe (or who believe wrongly) is "roused on account of... black bile."[72] Their love is diverted from God and perverted in human affairs. The speaker of *Pamphilia to Amphilanthus* is herself subject to the same bodily transformations that produce madness and misdirect her love: too much in the sun, she exhibits the effects of adust melancholy. But she also aligns herself with the burnt and brown bodies that are indicative of this melancholy. Like Jonson, Wroth self-consciously exploits the Neoplatonic tradition in order to invoke ideas of misdirected desire. Precisely because her speaker tries to set her desire outside of religious or communal sanction—she has chosen her own "sainte"—she is affiliated with bodies expelled from both faith and charity. When she is herself again, she is "pale, and white... w^t griefs store" but returned to a complexion and a context in which she can be "blest."

In the context of the humoral discourse of religious essentialism, the surface markings of Black bodies identify them as expelled from the *corpus Christianum*. Indeed, the marks on their bodies, produced by the worship of an idol god, the sun, makes their expulsion legible. In Pauline terms (explored at greater length in Chapter 4), the flesh that is scored by religious practice, such as circumcision, marks the practitioner as a follower of ritual rather than faith, of Law rather than spirit. "The Law of the Spirit of life *which is* in Christ Iesus, hathe freed me from the law of sinne and of death," Paul declares, "For... that [release] was impossible to the [Judaic] Law," or any other religious membership that is marked on the body, "in as muche as it was weake, because of the flesh" (Rom. 8:2–3). The individual claimed by a particular religious practice, and isolated by tribal ritual, follows the Law of the flesh but refuses the spiritual truth of Christ that is available to all. Such a condition is a "degeneration of righteous *amor Dei*, and its by-product charity, into sinful... *amor sui*."[73] Individuated rather than inclusive, these bodies are written outside of the love of Christian charity.[74] Catholics are among those bodies that are too much of the flesh, marked by ritual practice and afflicted by one of "two extremes of *Excesse* and *Defect*, impiety and Superstition, idolatry and Athisme."[75] But they might be reclaimed to the body of the Christian faithful with a change of complexion: the daughters of Niger sue for grace but are only promised receipt of it once they are cleared of their "rude defects" and "their beauties [are] scorched no more."

The rejection of black bodies from Christian communion makes good sense of the European pageants that stage the expelling forces of Protestantism. In his ironic appropriation of the conceit, however, Jonson also demonstrates a difference in blackness (distinctions not always visible in Burton, whose polemical position will not permit them). Jonson imagines bodies reformed for redemption. The black melancholy of the Ethiopian princesses is not enduring. But this also imagines another category of human indelibly marked by bad faith. The works of Jonson and Wroth reveal not only a complexion to right religion but also that for some, the stain of error is not eradicable. The black bile that is the supposed source of their dark skin is indelible "proof" of the madness of irreligion that attends it. Both Jonson and Wroth imagine melancholy bodies as barred from divine love—but for actual Black and brown bodies, like the expulsion from Paradise itself, the eviction is permanent.

CHAPTER 3

Moral Constitution

The Color of Blood in Elizabeth Cary's *Tragedy of Mariam* and the New English Tracts

> For greatest perills do attend the faire,
> When men do seeke, attempt, plot and devise,
> How they may overthrow the chastest Dame,
> Whose Beautie is the White whereat they aime.
> —Aemilia Lanyer, *Salve Deus Rex Judæorum*

Jean Feerick has argued that racial discrimination grounded in chromatic distinction emerges "in dialectical relation to social rank, [and allows for] social tensions originating with the difference of rank to be resolved, mitigated, or exploited with reference to this emerging difference of colour."[1] My argument inverts this claim: color in this case does not accrue value as a marker of difference in cooperative relation with an emergent system of racialization. Rather the surface markings of the body are read and interpreted through an earlier system of racial encoding—one of rank—that read the body in terms of moral taxonomy.[2] I have so far focused upon melancholy as a form of madness and an index of bad faith. But notions of paganism as an *inherited* trait derive from the ideology of the superior humoral constitution that secured the birthright of power and privilege for the ruling class. As I argue in the Introduction, the English colonial project demanded subjects that were not capable of conversion to Christianity. In the previous two chapters, we have seen how Catholics are scored as pagan, but Jonson's *Masque of Blackness* indicates that they are not past reform: to the contrary, the reformation of Black subjects to White Christianity is the promise that the masque (with)holds. But the reformation of Irish Catholics, for example, would not give room to colonial ambitions for Irish land.

If race in the early modern period is a concept with intersecting vectors of lineage, religion, and nation, Spenser's *View of the Present State of Ireland* (1596) reveals the complicated cross-channels by which all three ideologies interact and combine at this time.[3] Since notions of lineage and superior humoral composition license the political authority of ruling families, Spenser is attempting to detach Anglo-Irish lords in Ireland from their land and their rule by these means.[4] Certainly, the degeneracy for which Spenser argues had been deployed as a nationalist strategy in political histories that sought to explain the intractability of the Irish problem—including those written by Catholics such as Edmund Campion. And degeneracy as an explanation had been pressed into the service of this strategy since Gerald of Wales. But the debates concerning subjectivity and the status of the soul in England in the late sixteenth century altered these arguments. The ambition for Irish land revised fictions of lineal descent—fictions that were well supported by conduct literature, political tracts, and medical treatises—to fantasies of faith transmitted through blood.

Color functions as an index of moral character in the historically older ideology of hereditary blood, fastening to status as the crucial category of difference.[5] Patricia Akhimie has set this fact at the center of her analysis of early modern racial constructions that rely upon "somatic marker[s]" as a "signal . . . [of] indelible social difference."[6] But Akhimie also notices the paradox of a social system in which "social identity is understood as both fixed and fluid." Medical tracts and political polemics make clear that the humoral constitution of noble subjects must be cultivated and maintained. While the superior qualities of the nobility are apprehended as a set of heritable traits, the evidence of conduct literature reveals these traits to be unstable. The instabilities of the humoral model, however, do not undermine the political force of these narratives. Indeed, conduct books and political tracts, as Akhimie has shown, do precisely the work of fixing these traits. But Akhimie has also demonstrated not only how the moral differences perceived in status relations are treated as inherited and inherent facts but also how subjects who are raced in these terms are color-coded.[7]

Understanding early modern race in terms of hereditary blood and the constitution of noble subjects reveals how moral rectitude is appreciated in essentialist terms: the body is literally the original site of moral capacity. The historically older construction of race as lineage, or rank, understands the body as a hydraulic machine—and as the site of moral production. To apprehend racial logic in this way puts a particular field of early modern medical knowledge—and its application to social arrangements—open to our inspection. Such intellectual histories often lack the subjects for whom the ideological discourses are produced. Elizabeth Cary's *Tragedy of Mariam* places an actor within the discursive field of race at this early modern moment and shows how it colors her imagination.[8]

Years ago, Dympna Callaghan wrote brilliantly about how Cary "deploys and manipulates the concept [of race] as a vital aspect of her construction and interrogation of femininity" in her drama.[9] I revisit this observation because, as much as I admire the piece, I believe that a contemporary—which is to say, early modern—application of the concept of race needs to be applied to Cary's interrogation.[10] The embodiment of moral differences in the play, color-coded in black and white, are grounded in prevailing medical theory as it attaches to rank and lineage. *The Tragedy of Mariam* is about rank, and inherent moral superiority as a feature of the blood. And crucially, this superiority attaches to Mariam. Margaret Ferguson has noted that Cary's drama represents one of the key problems between Herod and Mariam as a "serious, though occluded, competition for the throne."[11] Mariam's whiteness marks her as the natural superior to the dark figures of Salome and Herod. In the competing claims of gender and status, Mariam's rank ratifies her moral authority and alters her position as gendered subject within the drama.

Since race as both category and political concept is imbricated, it seems unsophisticated to make the distinction between rank and nation at all.[12] The manner in which raced subjects are encoded in the drama, however, helps us to perceive the black/white binary deployed as something other than Christian typology or the evaluation of an external hue. M. Lindsay Kaplan has observed how black melancholy scores the bodies of Jewish subjects in Cary's drama. Kaplan rightly points to melancholy Jewish bodies in medieval thought as the origin of the idea: "[The] desire to distinguish Jews from Christians might also account for the development of the medieval concept of the melancholy Jewish body."[13] But it is the desire to distinguish colonial *Christian* subjects from others of the Christian communion that scores bodies as black with melancholy in early modern England. Cary's *Tragedy of Mariam* shows how moral authority is invested in governing noble bodies and how this ideology of hereditary superiority—and degeneracy—crosses over to notions of inherited depravity.

In *The boke named the governour*, Thomas Elyot demonstrates the extent to which bloodlines and blood relations determine the physiological and moral temperament of human subjects. His instruction on the rearing of the infant children of English nobles concentrates upon the careful maintenance of their inherited moral constitution. Elyot pays particular attention to the choice of a wet nurse, advising that the selection for noble children must be dictated by her "complection"—or the distribution of the humors expressed in her milk. His concerns about the humoral complexion of the nurse demonstrate the extent to which blood was believed to direct character. He says that the "nourise ... shulde be of no seruile condition, or vice notable. For as some aunciente writers do suppose often times the childe soukethe the vice of his nouryse, with the milke of her pappe." Rather, "her complection most be of the right and pure sanguine."[14] Since a nurse of noble rank was usually out of the question, Elyot tries to safeguard against the pollution of noble blood through its mingling with the blood of the servant (breast milk was blood in concocted form). The nurse, therefore, must not be "seruile," or of very low status, must be of a young and healthy age, and must demonstrate a strong moral character—the grounding of which was thought to be the quality of her blood.[15]

While Elyot's fixation upon blood as a source of moral corruption might appear strange to us, his advice is ultimately derived from an inherited set of physiological assumptions. This advice has classical origins but is a commonplace within sixteenth- and seventeenth-century Galenic medical philosophy. Elyot explains the susceptibility of noble children to their wet nurse in the following way: "the braynes and hertes of children, whiche be membres spirituall, whiles they be tender, and the litle slippes of reason begynne in them to burgine, ther may happe by iuel custome some ... vice to perse the sayd membres, and infecte and corupt the softe and tender buddes, whereby the frute may growe wylde."[16] Elyot situates the mind among the higher faculties of the rational soul as one of the "membres spirituall." This would seem to put it out of reach of the body's operations, thereby rendering it invulnerable to the quality of milk that the wet nurse dispenses or to other impressions from her weakness of character. And yet virtually every medical treatise of the sixteenth century grappled with the proximity of the body to the soul—and to what extent the body could affect the soul, and vice versa.

The humors are the product of digestion, but these concoctions of the body are vulnerable to internal and external conditions of diet and climate and even psychic and emotional states. The ingredients of such a complicated mixture make the brew of noble blood susceptible to the impression of the immediate environment. The fact that affected humors also disturb the operation of the rational mind—and consequently, the soul—renders the moral constitution of human subjects pliant to outside forces. Elyot's preoccupation with noble blood demonstrates not only its perceived vulnerability but also its value in relation to the blood of others. The assumption regarding the superiority of noble blood—and the physical, intellectual, and moral supremacy that attended it—offered stability to the social hierarchy that it naturalized (hence, Elyot perceives the "destruction of a realme" in the poor selection of a nurse).[17]

Similar to other forms of racial logic, race as family lineage in the early modern period buttressed a political arrangement with a fantasy of the body. Similarly too, this concept of race bore a signature of color expressed in the face. Shakespeare plays upon these contemporary apprehensions of race in *II Henry IV*:

> *Prince Henry:* Before God, I am exceeding weary.
> *POINS:* Is't come to that? I had thought weariness durst not have attached one of so high blood.
>
> *Prince Henry:* Faith, it does me; though it discolours the complexion of my greatness to acknowledge it.
>
> (II.ii.1–5)[18]

Of course, Henry simply means that it discredits his rank to admit that he is physiologically (humorally) as weak as other men. But his terms are no accident: Elyot maintains in *The castel of helthe* that those possessed of "equalytie of humours" are visually marked by "redde and white" skin, whereas those with an "inequalyte of humours" have skin that is "blacke, sallow, or whyte onely."[19] "Complexion" in Henry's phrasing refers to both the humoral constitution of an individual and the external hue that is a sign of inner disposition. He is therefore suggesting that his admission sullies his noble status, but he is also punning on the visible marker of his noble blood: the color of his skin.

The assumptions that underwrite power are naturalized in Cary's culture and reproduced in graphic terms in her play. *The Tragedy of Mariam* also demonstrates the availability of the humoral system as a scheme for reading moral difference. The color differences that distinguish Mariam from Salome and Herod signify her authority over them—in both moral and political terms. While patriarchal control is asserted with force at the end of the play, for much of it, Mariam is imagined as the legitimate ruler. But significantly, the play reproduces the judgments of the history from which it draws. In Thomas Lodge's translation of Josephus's *Antiquities of the Jews*, the narrative constantly affirms the illegitimacy of Herod's rule due to his low birth—having deposed Judea's "rightful king[s] and priest[s]" (Argument, 67). Complaints against Herod extend to his appointment of "certaine [men] of bace condition" to the priesthood and to high levels of government.[20] Cary's assertion that Herod desired Mariam in the first place for "her high blood" (Argument, 67) suggests that she principally understands the differences drawn in her play in terms of rank. The claim not only sets Mariam's lineage at a higher premium than that of Herod or Salome, it underscores the distinction between them as one of rank. The play insists, as does the history, upon Mariam's "purest blood" (I.vi.489).[21] The effect is to delegitimize the rule of Herod and to elevate Mariam to a position that neither her sex nor gender would permit. This reordering rests upon a racial ideology—that of rank—so culturally visible that its representation is rendered in color.

"Race" can refer to either rank or nation in the early modern period. The distinction that I am making between concepts, and how they are employed in *The Tragedy of Mariam*, requires a careful separation of terms and ideas. For one thing, noble families were not easily separable from the nation(s) they ruled. But in Josephus's history, Herod and his kin are persistently represented as outliers and usurpers to the rule of Judea—and their place of origin has little to do with this appraisal. Rather, it is their social situation that constantly affirms their rule as illegitimate. Cary replicates this logic, and rank is the key term around which the power struggle depicted in her drama turns. The first confrontation of the play is between Mariam and Salome, Herod's sister.

> *Mariam:* My birth thy baser birth so far excell'd,
> I had to both . . . you [and Herod] the princess been.
> Thou parti-Jew, and parti-Edomite,
> Thou mongrel: issu'd from rejected race.
> . . . .
> *Salome:* Still twit you me with nothing but my birth,
> What odds betwixt your ancestors and mine?
> Both born of Adam, both were made of earth,
> And both did come from holy Abraham's line.
> (I.iii.233–42)

Mariam appears to be drawing lines of separation based on tribal inheritance, particularly with slurs such as "mongrel: issu'd from rejected race." But I will insist that the race that she intends here is a rejected family line. (The animalistic imagery should not surprise us if indeed the concept of the superior blood of rank descends from tracts on breeding and animal husbandry.)[22] As Salome points out, she and Mariam ultimately share an ancestry. Esau, the supposed progenitor of the Idumeans, or Edomites, sold his birthright as the elder of two sons to his younger brother Jacob for pottage. On first feeling her twins fighting inside of her, Rebekah is told by God that "two nations *are* in thy wombe, and two maner of people shalbe deuided out of thy bowels" (Gen. 25:23). This pronouncement supports the division of nations as the principal category of distinction. But the Lord further declares, "the elder *shal serue* the yonger" (my emphasis). The Hasmonean dynasty, from which Mariam descends, had ruled Judea for over one hundred years before yielding to the Herodian dynasty in 37 BCE. But the Idumeans had already been part of the Jewish nation for eighty-eight years—nearly the full term of Hasmonean rule. Their assimilation was complete: they were integrated in the governing structure, and Herod's father was close enough to power to grab it. The displacement of the Hasmoneans was facilitated by the machinations of Antipater but was secured by Herod and his marriage to Mariam. Which is to say that the struggle represented in the play is an internal one for rule of Judea, not an external one involving the conquest of one nation over another. Herod's assassination of Mariam's remaining male relatives was a political gesture: its motivation was the elimination of political competition, not any kind of ethnic rivalry.

In Lodge's translation of the *Antiquities of the Iews*, "race" is used to denote "nation" only once over the history that traces Herod's rise to power. In the list of the contents to Book 14, Josephus includes a heading, "Of the race of *Antipater*, and how he purchaseth renowme, great power and authoritie both to himselfe and his children."[23] The subsequent introduction of Antipater indicates that "race" here refers to "nation": he is described as "a certaine friend of *Hircanus* (by nation an Idumean, and by name *Antipater*)."[24] This is the single instance in the account, which spans over eighty-five pages, where the term "race" appears to invoke Antipater's place of origin and not his ignoble birth. The term is put to use often throughout the history, but in all other occasions (in the particular story of Herod) it refers to lineage and family line. Further, the next sentence illuminates the real problem concerning Antipater's Idumean ancestry: "*Nicholas Damascene* writeth of [Antipater], that he was descended from the noblest amongst those Iewes who returned from out of Babylon into Iury: but this he did of set purpose to gratifie *Herode Antipaters* sonne, who ... became afterwards King of the Iewes."[25] Herod compels the rewriting of family history to achieve a nobler heritage, where he is descended from among the ancient families of Jews taken into Babylonian captivity. This revised account served two purposes: elevating Herod's status and legitimizing his religious affiliation. Antipater's origins complicated Herod's rule because he had no claim to an ancient line. Further, since Idumeans had been compelled to convert under John Hircanus (the great-great-grandfather of Hircanus), and forced conversion was not recognized, the religious commitment of Herod's family was suspect. In Josephus's narrative, the Hasmonean dynasty is largely overthrown by themselves and their own infighting. But the principal objection to Herodian rule is their mean descent and questionable religion: "For [the Jews] haue lost [their] liberty, and haue beene subdued by the Romanes... and the roialty which before time was an honour reserued for those that were of the race of the high priests, hath been bestowed on men of obscuritie and communitie."[26]

Josephus consistently emphasizes Mariam's rank, not her nation—and, by contrast, that of Herod and his kin. Indeed, Josephus attributes Salome's hostility to the tendency of Mariam to taunt her for the mean quality of her birth. Cary's drama conflates two episodes where Herod travels abroad in order to maintain his political alliances with Rome. Upon his return from the first trip, Salome implies that her husband, Joseph, to whom Herod had committed "the gouernment both of the kingdome and his priuate estate," had been too familiar with Mariam.[27] Josephus makes the policy of Salome clear but emphasizes that her hatred is directed more to Mariam than her husband: "she spake thorow the malice she had long time conceiued... for that in a certaine debate *Mariamme* had in her rage despitefully hit them in the teeth with their obscure birth."[28] In the history, it is both Salome and Herod's mother who accuse Mariam—and it is implied that Mariam denigrates the birth of the entire family, including Herod, just as she does in the play. Indeed, Mariam's tendency to "[upbraid] and publikely [reproach] both the kings mother and sister, [and to] tell ... them that they [are] but abiectly and basely borne," is represented as something of a habit in Josephus's narrative.[29] Mariam's slur of Salome as "parti-Jew, and parti-Edomite" in their dramatic encounter is consistent with Cary's source: "parti-Jew" reminds Salome that Mariam's grandsire forced the conversion of her family, and "parti-Edomite" insists that she is a political intruder.

Mariam's insults against Salome ultimately concern the hierarchy of families and not nations: Mariam invokes the politics of a past; Salome, those of the present. But both resort to the status of family line to declare their superiority over the other. Cary is depicting a family drama—the conflict between a ruling family in decline and one in ascension. She shrinks the political conflict to the proportions of a domestic struggle. That women should be at the center of this struggle is entirely appropriate to the genre of a closet drama. But it is also apposite to the nature of the conflict itself: where internal strife weeds political rivals, the women of the family are ultimately the members who survive. Hence, the opening scenes of the play pit Alexandra and Mariam against Salome: the "Hebrew women [are] now transformed to men" (I.vi.421), engaging in a battle of words where men are absent. We should not lose sight of the fact that this is a contest between two families in a shifting political order. The women ultimately seek to have the authority of their family recognized.

That Cary chooses sides in this conflict is starkly apparent. None of my observations thus far counter Kim Hall's claim that "the use of complexion to accentuate status, cultural, and religious differences is quite striking in *Mariam*."[30] What is different in my analysis is the shift of attention from exterior to interior complexion. The humoral theory that grounds moral production is the ground on which early modern government is laid—and for that reason, the theory is particularly rigorous and well disseminated.[31] Mariam's moral authority is signaled by the white images used to describe her, a signal that a contemporary audience or readership would have recognized as a privilege of rank. A cluster of brilliant images around Mariam increases as the play progresses and is set against the darker aspect of Salome and Herod. At the conclusion of Mariam's argument with Salome she says that she will "not pollute [her] breath" with the "black acts" that Salome has committed (I.iii.44). Salome is painted black by other characters as well: her husband tells her that he blushes for her because she has lost the capacity (I.vi.378). Even Salome speaks of her "tainted brow" (I.iv.283) that obscures blushing. But her "darkness" is thrown into particular contrast against the superior color of Mariam. Herod is most inclined to the comparison; Salome is "so unlike . . . Mariam in [her] shape":

That when to her you have approachèd near,
Myself hath often ta'en you for an ape.
. . . .
You are to her a sun-burnt blackamoor.
              (IV.vii.458–62)

He calls Salome his "black tormentor" (IV.vii.513). She is "outmatchèd in [her] sex" (V.i.162) when placed in contradistinction to the "white" Mariam:

> [Mariam] was fair,
> Oh, what a hand she had, it was so white,
> It did the whiteness of the snow impair.
> (V.i.149–51)

Mariam's whiteness is an index of her higher rank and of her fitness to rule. It marks her as constitutionally—physically and, particularly, morally—superior. While moral differences—or, rather, the construction of moral differences—are plotted along the lines of Christian semiotics in Cary's *Mariam*, we can see how these readings of moral character begin in the blood. The superior quality of blood itself accounts for the superior moral character of the human subjects of the play.

Perhaps the strongest evidence that Cary ascribes a moral constitution to rank lies in her rewriting of the history of England, not Judea. Cary opens her *History of the Life, Reign, and Death of Edward II, King of England* with this assessment of Edward's moral character: "He could not have been so unworthy a Son of so noble a Father ... if either Vertue or Vice had been hereditary."[32] But in spite of the conditional clause with which it begins, the history affirms throughout—relentlessly so—that "Vertue [and] Vice" *are* indeed "hereditary." Edward is quickly marked as "a meer Imposture" to the "honour of his Birthright" and the rest of the history is an anatomy of political corruption.[33] Cary attributes Edward's "degenerate" nature to having been "mis-led [in] his unripe knowledge" by "Gaveston his Ganymede, a man as base in Birth as in Condition."[34] Edward's temperament is obviously affected by his "diseased Passion" for Gaveston, but it is principally the fact that he surrounds himself with people of inferior birth (at Gaveston's urging) that effects his full alteration.[35] Further, Gaveston, "advance[d] ... beyond proportion, or his birth and merit," remakes the kingdom in his own image: "the sacred Rules of Justice were subverted, the Laws integrity abused, the Judge corrupted or inforc'd, and all the Types of Honour due to Vertue, Valour, Goodness, were like the Pedlers pack, made Ware for Chapmen."[36] *The History of . . . Edward II* reads as a cautionary tale of the hazard of surrendering government to those constitutionally unfit to rule. Edward turns over government of his kingdom to "Sycophants and Favorites" of base heritage, until he himself becomes "a meer stranger to those Abilities that are proper to Rule."[37] The king's natural temper is corrupted through these influences, and the whole kingdom mimics his degenerate nature: "The intemperate and indiscreet Government had alien'd the hearts of this People ... the Ulcers fester'd dayly more and more." The outbreaks of internal revolt are characterized as humoral disease (literally distemper), mapped onto the king's body, for "it is a very dangerous thing when the Head is ill, and all the Members suffer by his infirmity."[38]

Cary's chromatic contrast of Salome and Mariam denotes the social hierarchies that the play itself naturalizes. Alexandra concludes her argument with Salome with the dismissal: "let us go: it is no boot / To let the head contend against the foot" (I.iii.259-60). This declaration forms the central argument of the play. Elyot's contention that the corruption of noble blood risks the "destruction of [the] realme" is writ large—although the corruption lies in the exchange of families. While the principal distinction of the play is made between "The King of Jewry's fair and spotless wife" (V.i.198) and Salome, his sister, whose spots are acknowledged even by her ("Had I affected an unspotted life / Josephus' veins had still been stuff'd with blood" I.iv.286-87), the differences in the blood of families is identified by the tincture of the skin. Herod and Salome are dark. They are marked as usurpers, and not the "natural" rulers of Judea. Herod is a "Base Edomite, the damnèd Esau's heir"; "must he," Alexandra asks, "ere Jacob's child [Mariam] the crown inherit?" (I.ii.84-85). Family affiliation is identified by color, and Herod is red because he descends from another branch of the family tree. Because Esau "despised his birthright" and sold it for a stew of red lentils (and, by consequence, constrained his descendants to a position subordinate to Jacob's line), the Idumeans are associated with the color red (Gen. 25:30-34).

> *Alexandra:* His cruel nature which with blood is fed:
> That made him me of sire and son deprive,
> He ever thirsts for blood, and blood is red.
> (I.ii.104-6)

Herod's excess of choler shows in his face, but it is also evident in his rule: he is rash and impressionable, bloody-minded and easily led. He seems unable to rule, and even less so after he kills Mariam: as he complains, "She was my graceful moiety; me accurs'd, / To slay my better half and save my worst" (V.i.133-34). What is noble in him, or at least about him, dies with his wife.

It is because Mariam is the "natural" ruler of Herod that she is permitted (within certain terms of the play) to break the codes of female behavior and still retain her moral superiority. Salome, by contrast, cannot. Her defiance of her husband(s) and presumption that she shares in the rights and privileges afforded to men, such as the right of divorce, are chief among the "black acts" with which she is charged. When she is found in conference with another man, her husband upbraids her:

> Oh Salome, how much you wrong your name
> Your race, your country, and your husband most!
> . . . .
> I blush for you, that have your blushing lost.
> (I.vi.375–78)

"Race" here does not refer to nation or tribe. It instead invokes her family, now elevated politically (as in "lineage, nation, and husband"). Constabarus is also Idumean. But he is morally approved in the logic of the play. This is, in large measure, because his "natural" position has been seized by Salome; his words to her are "intended for [her] good, / To raise [her] honour and to stop disgrace" (I.vi.412–13). But Constabarus is, crucially, also noble, "one of the greatest account" among the Idumeans.[39] Whereas the race of Antipater, and subsequently, Herod, is consistently affirmed as base or common in Josephus, the nobility of Salome's husband is underscored. While Constabarus's descent from Idumean priests would not be recognized within the Jewish tradition, his moral role in the play seems to draw from his noble heritage.[40] Indeed, Constabarus might be the case in point that rank prevails as the moral determinate in *Mariam*.

It also seems clear from Constabarus's subsequent railing against Hebrew women, among whom he counts Salome, that he means the nation of the Jews, and that he is not setting the Idumeans apart. Salome is blackened and "damnèd" (IV.vi.295) by her own bad actions. But it is Salome alone who is restricted by this "natural" order, not Mariam. While Constabarus's description of a world turned upside down by women ruling men also seems to receive the approbation of the play (I.vi.421–32), Mariam is accounted the rightful ruler of the men around her, even by him. Mariam also divorces her husband, in that she refuses conjugal relations with him, but she remains unique among women. Women are a "wavering crew" whom Constabarus curses to the end; but Mariam is the "one to give [women] any grace" (IV.vi.311–12). Even Herod claims that Mariam cannot be "darken[ed]" because she is by

"Heaven made so bright" (V.i.38). Those whose rule is accepted as "natural" are brilliant; those who "unnaturally" seize power are dark.

The only characters colored against type are Graphina and Cleopatra. Graphina is a slave girl, and Cleopatra, a queen. And yet, "Graphina's brow's as white, her cheeks as red" (II.i.40) as Mariam's, and Cleopatra is a "brown Egyptian" (I.ii.190) whose face cannot compare. In both cases, color seems to signal moral judgments about the appropriate rule of (certain) women. Cleopatra often seems to overrule Antony in Josephus, whereas Graphina is a model of female subordination of Cary's own making.[41] While much of the critical tradition concerning *The Tragedy of Mariam* has emphasized Cary's own defiance of her husband for the cause of religion, we should also bear in mind the extent to which she wished to appear subordinate.[42] *The Lady Falkland: Her Life* goes to great lengths to stress that "though she had a strong will, she had learnt to make it obey [her husband's]."[43] The author (one of Cary's daughters) insists that "where his intressted was concerned, she seemed not able to haue any consideration of her owne"—with the notable exception of questions of conscience and religion: "she seemed to preferre nothing *but religion and her duty to God*, before his will."[44] As Alison Shell points out, while we should treat the presentation of Cary in *Her Life* with suspicion, "such texts can provide potentially excellent evidence of the moral and religious ideals most valued by their subjects."[45] If female subordination is similarly represented in *Mariam*, then only moral imperatives license female rule.

Clearly, the gravity of political power bears upon Mariam as a sexed subject in the play: her husband executes her. But what precisely is interesting about *The Tragedy of Mariam* is the extent to which this position is ameliorated by other material conditions. The "natural" hierarchies of the play are appreciated through a system of color, but this is not (or not only) metaphor. Color marks the humoral equilibrium—the superior moral disposition—of the social superiors of the play. The play supplies us with a representation of a political order naturalized by a fantasy of physiological supremacy, and this distinction reorganizes the social relations within it. Mariam can assume the rights and privileges of men and retain her moral authority because she is—or so the play would have it—inherently superior to her husband. Indeed, Herod declares that "if she had been like an Egyptian black, / And not so fair, she had been longer liv'd" (V.i.239–40). His argument is that if she had not "pass'd [all women] / In every gift, in every property" (V.i.227–28) she would not have provoked such an extremity of feeling. This would have spared her both Salome's jealousy and his own. It is clear, however, that in his contrast of "black" and "fair" he is not simply speaking of an exterior quality; rather he says that "her excellencies [in every gift, in every property] wrought her timeless fall" (V.i.228–29).

What we witness in *Tragedy of Mariam* are signs of an internal disposition that are rendered in binaries of black and white. While they exhibit an effort to, in Hall's phrase, blacken "groups that needed to be marked as 'other,'" their application is not topical.[46] Rather, the ideology at work is a medically affirmed moral dispensation of human beings. Ferguson has argued that in *Mariam* "we can see some of the early complexities of racialist thinking," which she describes as an ideological formation whereby "some invisible quality [is] carried by the blood in one's veins." This prior mode of racialist thinking "become[s] yoked to ideas about nation and about hidden religious belief."[47] I have resisted yoking this ideological thinking to concepts of nation in the play precisely because I think that by refusing the attachment we render visible *how* these qualities are transmitted through the blood. Lineage, nation, and religious identity intertwine because humoral theory underwrites the production of all of these ideologies. But privileging one line of ideological production permits us to view its operations more clearly. The medical theory that guarantees the transmission of certain characteristics as a privilege of rank conveys to later formations of racial logic. But a system of social arrangements and discriminations articulated through a language of the body, and defined by a medical scheme, precedes the development of biological science—and this fact has raised an increasingly vexed set of questions for early modern scholarship. Cary's *Mariam* allows us to see how social prejudice informs a particular dramatic imagination; and it is perhaps useful to notice (once more) how a political construct is naturalized in its fantasy. If race is rewritten and redeployed for occasion—answering the political and economic interests of a particular time—then each instance where the fiction is produced has value in terms of both what it conveys about its cultural moment and what it predicts about the strategies of production for other occasions. Taken in this context, the play serves as both a reiteration of early modern racial logic and a site of its manufacture. *The Tragedy of Mariam* vividly portrays how the early modern humoral model underwrites a reading of the skin as an expression of interior disposition—the semiotics of black and white utilized throughout the play mark territory that is more than skin deep.

"Transmitted down"

Notions of moral superiority as a hereditary fact, transmitted through the blood in the form of humoral disposition, is the very idea upon which Temple builds his case concerning the inherent inferiority of Irish subjects in *The Irish Rebellion* (1646). Temple trades upon conceptions of hereditary blood, and the physical and moral virtue that noble blood was thought to transmit through family lines, in order to argue for the moral degeneracy and irreligion that he claims the Irish convey through family descent. "The perverse dispositions of the Irish ... the malignant impressions of irreligion and barbarism ... [are] transmitted down," Temple writes, "whether by infusion from their ancestors, or naturall generation ... [this disposition] had irrefragably stiffned their necks, and hardned their hearts against all the most powerfull endevours of Reformation."[48] While previous New English tracts cite Irish constitution as the source of the intractable Irish problem, many provide multiple sources of corruption. Spenser swears that "no purposes whatsoeuer ... mente for [the] good [of Ireland] will ... prosper or take good effecte" but claims that the cause might "proceed from the *very Genius* of the soile, or influence of the starres" as well as from hereditary blood.[49] But the idea that religion is derived through parental descent has both a context and a complicated history, so that it is worth tracing (at least some of) the steps that lead to Temple.

The Old English Lords in Ireland, in the narratives of the New English tracts, neglected their constitutions and degenerated from themselves. In explaining how English lords failed to be "defenders of theire bloodlines," the author of *The Supplication of the Blood of the English* provides a précis of the account recurrent in New English tracts of how the English were converted "from men to monsters."[50] Early English statutes "forbadd the Englishe to intangle themselves with Irishe woemen ... but [to assure that] these with whom wee marry, are of the race of the Englishe: are spronge of them." But the "predecessors" of the Old English Lords "drowned themselves in Irishe puddells ... [and] gave theire children nothing but theire names." The children themselves both "drewe theire nature from the corruption of their mothers ... [and] suckte theire conditions from the teates of their Irish nurses."[51] The English have joined with the Irish in blood, and like Elyot, the author of *The Supplication* sees the "utter destruction of [the] realme" in the alteration of the noble constitution of the Irish governors.[52] But if they have "drowned" their superior complexions in the fluids of Irish women, the humor that they seem to have imbibed the most is the "monstrous melancholy" of wrong belief.⁵³ The Old English nobles are absent all of the traits that faith would produce: "love," "humanytie," "conscience," and "religion."⁵⁴

Evidence that religion, or wrong religion, is the chief source of corruption that the Old English Lords drew from the Irish lies not in the description of the majority as "hereticks, infidells, doggs," and their children as "the seede of an hatefull generation,"⁵⁵ but in the depiction of the lone Protestant lord in Ireland, the Earl of Ormond: "He is not Irishe howsoever his honor hath wrought him into an Irish Erldome: His hart hath not a droppe of Irishe bloode, not a point of Irishe condicons in it . . . his behaviour shewes him ours not theirs; faithful not treacherous; Englishe not Irishe."⁵⁶ Ormond surely had every bit as much "Irishe bloode" in his heritage as any other Anglo-Irish lord. But his body was "Englishe not Irishe" if he was Protestant.⁵⁷ Religion, rather than rank, becomes the guarantee of moral inheritance in Ireland. And like Cary's *Tragedy of Mariam*, moral differences are drawn in color.

> [The Irish] are blacke Moores . . . wash them as long as you will, you shall never alter their hue. [Our] mercy will not change theire manners; [our] benefitts be they never soe aboundantly powred upon them, will never wash away the corruption of their nature; nor . . . move them to forsake the rebellion that buddes from their supersticious Idolatry. It is the fruite of their religion.⁵⁸

The moral differences that are being marked, I have insisted throughout, are understood in somatic terms: the excess of black bile that assures the religious corruption of the Irish is expressed in a discourse of blackness. Sujata Iyengar has written that in the New English tracts generally (and Spenser's *View of the Present State of Ireland* in particular), "skin color is, if not irrelevant, certainly far less important than . . . religious affiliation . . . national origin . . . language and culture."⁵⁹ But while skin color is certainly not the point, the blackness that covers the Irish in these descriptions *is* pointing to their shared humoral complexion. Nuanced studies have been produced in the wake of Hall's *Things of Darkness* that explore the racializing potency of color-coding; but unless it is aligned with black skin, blackness is often understood as signifying something that is not somatic, but semiotic, in its terms. The estrangement of religion from humoral complexion in many of these studies renders the somatic terms separate from the cultural discourse that describes them. The New English tracts demonstrate a fantasy of an interiority that—like the ideology of hereditary blood that upholds lineage—marks the Irish and their descendants.

These discourses are both technically descriptive *and* discursive. The blackening of the Irish invokes both their shared pagan nature and shared constitution. It further assures that they are all indelibly one color. If the constitution of rank vacillates in a colonial context, the constitution of religion is written as a stable, unwavering fact: both Anglo and Gaelic Irish are marked as constitutionally inured to reform. Permanence is the point: if Jonson shows the climate (and prevailing sun) under which reform is possible, the intention of the New English tracts is to show that reform is impossible in Ireland. A discourse that racializes the Irish—and that produces their religious nature as an inherited trait—becomes part of the argument that pressed for escalation of English military activities in Ireland in the latter part of the sixteenth century.[60] One can glimpse the production of this discourse as early as 1581 in John Derricke's *Image of Ireland*, but as Iyengar notices, Derricke first distinguishes the Irish descended from "English race" (Plate II) from their Gaelic countrymen, before grouping all Irish Catholics under the rubric of "deuilles sonnes" (Plate IV).[61] Treatises that argue in these terms, racializing the Irish according to religious affiliation and not national descent, increase correspondingly with English-Irish tensions.[62]

Which is also to say that political agendas color the discourse. In 1594, Richard Beacon proposes a treatment regimen to cure the humorous body politic of Ireland.[63] In *Solon his Follie*, Beacon writes that

> Reformation of a declined commonweale, is nothing els but an happy restitution unto his first perfection: this worde Reformation being thus described, may in like sorte be devided into two parts and members: the one may bee termed an absolute and a thorough reformation of the whole bodye of the common-weale, namely of the manners of the people: the other way may be termed a reformation of particular mischiefes and inconveniences onely, which like unto evill and superfluous humors dailie arise to the annoyance and disturbance of this politicke body.[64]

But Beacon's prescription changes radically within a year of the publication of his treatise. In 1595, he wrote to the Keeper of the Great Seal that the government should "Leave . . . noe matter in the bodye of this common welthe for soe pestelent humors, or the Spanishe phesicion to work vppon: but with sword and famen remove the same: for so shall her majestie vphould the bodye of this her kingedome in safetye."⁶⁵

Beacon's later diagnosis is that Ireland must be purged so that corruption cannot spread by foreign agents. There were two prevailing treatments for Irish political disorder, and Beacon represents both sides within the space of a year: as the anonymous author of "A treatise of Irlande" (c. 1588) outlines, one argument "vundertake[s] to procure [Ireland] by Conqueste and by peoplinge of Contres with english inhabitantes," another, "wherein is vndertaken to make reformacion by publique establishment of Iustice."⁶⁶ The Old English of the Pale argued for legal reform because it would enlarge their control in Ireland and not jeopardize their property.⁶⁷ But New English settlers had no such foothold, and no such concern: as they competed with the Old English for positions and land, a discourse emerged that advocated conquest and colonization as English policy. The alteration of Beacon's mood and method in response to Irish insurrection in many ways captures a moment when the cultural narrative shifts: his *Solon* was a tract that largely stated the position of the Old English, but it was composed before the Nine Years' War (1594–1603).⁶⁸

The emergent racial discourse that these tensions produced inhabits the contradiction of inscribing essential difference upon bodies that are inherently, humorally, unstable. All of them, as a consequence, insist that there are stable programs for restitution. "Neuerthelesse [would] I persuade in no wise anie more to mixe English with the Irish in replanting [Ireland] with English inhabitants," the anonymous author of the 1599 "Discourse of Ireland" writes, "which must be a course necessary to be helde yet I would not the bloud of [the Irish] should be extinct, but all the race of them to be translated out of Ireland . . . The removing of the Irish maye happily alter their disposition when they Shall be planted in another Soyle."⁶⁹

The alteration of the Irish, their potential to grow into another sort of human, depends in this racial fantasy upon a change in environment and influence. The Irish would be transplanted in England as servants until climate and religious conversion wrought a change in them. The susceptibility of the humoral temperament to external non-naturals renders such programs possible. But while the author of "A Discourse of Ireland" attributes physical difference to entire populations—asserting that "some Flemmings" might be "planted in [the] Roomes" of the Irish because they are "of more propinquity to our Nature"—he nonetheless assumes that the Irish body will reform in a different habitat, over successive generations.⁷⁰ Of course, this is all in the service of the English. And England, of course, supplies the perfect climate for right religion. The contradictions captured in this prescription for the restoration of the Irish to health show the extent to which essentialism ("all the race of [Irish]") is consistent with humoral theory.

In the humoral language that flows through both the discourse on policy and the New English tracts that try to influence it, blood and inheritance become the argument. But while these tracts argue that the degeneracy of Old English Lords in Ireland alienates them from the land that they oversee, their degeneration seems to derive more from the wrong religion than from other colonial pressures of displacement. As the stability of notions of hereditary blood begins to disintegrate under the pressure of colonial activity, and the revised political and economic agendas that attend it, we can perceive in these writings the altered somatic conditions of moral authority. If the moral authority to rule is conveyed through bloodlines, and the virtue of nobility is perceived to be in decline, it is refused in favor of a revised category of virtue, captured in religious affiliation. Presumptions of hereditary virtue break down at the same moment that a different system of virtue supplants it. Religion emerges at this time as a key term in affirmations of who should rule—and will emerge, as we will see in Chapter 5, as a key term in assertions of who must serve.

"For the first hundred years after their arrival," Temple claims, the English "kept themselves in entire bodies ... not suffering the Irish to live promiscuously among them." Their decline begins in close contact "when afterwards they began to be more carelesse of their habitation, and to suffer the Irish to intermingle with them."[71] But while the breakdown of the English body seems to clearly come through the traffic of flesh and fluid, and the English clearly assume "the perverse dispositions of the Irish" at the time of comingling, "the malignant impressions of irreligion and barbarism" appear to be the chief bequest of Irish constitution. The moral degeneracy of the Old English Lords is expressed in irreligion, but it is an Irish inheritance. The Irish are so poorly inclined to religion that "the power of holinesse decay[s] in the land": "the name [is] soon lost, and even the very prints and characters thereof ... obliterated."[72] The discourse of the New English tracts render religious difference as disease: Catholicism is either a moral pathogen that breaks down the humoral body or an expression of the body's corrupted state. But in its passage from parent to child, or through the blood of the nurse, the disease is congenital.

CHAPTER 4

"Soule is Forme"

The (Re)formation of the Body in Edmund Spenser's *The Faerie Queene*

> For we are members of his bodie, of his flesh, and of his bones.
>
> —Eph. 5:30, Geneva Bible

Toni Morrison has written that "the act of enforcing racelessness in literary discourse is itself a racial act."[1] While there have been a few excellent studies of race in Spenser—notably, Dennis Britton's examination of the racialization of religion in early modern English Romance—the "racecraft" deployed in the religious allegory of Spenser's *Faerie Queene* has received limited attention.[2] Arguments against such a focus have ranged from pointing to the highly artificial nature of poetry, to the allegorical terms in which the work is written, to Spenser's sustained engagement with prior literary source material that is not situated in his historical context.[3] But the manner in which Spenser uses his source material, and the context in which it is applied, is precisely the act of racecraft. As Britton and I have written elsewhere, "Those who argue that it is historically inaccurate to analyze the Christian typology of black and white in *The Faerie Queene* in terms of chromatic race miss the point: this is a cultural moment in which that history is written."[4] Spenser is one of the chief authors of English colonial policy and one of the principal architects of race-thinking in English poetry.[5] The allegorical figures in his long poem, scored in black and white, are marked with a purpose: the grotesque configurations of allegorical Catholic subjects in Spenser's epic poem represent them as figures that literally cannot (re)form.[6]

In his study of how categories of Christian thought shaped racial science, Terence Keel notes that "we must see that Christian universalism entails a series of conceptual negotiations with racial difference, negotiations that simultaneously 'other' specific populations and shore up the boundaries of Christian European identity."[7] But the renewed interest in Christian, or Pauline, universalism in early modern literary studies has only recently brought attention to how it was used as an instrument of early modern theorizing about race and physiological difference. In his study on the religious and racial diversity of Spain before the expulsion, and before contact with the New World, Jonathan Boyarin argues that it was Jewish difference, not the colonial encounter, that molded how Christian Europeans thought of themselves in relation to Pauline universalism.[8] Gregory Kneidel has argued that the communally oriented Paul of the messianic tradition, interested in bringing diverse social groups together in a corporate church, was the figure more recognizable to early moderns—and is the one that animates the work of writers such as Spenser, Donne, and Milton.[9] Julia Reinhard Lupton affirms this Paul as the precedent to a cohort of early modern literary progeny. But embedded within the universalism of Paul's teaching was the assumption of embodied difference that marked religious membership. Paul's distinction between flesh and spirit focused on the marking of the body through circumcision—or the demarcation of Judaic flesh against Christian spirit. Both Kneidel and Lupton maintain that Paul as a civic actor required that social identity and religious affiliation be subordinated to universalism, that the "peculiar practices" of Jewish law "must be subsumed and refigured by the universal order promised by the Messiah to all nations."[10] Circumcision, the physical mark on every male follower of Jewish law, is set against baptism—a ritual available to all that leaves no surface marking.[11] Jewish bodies marked the boundaries that delimited Christian universalism—as communities are legitimated by exclusion. Jane Degenhardt perceives, as Keel does, the strategies of race in such demarcation and sees early modern English drama as a proving ground for such identity practices.[12] Edmund Spenser's *Faerie Queene* participates in this project as well, relegating religious others to the outskirts of Christian community—but it is Catholics in particular whose carnal commitments configure them as Jews by a different name and situate them outside of the *corpus Christianum*.

To understand how Christian universalism functions as a mechanism of exclusion in Spenser's epic romance, it is necessary to at first recognize how the entire work is deeply invested in the material effects of religious belief. In the Castle Alma episode of Book II of the *Faerie Queene*, Spenser seems to imply that the careful regulation of the body is required for the healthy habitation of the soul. The "house of Temperaunce" in which Alma resides is a model of humoral regulation, in which intake and expulsion are carefully monitored.[13] The chief enemy of Alma's castle of health, the "badly sick" Maleger, is marked as a melancholic by his cold and dry humoral condition. When the melancholic figures of Maleger's army storm the castle, the assault upon the rational soul (Alma) seems a physical one. And yet, in his final defeat, Maleger is not killed by sword or suffocation (both are tried by Arthur) but by baptism. After exhausting other options, Arthur throws Maleger into a lake and finally overcomes him. This oddity renders the treatment of the melancholy that afflicts Maleger unclear, as well as the state of the affliction itself. Whether melancholy is a physical imbalance or spiritual crisis is a current and significant debate at the time of Spenser's writing (as we saw in Chapter 1). According to both Aristotelians and Galenists contemporary to Spenser, the question is not whether the soul is affected when the body's qualities are altered; certainly, it is. The question is what this tells us about the status of the soul in the body.

Spenser's understanding of the operation of the soul is deeply implicated in matter. In spite of this, Spenser struggles, like his contemporary John Donne, to reconcile belief in election with a materialist idea of the soul.[14] The conflict of this position with central principles of Calvinist thought is made clear with the rehearsal of the strategies of Calvinists such as Timothy Bright in his *Treatise of melancholie*. Regardless of how, or how much, contemporary treatments for melancholy had appeared to put the mind, and therefore the rational soul, within the compass of medical remedy, Bright's treatise is entirely occupied with driving a wedge between body and soul in psychosomatic relations. The notion that a condition of the body could restrict—or even obstruct—the reception of grace had to be conclusively refused. But as both Angus Gowland and Beth Quitslund have argued, the separation that the Calvinists attempt to force was in many ways blurred by their own use of medical terminology in manuals that prescribe for the treatment of spiritual affliction.[15] I have argued that the intended purpose of pressing medical language into the service of spiritual treatment was in part to evacuate the terms of their material and medical specificity. But the effect, Gowland

and Quitslund both observe, was instead to render the distinction between mental and spiritual affliction obscure, to "bind . . . together body and soul and redefine . . . their interactions."[16] Further, Luther had previously affirmed the spiritual melancholy that the Calvinists eschewed. While the recovery of spiritual crisis (against physical melancholy) was an urgent theological problem for Calvinists, Christian physicians on the continent such as Felix Platter and Ercole Sassonia follow Luther in citing spiritual melancholy as their most persistent problem.[17]

If Bright's construction uses the spirit as a bulwark to keep the soul apart from the organic operations of the body, Spenser seems to afford the body access to, and corruption of, the rational soul. Spenser's literary doppelganger in *A discourse of ciuill life*, "Maister Spenser," asks how the "soule being immortall" can be "troubled with Lethargies, Phrensies, Melancholie, drunkennesse, and such other passions, by which we see her ouercome, and to be debarred from her office and function."[18] The character of Spenser in Ludowick Bryskett's fictional discussion finds, as Donne does, "no opinion in Philosophy [or] Divinity . . . [that] constrains [one] to beleeve, both that the soul is immortall, and that every particular man hath such a soul,"[19] "ffor the minde," Spenser declares in his *View of the Present State of Ireland*, "followethe muche the Temparature of the bodye."[20]

These contemporary arguments bear particularly upon the two cantos in Book II of Spenser's *The Faerie Queene* that deal with the regulation of the body and the maintenance of the (rational) soul. The Castle Alma episode(s) of cantos 9 and 11 show the body subject to the attack of the forces of melancholy. Maleger is the desperately diseased "cruell Capitaine" (II.ix.15) of the ruined band that assails the rational soul. The spelling of "Capitaine," as A. C. Hamilton observes, not only serves the meter but emphasizes "Maleger's role as head of the troops that assault the head of the temperate body" (II.ix.15, 3n). The higher faculty of the intellective soul—of reason and will—is subjected to a "swarme" (II.ix.16) of phantasms that "though they bodies seeme, yet substance from them fades" (II.ix.15) when they are put under the pressure of examination. This implies the fantasies of the mind that melancholy produces. But it is the figure of Maleger himself that provides the greatest evidence of melancholy as the chief assailant against the rational soul.[21] He is "pale and wan," "leane and meagre," and wears a helmet "Made of a dead mans skull" (II.xi.22); he is a figure of death himself, or the prefiguration of inevitable demise. His bodily humor is cold and dry, his skin "withered like a dryed rooke" and "as cold and drery as a Snake" (II.xi.22), the physiological disposition of melancholy. He appears to be the melancholy humor brought on by the consideration of salvation.

Canto 9 largely contends with how the mind is kept in health: Alma is not simply the soul of man but the higher, rational soul that controls the body (II.ix.18, 1n.). Her residence in the heart (II.ix.33) indicates that she inhabits the body, rather than simply occupying it as a vehicle or instrument. This is one of the chief departures of Aristotle from Plato in *De Anima*: that reason, the highest principle, was associated with the heart, from which it spread its influence through the body as its form.[22] In Alma's castle, it is clearly implied that reason and judgment are affected by the body's humoral disposition.[23] When the rational soul seems so much within the scope of the body's organic character, however, it comes as a surprise that Maleger's melancholy state is ultimately eradicated by baptism. In his battle with Arthur, Maleger continually arises with fresh vigor "From th'earth" (II.xi.44), his melancholic humor ("spirits") renewed from the element of earth from which it is derived. After several attempts to kill him (II.xi.44–45), Arthur finally drops him into a "standing lake" (II.xi.46) from which he does not rise. What is startling about this conclusion is that Spenser ultimately suggests that Maleger's disease is spiritual sickness—with a spiritual remedy. The moment produces the very collapse in terms that the Calvinist Platonists abhor. Maleger's sickness is clearly a physical malady, a humoral imbalance, for much of the two cantos; however, in the final struggle, his illness is ultimately eradicated by a spiritual salve. Spenser appears to be claiming that baptism will forestall melancholy.

Spenser seems to want to follow the Calvinist scheme of a spiritual crisis without medical therapy: the arrows with which Maleger is supplied are tipped with a poison that has no cure ("Ne was their salue, ne was their medicine, / That mote recure their wounds: so inly they did tine" [II.xi.21]). But Maleger is himself a figure of humorally "vnsound" "substance" (II.xi.20): his name (meaning "badly sick") and his imbalanced constitution are introduced concurrently in the poem. The assault that he leads is against a body—the fortress of Alma. Spenser's conflation serves as more than an index of the brand of Galenic materialism that Bright sought to counter. Spenser does not understand the soul as an accident of the body, but he clearly perceives it as part of the body's substantial form. It gives specific existence to the living body. As Spenser puts it in another work: "For of the soule the bodie forme doth take: / For soule is forme, and doth the bodie make" (*An Hymne in Honour of Beautie*, 132–33).[24] Spenser's composite of physical and spiritual ailments reveals how he understands this fashioning to take place. It underscores that he perceived religious affliction as a physical *and* spiritual problem. And it strongly suggests that Spenser saw the conditions of body and soul as sympathetic and reinforcing.

Of course, this makes no sense at all. The metaphor of the body as a castle is derived from Plato, and the tripartite hierarchy of powers that Plato describes as three ascending levels of vision and desire seems at large in Alma's castle. But Platonic (and Neoplatonic) formulations fall apart if reason can be attacked by a physical malady—and if a physical malady can be resolved by a spiritual exercise.[25] Spenser's image of the natural body as a castle is not Plato's. As Robert Reid observes, the frame of Spenser's figurative body "is informed by the Platonic hierarchy," but in its constitutive parts—"the ... lower 'nutritive' parts of the castle," the "dichotomy of pleasant-painful emotions in the heart," and most particularly the "diverse portrayal of rational activity both in the brain and elsewhere"—the body operates according to Aristotle's system.[26] Which is to say that Plato provides the skeleton, but Aristotle largely supplies the corpus of the representation. Spenser's configuration is a synthesis of the Platonic and Aristotelian schemes.

The image of the natural body in Alma's castle is the most sustained and carefully constructed in a long literary history of the figurative castle. The Castle Alma episode is an attempt to answer how the "soule [can be] immortall" and yet can still be "troubled with Lethargies, Phrensies, Melancholie, drunkennesse, and such other passions, by which we see her ouercome, and to be debarred from her office and function." Like Furor, who is not an opponent that "steel can wound, or strength can ouerthroe" (II.iv.10), Maleger cannot be overcome by the usual means, and Arthur is forced to throw away "His own good sword *Morddure*, that neuer fayld ... And with his naked hands him forcibly assa[yl]" (II.xi.41). The resort to hands as weapons recalls the physical nature of the struggle, and Arthur, like Guyon before him, is left to wrestle Maleger into submission.[27] The parallels between these two poetic moments call attention to the physiological and psychological nature of temperance. But they also serve to remind us of the nature of the challenge: the characters of Furor and Maleger are among the "Phrensies [and] Melancholie" that daily overcome the soul. This reading gives new dimension to Maleger as a figure of old Adam. Indeed, he represents how the body, and the sins that it carries and sustains, can impair and imperil the soul. In the *Faerie Queene*, particularly in the Castle Alma episode, reason seems highly susceptible to the body's organic temper in Spenser's construction. Maleger, as a figure of melancholy, enacts the challenge that the body poses to the soul's direction.

No one would claim that Book II of the *Faerie Queene* does not cast the virtue of temperance in terms of psychosomatic relations. Nor has the implication of the soul in this transaction been absent in scholarship on Spenser for sixty years: since A. S. P. Woodhouse argued for the division of nature and grace between the second and the first books, scholarship has continued to trouble this binary.[28] But while there are numerous arguments that perceive Spenser's view of temperance in Christian terms, the arguments concerning temperance as the ground of Christian belief do not inhabit the flesh. This is to say that temperance has been understood in critical terms as producing Christian virtues, or as preparing the individual to receive God. Religion itself has not been reckoned a product of humoral constitution. But both right and wrong religion, as we have seen throughout this book, were often understood to issue from the body's humoral temperament in the early modern period. Early modern moralists and physicians, as we have seen, resorted to Galen "as a physiological model for understanding the relationship between the immaterial soul and the physical world as they were connected to one another within and through the human body."[29]

Indeed, we are promised such an exposition at the start of canto 9:

> Of all Gods workes, which do this world adorne,
> There is no one more faire and excellent,
> Then is mans body both for power and forme,
> Whiles it is kept in sober gouernment;
> But none then it, more fowle and indecent,
> Distempered through misrule and passions bace:
> It growes a Monster, and incontinent
> Doth loose his dignitie and natiue grace.
>
> (II.ix.1)

Central to Galen's interpretation of body-soul interaction is the causal relationship between humoral constitution, or temperament, and the soul's capacities.[30] The "natiue grace," or character of God in a man, in Spenser's expression, becomes deformed and monstrous without proper and vigilant attention to humoral regulation. The means by which men grow monsters is revealed in Maleger's final contest with Arthur. Maleger's fatal power is exposed in a riddle "exceed[ing] reasons reach" (II.xi.40). He is

> Flesh without bloud, a person without spright,
> Wounds without hurt, a bodie without might,
> That could doe harme, yet could not harmed bee,
> That could not die, yet seem'd a mortall wight,
> That was most strong in most infirmitee.
> (II.xi.40)

This ultimate challenge to Arthur has been interpreted as man's struggle with the mortal problem of concupiscence. But while this is undoubtedly true, I want to focus attention on the subject of Maleger himself. "A bodie without might, / That could doe harme, yet could not [be] harmed" sounds less like the exterior corpus and more like the internal workings of a man. "Flesh without bloud," or the spirits that rise from blood to knit body to soul, leaves nothing but a hydraulic machine. But it is that appliance, strongest when it is at its weakest and most diseased, with which Arthur must wrestle.

If we see Maleger through this optic—as the distempered, melancholic body assaulting the rational soul and (potentially) changing its ultimate course—then an altered reading of Book II also comes into focus. The "natiue grace" that is threatened in man is not simply the image of God in him but the religious belief that is indigenous to him. Arthur's defeat of Maleger in water indicates that the melancholy he is battling is spiritual and not purely physical. The melancholy that Arthur ultimately defeats is the "grand sinne of Atheisme, or impiety, [or as] *Melancthon* calls it . . . monstrous melancholy."[31] But as Burton's declaration makes clear, atheism, in its early modern sense, means wrong belief—or those who do not hold to the moral tenets of Christianity—as well as those who do not believe in God. The extent to which Spenser believed the soul to be material is impossible to say. The single source of evidence for this lies with Bryskett's sketch based upon a treatise by Baptista Giraldo; and while it would make sense for Bryskett to match the people he knew to Giraldo's speakers, we cannot know how much of the conversation is shaped by Giraldo's text or is configured to it. But within the fictional narrative, Spenser not only is entreated by his host to hold forth on the moral philosophy of Plato and Aristotle, he demurs that he has already done so in the *Faerie Queene*.

At the conclusion of Bryskett's *Discourse*, the conversation among himself and his interlocutors turns to the ontology of the soul.[32]

> Because that diuine part of the Intellectiue soule which is in vs, is to haue consideration not onely of our present state of life, but also

to . . . eternitie . . . Therfore did *Aristotle* fitly teach, that men ought to bend and frame their minds wholy to that true and absolute end: for that the minde being diuine, it is his proper office to seeke to vnite it selfe to his first principle or beginning, which is God[.] . . . [God] hath bestowed on him a soule made to his own likenes, so he should therewith bend his endeuour to be like him in all his actions, *as farre as the corruption contracted by the communion of the bodie will permit.*[33]

Because the character of Spenser speaks to the point of corruption, in asking how the soul can be both immortal and fatally disturbed by the "Phrensies, Melancholie . . . and such other passions," this section of Bryskett's *Discourse* has been the subject of much critical discussion. Yet most scholars, even one as alert as Michael Schoenfeldt, have largely passed over "Spenser's" inquiry into the essence of the soul itself. While Schoenfeldt admits that the moment is part of an investigation of the "close relationship between bodies and souls," he avers that "Spenser's" question goes to "how body affects spirit."[34] But spirit is not soul: as we have seen through Bright's treatment of the spirit in his *Treatise*, the spirit(s) can be perceived as either a conduit for the exchange between body and soul or as a barricade against their transaction. "Spenser" is interrogating the nature of the soul and how, if it is "debarred from [its] office and function," and frustrated in its path to salvation through the operations of the body, it can be counted immortal. Bryskett's *Discourse* is an index of not only how preoccupying the argument was at the end of the sixteenth century but also how available. Characterizing the controversy in terms of the role that temperance plays in the maintenance of virtue fails to fully capture either the debate or its consequences. Temperance is part of the discussion, to be sure. But the extent to which the process of intellection involves the rational soul in matter has implications far beyond the limits of the body. If the rational soul relies upon the sensitive for intellection, does it die with the instrument of apprehension?[35] Even if the soul can be counted immortal, to what extent does the body have the power to corrupt it?

The *Discourse* shows the currency of the controversy in Spenser's time, and while Bryskett tries to represent the triumph of his opinion in the discussion, he is mostly met with skepticism. Indeed, "Spenser" does not seem persuaded: "Let me ask you this question," he says, "if the vnderstanding be immortall, and multiplied still to the number of all the men that haue bene, are, and shall be, how can it stand with that which *Aristotle* telleth vs of multiplication, which (saith he) proceedeth from the matter; and things materiall are always corruptible?"[36] If every individual has a particular soul (as Avicenna theorized and many accepted), then, "Spenser" reasons, the multiplication of souls suggests that the soul must be matter, or must proceed from matter.[37] Far from accepting Bryskett's arguments, "Spenser" seems to be saying that the soul has its beginning with a specific body, and that it is indivisible from matter.[38] Of course, Bryskett's account cannot be counted as Spenser's position. But we see in Bryskett's account a position that is consistent with the embodied terms of Spenser's religious allegory.

That Alma directs her rational activities from the heart of her castle tells us a good deal about how Spenser imagines the body of the elect. Daniel T. Lochman has observed that Melanchthon, like Spenser, follows the philosophers who put the seat of the rational soul in the heart.[39] But this is in no small measure due to the idea that love of God is natural to all human beings: Calvin writes that the "seed of religion," belief in God, is a "natural disposition" that "tenaciously ... inhere[s] ... in the hearts of all."[40] In resolving upon the situation of the rational soul, Melanchthon cites the authority of the prophets and apostles, who identified the heart as the source of cognition, not the sentiment.[41] But he obtains his conviction from Paul, who wrote that men have "the Law written in [their] hearts" (Rom. 2:15).[42] Paul is, at this moment in Romans, arguing for the inclusion of the Gentiles in the Christian faith: they have no need of Jewish law because they "do by nature the things *conteined* in the Law, they hauing not the Law, are a Law vnto themselues" (Rom. 2:14). They follow by nature what the Jews adhere to by authority, for "the Spirit of ... God [is written] not in tables of stone, but in fleshlie tables of the heart" (2 Cor. 3:3). This is a cornerstone of Paul's radical doctrine of inclusion—that all have access to the universal truth of Christian faith because it is inscribed in the heart. It is the premise of the Pauline conception of a universal church. I want to suggest that Spenser invokes the same Pauline idea in settling on the heart as the seat of the soul.[43] But for Spenser, for whom the separation of body and soul was not assured and for whom belief had material consequences, Christian universalism cannot be achieved without bodily incorporation. Reform therefore lay in the body itself. Because of close contact between body and soul, belief could not reform until the body was re-formed.

One Catholic Body

The conclusion of Book I of *The Faerie Queene* promises a marriage that is not performed. Una and Redcrosse are finally joined in "holy knots . . . / That none but death for euer can deuide" (I.xii.37). But they are soon separated. We discover that the bonds are only "signs," or tokens, for a future "knitting of loues band" (I.xii.40). The *Book of Common Prayer* holds the rite of "holy matrimonie" as significant of "the misticall vnion, that is betwixte Christ and his Churche."[44] The image is put to different employment in Spenser's poetic celebration of his own marriage. In the *Epithalamion* (1595), Spenser's concerns are aimed at the personal, even if the "endlesse matrimony" (217) that he imagines gestures in the direction of both the immediate and the eternal.[45] At the conclusion of the 1590 *Faerie Queene*, Spenser looks beyond the immediate and personal to what is enduring and communal; he looks beyond the chronology of the body to the eternal, and universal, body of the church. But the church is an earthly construct (with spiritual implications), and Spenser's concern is precisely how, in a material world, one is able to forge communion.

The union deferred at the end of Book I is effected at the end of Book III. It concludes the work in its original orientation of 1590:

> Lightly he clipt her twixt his armes twaine,
> And streightly did embrace her body bright,
> Her body, late the prison of sad paine,
> Now the sweet lodge of loue and deare delight:
> But she faire Lady ouercommen quight
> Of huge affection, did in pleasure melt,
> And in sweete rauishment pourd out her spright:
> No word they spake, nor earthly thing they felt,
> But like two senceles stocks in long embracement dwelt.
>
> Had ye them seene, ye would haue surely thought,
> That they had been that faire *Hermaphrodite*,
> . . . .
> So seemd those two, as growne together quite.
> (III.xii.45–46)

Gendered pronouns ("he," "she") in the description give way to a gender-neutral plural identity ("they," "them"). The moment in which Amoret and

Scudamour lose the integrity of their borders and become one creature recalls accounts of the androgyne as a figure of the union of the two sexes in marriage. Indeed, the image, in which individual subjectivity is abandoned for a new form of being, is commonly read as an allusion to marriage as represented in Genesis 2:24: "Therefore shal man leaue his father and his mother, and shal cleaue to his wife, and they shalbe one flesh."

Spenser's hermaphrodite in the 1590 *Faerie Queene* has been both celebrated and denigrated as an emblem of ideal marriage.[46] But it is not a depiction of marriage at all, at least in terms of heteronormative relations. The union of Redcrosse and Una is the most direct version of the allegorical construction of marriage as a mystical union in the *Faerie Queene*—which nonetheless remains unrealized. The more secularized vision of Scudamour and Amoret refuses the gendered and sexual differences of marriage in favor of a unitary hermaphrodite as the figure for "one flesh"; that is, the universalism of the Pauline church is expressed in the hermaphrodite.

This moment represents instead the denial of heteronormative coupling, of reproduction, and of gender itself. The association of the image with mystical marriage—of that of Christ with his church—is readily available in the injunction from Genesis, that husband and wife "cleaue" and "be one flesh," repeated in Ephesians 5:31. The correlation in Ephesians (5:30) of man and woman as one flesh to our own incorporation as "members of [Christ's] bodie" almost forces the conclusion that, as Jonathan Goldberg observes, "Christian materialism in Paul is insistently registered in socioerotic terms."[47] This assessment is not wrong, but the gendered affiliations usually associated with such a project are eschewed at this moment. Instead of a vision of heterosexual cleaving, we are provided a picture of indeterminate gender and subjectivity. Indeed, the figure of the hermaphrodite calls these sexual arrangements into question: the reproductive relationship is refused in favor of self-containment. Subjectivity, and the claims by which it is defined, is rendered diffuse in a creature that has no integral subject. And the body's plans—its pleasures, its needs, its chronology, and the reproductive impulses that are housed within it—are set aside.

Scholarship in queer studies has pointed to the central role of the reproductive agenda in our conceptions of time.[48] The awareness of the degradation of the human body over time—an awareness that has been historically asserted as uniquely human—has resulted in sustained cultural attention upon procreative sexual practice as the means to stave it off. But the hermaphrodite stages another solution to time's ravages. As Amoret's body dissolves in "pleasure," and her vital "spright" is "pourd out," the lovers become no longer human but "two senceles stocks" that lose distinction entirely and "[grow] together" in one trunk. They form a new self "that moves directly from time into eternity on the basis of its mutual devotion, rather than its production of progeny."⁴⁹ I want to suggest that this moment of intimate transcendence provides a radical vision, one more closely aligned with Pauline prescription than the ordering of the world according to normative sexual relationships allows. It imagines the obstructive definitions of the body giving way to a corporate church: "For all ye [that] are baptized into Christ, haue put on Christ. There is nether Iewe nor Grecian: there is nether bonde nor fre: there is nether male nor female: for ye are all one in Christ Iesus" (Gal. 3:27–28).

Principal terms of identity—religion, nation, social status, gender—are erased in Paul's radical declaration in favor of a universal truth. That the universal truth is equally accessible to all is Paul's principal contribution to Christian faith. But "[putting] on the new man" (Eph. 4:24) requires putting off old habits. Alain Badiou summarizes the terms of Paul's universalism in the following way: "The Christian subject does not preexist the event he declares (Christ's resurrection). Thus, the extrinsic conditions of his existence or identity will be argued against [by Paul]. He will be required to be neither Jewish (or circumcised), nor Greek (or wise). . . . No more than he will be required to be from this or that social class (theory of equality before truth), or this or that sex (theory of women)."⁵⁰ Rites and external markings that signal inclusion in a community, and observance of the law, cannot be a qualification to declare the founding event of the new religion—it "can only *fix* the Good News within the communitarian space, blocking its universal deployment."⁵¹ For Paul, there are no visible signs that mark those called to witness the event: "circumcision is nothing, and vncircumcision is nothing" (1 Cor. 7:19). The markings and ritual practices of a community indicate degrees of belonging to the community and do not signal one's relationship to the "universal singularity," or truth of the founding event, Christ's resurrection. A "truth procedure" must be universal—it must be *real*, and therefore its truth claims must be accessible and recognizable to all.⁵² But the law calls to mind alliances that demarcate and define the Christian subject—and that obstruct the subject's relationship to the "universal singularity." Paul understands the evacuation of material specificity, the categories of subjectivity, as the premise upon which Christian universalism is founded. "The letter killeth" (2 Cor. 3:6) because the subject who identifies with the law, identifies with the flesh and not with the spirit—or the truth. "The Spirit of the liuing God [is written] not in tables of stone"—or the laws of Moses—"but in fleshlie tables of the heart." Pauline materialism is divested not of materiality but of its categorical distinctions.

The image of the ideal church, then, is at the conclusion of Book III, and the image is both corporeal and corporate. But in order to be so, it is stripped of its gender-specific terms. This is also to say that the objective to which the three books tend is the denial of material categories of subjectivity, like gender, that define and divide us. Such a claim is consistent with studies that examine the ethical practices of gendered bodies in Spenser—and where the particular *ethos* applied is spiritual.[53] What if the demand of spiritual ethics is for Spenser what it is for Paul: the neglect, or setting aside, of the particular claims of the body—its pleasures, its desires, its *sex*—in favor of one catholic body? Spenser's radical refiguring of a unified church is routed through the image of mystical marriage so that "one flesh" is reimagined as one mystical body. But in order to be incorporated, the body must be divested of all signatures of its identity so that the flesh bears no marks of ethnospiritual distinction.

The connection between the ritual law and sin, and between sin and death, is widely available in Paul's letters to followers: "For sinne toke occasion by the commandement [or law], and deceiued me, and thereby slew *me*" (Rom. 7:11). Paul insists that the law is "iust, and good" (Rom. 7:12) but that communal rituals fix the subjective identity, even mark it, as separate and apart from the universal. This is death to faith—or the belief that the truth (Christ's resurrection) is universally available. This is what Paul means when he says that the law kills: it fixes the subject within a communal identity and outside of the universal communion that is "iustified by faith" (Rom. 3:28). "For as many as are of the works of the Lawe, are vnder the curse," he writes, but "Christ hath redemed vs from the curse of the Law" (Gal. 3:10–13). Sin is a life of the body as an autonomous, and therefore desiring, subject; ritual law fixes the body within a set of practices that precisely make it separate and autonomous. Paul puts it bluntly: "the Law is not of faith" (Gal. 3:12). But what can redeem this process of self-enclosure (through ritual self-identification) is charity—or, in Pauline terms, love.

A. C. Hamilton summarizes critical opinion on the allocation of Books I and II of the 1590 *Faerie Queene* in the following way: "Holiness is the bedrock on which ... virtues are founded," and "Temperance is the basis of the virtues themselves."[54] I would argue this differently—that rather, the "Booke ... *Of Temperaunce*" demonstrates how the signature virtue of the former book is effected. In context, this formulation makes good sense: "Temperaunce" is the means by which "Holinesse" is achieved; and "Chastitie" is the virtue that "farre aboue the rest" (III.i.1) ensures temperance. The reading also understands all three books of the 1590 *Faerie Queene* as working toward the ultimate ideal of "Holinesse." I am proposing that Spenser's "*Chastitie*" represents the virtue of charity and that at the conclusion of the book dedicated to it, we see the virtue realized in its ideal form. Chastity is a love that exceeds the body: it "[shatters] that death wherein the subject, under the law, had exiled himself in the closed form of the Self."[55] It permits us to see ourselves as members of a universal union that is not part but in excess of us. Neither abstinent nor heteronormative, it surpasses the bonds of human attachment. It is not human but the force of love itself—Amoret and Scudamour therefore feel no "earthly thing" (III.xii.45). The hermaphrodite is the emblem of agape, or charity, by which both man and woman are loved equally and by which we are bound together. But as Badiou makes clear, the annihilation of self-interest requisite to faith is material in its terms, at least on a terrestrial plain. I have been arguing that all three books of the 1590 *Faerie Queene* are organized toward the ultimate ideal of "Holinesse." "Temperaunce" is the means by which the body is re-formed so that "Holinesse" can be achieved; "Chastitie" is the virtue that assures such reformation. In fact, I am arguing that all three books of the 1590 *Faerie Queene* are arranged according to Pauline prescription of what is left to us in the material world: "now abideth faith, hope and loue . . . these thre: but the chiefest of these *is* loue" (1 Cor. 13:13). "Faith" is the commitment to the universal truth of resurrection; "hope" is the process by which the self is reformed in faith, once this conviction is accepted; and "charity" is the means by which the process is effected.[56] As Paul says, "Faith . . . [works] by loue" (Gal. 5:6).

It would be hard to think of a context more appropriate to Spenser, or a framework more relevant to his time, than the text of 1 Corinthians 13:13. Spenser declares "the armour of a Christian man specified by Saint Paul" (Eph. 6:11–17) as the outfit of the knight who first comes "pricking on the plaine" (I.i.1, 1) in defense of "Holinesse."[57] But of the three operations that Paul declares essential to the new man, a female knight in *The Faerie Queene* defends the virtue to which he assigns the greatest importance. The truth is—it must be—universal. But "what makes it exist in the world . . . is identical to its universality." This cause is a call to arms in Paul, the meaning of the militant Christian: under the "name of love" it is a virtue that "consists in its tirelessly addressing [the truth] to all . . . others" without discrimination or bar.[58] Spenser's central concern in *The Faerie Queene* is how to make virtue active in the world; and for him, as for Paul, both men and women are called to Christian militancy.

The description of the love that motivates Britomart's quest is plainly Pauline in its terms (in spite of Neoplatonic infiltration).

> Most sacred fire, that burnest mightily
> In liuing brests, ykindled first aboue,
> Emongst th'eternall spheres and lamping sky,
> And thence pourd into men, which men call Loue;
> Not that same, which doth base affections moue
> In brutish minds, and filthy lust inflame,
> But that sweet fit, that doth true beautie loue,
> And choseth vertue for his dearest Dame,
> Whence spring all noble deeds and neuer dying fame.
> (III.iii.1)

Immune to the ritual charms of Glauce (III.ii.49–51) or Busirane (III.xii.29), and not conceived in the "base affections" that particularize human sexual relations, the capital "Loue" to which Britomart is called is a transcendent union, emanating "first aboue" and equally available to all. It will be objected at this point that Britomart seeks a particular "Paramoure" and the "fruits" of a "matrimoniall bowre" (III.iii.3). Even I have argued elsewhere that her quest is one of marriage and reproduction. The narrative fixation of the book is undeniably upon family generation (and this is appropriate in terms of Spenser's critique of the family practices of Elizabeth I).[59] But the aborted conclusion to Merlin's Virgilian prophecy in Book III (III.iii.50) points not only to the dynastic disappointment of Elizabeth's reign but also to the uncertain future of the English Church. Colin Burrow has observed that the descent of Britomart into the cave of Merlin invokes the episode in which Aeneas receives the prophecy concerning the future of Rome in the underworld, and the political insecurity registered in the *Aeneid* is revisited here.[60] Concentration upon the universal church imagines a future that contemplation of the English Church forecloses. So long as Spenser's Protestant epic remains fixed upon dynastic concerns, its structure fails. Like the *Aeneid*, Spenser's epic must reject a woman for its story to continue. The founding of the Protestant Church can only be imagined by looking beyond the body of Elizabeth, beyond the production of progeny, and beyond the present time.

The pursuits of Spenser's book "*Of Chastitie*" are not disembodied—quite the opposite. Rather, the quest that the gendered bodies of the book anatomize is the conquest of the body's claims. This is not to say that Spenser favors abstinence: the victims of both an excess of appetitive desire (Verdant) and abstinent refusal (Timias) are similarly prone in the vulnerable attitudes of their bodies; Spenser clearly sees both behaviors as detrimental to body. But before we read the virtue of chastity as normative and procreative, we should be attentive to the reproduction that takes place in the book dedicated to it. While the book "*Of Chastitie*" might be about conception, love is its ultimate end. If Britomart is the champion of chastity, Amoret is its hero. Amoret is stolen from her wedding feast; and it is when the gendered—and generative—features of her body dissolve that she is dislodged from its "prison" (III.xii.45).[61] In fact, Book III curiously lacks depictions of human reproduction. The "formes" (III.vi.47) that Adonis fathers are benign impressions of Error's brood. The birth of Amoret and Belphoebe is made possible by immaculate conception. As Melissa Sanchez observes, Spenser was not persuaded that lust could be directed toward virtue, or rather, that sexual pleasure did not consistently invade, and ultimately corrupt, the act of reproductive sex.[62] Spenser cannot seem to view the products of that act, progeny, without an eye toward concupiscence.

Concupiscence is the point. The Greek word *epithumia*, meaning desire or yearning, is usually rendered as "concupiscence" in biblical translation.[63] This conflation captures the Christian presumption of desire as a product of the flesh. In Pauline construction, however, desire is a product of the automonous and descrete self, and self-enclosure is excited by the material distinctions that mark us as members of a religious sect or community, as free or unfree, as male or female. There is good evidence that Spenser similarly understands "concupiscence" in terms of such marked physical separation as well. The figure of Error is herself a monstrous image of generation. But the creatures issuing from Error, as Janet Adelman points out, seem initially unthreatening. As soon as the progeny flowing from her is identified as "partly male/And partly female" (I.i.21), however, as soon, Adelman claims, "as gender-difference emerges ... in language that ... does not distinguish between sorting each of the creatures separately into male and female ... [then] disgust at generation returns."[64] The "deformed monsters" (I.i.22) that Error emits might seem the mirror of the hermaphrodite; but the recurring strategy of the *Faerie Queene* is to depict the ideal and its opposite—every emblem has its travesty. They are, in fact, its inverted image: where the hermaphrodite loses gender distinction, Error's children grow malignant *as they achieve it*. That the production of Error's offspring would be directly opposed to the procedure that creates Spenser's ideal church makes good sense. Crucially, however, it is the acquisition of physical distinction that causes them to be counted as the heirs of a "heauen accurst" (I.i.26, 2).

The intervention of Greek and Christian philosophy had rendered Paul's distinction of flesh (*sarx*) and spirit (*pneuma*) as body and soul (a distinction more Platonic than Pauline in its terms).[65] But even in its Christian revision, Paul's persistent warning that the particularizing claims of fleshy existence actually *produced* the desiring subject (concupiscence) was still audible (Gal. 5:18–23). That Spenser heard the admonition is apparent in the episode that takes place in the castle of Medina (a parody of the house of Holinesse), which renders the separations among the individual sects of Christianity in terms of bodily distinction.

> Built on a rocke, adioyning to the seas;
> It was an auncient worke of antique fame,
> And wondrous strong by nature, and by skilfull frame.
> (II.ii.12)

The situation of the castle, "Built on a rocke, adioyning to the seas" (II.ii.12), suggests, as Hamilton claims, "the control of temperance over the temptations of land and sea"—and over the elements of earth and water (II.ii.12, 7n.). Its strength "by nature" indicates the body, and its "skilfull frame" is how the body is governed (II.ii.12). "Built on a rocke," it also suggests the foundation of the Church: "vpon this rocke will I build my Church: & the gates of hel shall not ouercome it" (Matt. 16:18). The moment reminds us that, just as Peter was the rock on which Christ built, the church is constructed from individual congregants. Frederick Padelford argued many decades ago that the three sisters dwelling in the castle represent three manifestations of the Christian church: the Puritan, Elissa; the Roman Catholic, Perissa; and the *via media* of the Church of England, Medina (II.ii.13, 7–9n.). The principal reason that Padelford's critique has been rejected is that the Platonic and Aristotelian elements of the episode, it has been assumed, are in contradiction to his argument. But such objections miss the point: bodily temperance, or the control, even the eradication, of the body's claims, is itself imagined as the remedy to the divisions of the Christian fellowship.

The elements of earth and water correspond to melancholic and phlegmatic humors. Melancholy has already received a fair rehearsal. A phlegmatic nature would be understood as unstable as water. Like Cymochles, such a person would be, in George Chapman's apt description, a "moist man . . . / That's ever flitting, ever ravishing."[66] These elements surround the placement of the castle within the terrain of temperance and are also paralleled in the position of Medina among her sisters. The sisters have been identified as the three faculties of the soul in Plato's tripartite division: the rational, irascible, and concupiscible. But while Medina's well-ordered appearance "and grauitie, / Aboue the reason of her youthly yeares" (II.ii.15) agrees with the rational figure she is meant to represent, and Perissa, "full of disport . . . [and] loosely light" (II.ii.36) consorts well with concupiscence, the eldest, Elissa, does not seem quite up to her part. She is admittedly malcontent, but hardly choleric, hot-tempered, or passionate. The alternate reading of the three sisters as representing the mean between two extremes of excess and defect—which reproduces the Aristotelian model of temperance in *Nicomachean Ethics*—is undercut by the battle between Guyon and the suitors. Scholarship has settled upon an amalgamation of Platonic and Aristotelian terms. But another reading becomes available when we view Medina as an extension of her castle: as a sound and temperate body straddling the rock of right religion in the midst of forces that threaten to destroy it.

As soon Guyon enters the castle, he is engaged in combat—which serves in place of introductions—with the champions of the two elder sisters. The suitor of Elissa, Sir Huddibras, is both hard and foolhardy, and his "sterne melancholy" surpasses his courage (II.ii.17). The lover of Perissa, Sansloy, was previously seen in Book I, "full of wrath" (I.iii.35) and encountering the Redcrosse knight. Now, the lust that caused him to carry off Una drives him into battle (II.ii.18). The nature of the champions is revealing of the identity of the women they serve. Huddibras, who shares his name with an English king, is most closely associated with England. His hard exterior indicates his unyielding nature, and his "errant armes" (II.ii.17) engage in a misguided fight. Samuel Butler later immortalizes him as the wayward champion of Presbyterian faith: "For he was of that stubborn crew / Of errant saints, whom all men grant / To be the true Church Militant" (*Hudibras*, I.i.192–94). Sansloy is one of three brothers who represent the perversion of religion, and in their association with Archimago in Book I, the brothers are aligned with the Catholic faith (I.ii.25).

Both suitors fall into "cruell combat ioyned in middle space" (II.ii.20), indicating their shared rejection of the temperate mean. When Guyon prepares to encounter them, his "sunbroad shield" (II.ii.21) recalls the "sunne-bright shield" (I.xi.40) of Redcrosse.[67] The knights engage in a "straunge sort of fight": "[a] triple warre with triple enmitee." The implication is that each knight wages war with an inner conflict as well as a pair of external combatants, so that "three combats ioyne in one" (II.ii.26). When Medina pleads for peace, she is reconciling a church at war with itself. But while this moment imagines an ideal conclusion where the Church of England negotiates a middle way for a divided Christian faith, it seems important to underscore that the divisions themselves are represented as a rupture of bodily forces—as a feature of temperament. Spenser's combatants embody a temperament of religious identity in Galenic terms. Thus Medina "attemper[s] her feast" (II.ii.39) in celebration of the concord struck: the "forward paire" of Perissa and Sansloy,

> she euer would asswage,
> When they would striue dew reason to exceed;
> But that same froward twaine [of Elissa and Huddibras] would
>   accourage,
> And of her plenty adde vnto their need:
> So she kept them in order, and her selfe in heed.
>   (II.ii.38)

The reconciliation in the castle of Medina is represented as a tempering of humoral extremes. But these extremes always threaten to reassert themselves and revive dis-ease.

Ruddymane, whose "cruell sport" (II.i.40) in his dying mother's blood recalls the acts of Error's brood, and who is permanently stained by his "bloudguiltinesse" (II.ii.4), or concupiscence, is given to the custody of Medina's "truth" for reform (II.iii.2). Which is to say that Medina negotiates one of the principal problems of concupiscence. Paul catalogues the "works of the flesh" as "adulterie, fornicacion, vnclennes, wantonnesse, [i]dolatrie, witchcraft, hatred, debate, emulacions, wrath, contentions, sedicions, heresies, [e]nuie, murthers, drunkennesse, gluttonie, and suche like" (Gal. 5:19–21). But the list appends a discussion of ritual circumcision and the affiliations that produce the autonomous and desiring subject. The "faith," "temperancie," and "loue" promised as "the frute of the Spirit" against the fault of ritual practices (Gal. 5:22–23) structure the strategies of Spenser's three knights in their collective quest for virtue. But it is love, finally, that is the requisite condition for the annihilation of the self. The conviction that the affiliations or categories that distinguish us must be eradicated in order to build a universal church can, as we know from Spenser, be put to darker purposes. But the conclusion of the 1590 *Faerie Queene* imagines love as the vehicle for reform. Amoret's spirit is "pourd out" of her in the same effusive terms applied to heaven's "sacred fire," and as she dissolves into Scudamour they lose both delimitation and subjectivity. Here, in this image, the new man is made through the re-formation of the body.

Members to Be Cut Off

Within the formal structure of the 1590 *Faerie Queene*, the book *Of Temperaunce* outlines the process by which the self is reformed in faith once the commitment to the universal truth, with its attendant obligations, has been accepted. The Medina episode epitomizes the process, where Medina's "truth" is the mechanism by which concupiscence is overcome. The religious affiliations of Huddibras and Sansloy are depicted as inclinations compelled by bodily disorder. Medina is able to temper these forces (at least temporarily) because she offers membership in the *corpus Christianum*—represented in her feast—that refuses individuation. Religious practices that reinforce sectarian participation deny access to the corpus: the law is weak because it inhabits the customs of the flesh; the claims of the flesh must be overcome if the law of the spirit is to be realized. The Book *Of Chastitie* shows how these fleshy prerogatives are revised through love. Chastity shows how the body can be prepared for grace—how its vegetable love can be redirected to vaster empires. Britomart embarks on a marriage quest, but the union that is ultimately achieved at the end of the book is that of liquid bodies resolving into a single corpus.

In Book IV of the 1596 *Faerie Queene*, the charity that cements the unified church of Spenser's imagining is shattered by the "disease[d] . . . soul[s]" and "depraved complexion[s]" that Ficino describes. Charity is the adjunct of love of God.[68] Corruption of the love of God, according to Augustine, corrupts the charity that proceeds from it. At the time of Spenser's writing the corruption of the soul that refused God, man, and woman had a somatic consequence, was manifest in the body as "a fault of humor."[69] Book IV is populated by figures who lack the predisposition to love God. Consequently, a different kind of hermaphrodite tries to take possession of Amoret.

It was to weet a wilde and saluage man,
Yet was no man, but onely like in shape,
And eke in stature higher by a span,
All ouergrowne with haire, that could awhape
An hardy hart, and his wide mouth did gape
With huge great teeth, like to a tusked Bore:
For he liu'd all on rauin and on rape
Of men and beasts; and fed on fleshly gore,
The signe whereof yet stain'd his bloudy lips afore.

His neather lip was not like man nor beast,
But like a wide deepe poke, downe hanging low,
In which he wont the relickes of his feast,
And cruell spoyle, which he had spard, to stow:
And ouer it his huge great nose did grow,
Full dreadfully empurpled all with bloud;
And downe both sides two wide long eares did glow,
And raught downe to his waste, when vp he stood,
More great then the'eares of Elephants by *Indus* flood.

His wast was with a wreath of yuie greene
Engirt about, ne other garment wore:
For all his haire was like a garment seene;
And in his hand a tall young oake he bore,
Whose knottie snags were sharpned all afore,
And beath'd in fire for steele to be in sted.
But whence he was, or of what wombe ybore,
Of beasts, or of the earth, I haue not red:
But certes was with milke of Wolues and Tygres fed.
                        (IV.vii.5–7)

William Oram was the first to point out the bisexed features of the figure of Lust.[70] "His huge great nose," "empurpled all with bloud" with elephantine ears on either side, was commonly read as the male sexual apparatus. But as Oram notices, the "neather lip" of Lust, "like a wide deepe poke, downe hanging low," invokes the female genitalia. Lust is the embodied figure of sexual distinction that contradicts the image that closes the 1590 *Faerie Queene*. Oram rightly perceives this episode as one that "recalls Orgoglio's imprisonment of the Redcrosse Knight in Book I: in both cases the human being is overmastered ... and deposited underground, in the dark; in both cases the progression suggests an imprisonment of the rational faculty by the sexual appetite."[71] But more needs to be said. Redcrosse is overtaken at a moment of "loosnesse" when his sexual energies are "pourd out ... on the grassy grownd" (I.vii.7), but what seizes him is not simply the occlusion of his reason. Rather, the overpowering of his rational faculty provides the occasion for spiritual crisis: he is captured by irreligion and imprisoned in the dungeon of the flesh. Redcrosse's slip leads to his immediate downfall: taken by a son of earth (I.vii.9), held by *Ignaro* (I.viii.31), he comes under the control of false religion.

The principal opposition to the life of the soul—to religion—is offered by sons of earth, by figures like Orgoglio and Maleger. The idea of the prison of the flesh is common to Christian discourse, derived from the conception that one can only perceive dimly while attached to earth available in 1 Corinthians 13:13. But the allegory does not require a specific context to make it legible. Whether the conceit is borrowed from Paul or from the dualism that marks later interpretations of Paul, the construction of the flesh as the chief challenger to the soul's condition operates across a range of traditions from classical antiquity through Christianity. What makes less sense in the context of Christian dualism is the fact that those who mediate the soul's salvation in the house of Holiness and the castle of Medina are committed to the *body's* reform. Redcrosse is first instructed in the miracles of faith (I.x.18–20). But he is subsequently seized by despair. Like Ficino's description of those who doubt religion, the knight is "soule-diseased" (I.x.24), but the procedure for cure addresses the "body's depraved complexion": Redcrosse is administered leaches (I.x.23) and then dieted to "tame his stubborne malady" (I.x.25) and to "abate" his "proud humors" (I.x.26). It is only when his body is reformed through the agency of hope (*Speranza*), the "superfluous flesh" (I.x.26) purged from him and his body's humoral balance restored, that he encounters charity (I.x.29). *Charissa* is "full of great loue" for all of God's children, but, "chast in worke and will" (I.x.30), her love proceeds from a perfected temperament. The intemperate body in these two episodes leads to wrong religion. But tempering the body does not merely produce Christian virtues; rather, the temperate body produces Christian charity, the sustaining spirit that resides in the love of both God and man. It is no accident, then, that the process that Redcrosse undergoes in the house of Holiness demonstrates in little what (I claim) the structure of the 1590 *Faerie Queene* does in large.

Both Redcrosse and Amoret are captured at moments when their own bodily desire is asserted. Amoret is seized when she walks the wood "for pleasure, or for need" (IV.vii.4).[72] The figure that claims her is a grotesque array of sexual organs. Lust is a travesty of the "faire *Hermaphrodite*" that integrates Amoret and Scudamour in a depiction of transcendent love. He is the embodiment of the physical distinction that creates the desiring subject. His exaggerated features mark him as a deformed monster similar to those that Error produces: consequently, he engages in an "vngodly trade / The heuens abhorre" (IV.vii.12), and his blood is the same "streame of coleblacke" (IV.vii.27) that flows from Error (I.i.24). Lust is the impediment to Love itself. His are the carnal impulses of those committed to the body and not to the spirit: of those unable to participate in Christian fellowship because unable to resist the claims of the body that sets them apart. These are the carnal impulses that govern the unbeliever.

That sexual license leads to sin is obvious enough, and it is not necessary to read beyond Lust's consumption of chastity to assume that his acts are not approved by heaven. To read these episodes as moments in which the passions occlude reason is sufficient to make sense of them. But these readings miss the extent to which Lust and Error are the same sign. Admittedly, one encounters the same signs repeatedly in the *Faerie Queene*; the repetition of signs is part of its didactic strategy—one learns to read the sign properly from recurrent exposure to it. But to perceive the recurrence of the androgyne in these terms alone is to overlook how the hermaphrodite operates in Spenser's construction of ideal love. It fails to make complete sense of the shared features of Error and Lust and how these are opposed to the fused form of Amoret and Scudamour or the Hermaphrodite that is the Goddess of Love herself (IV.x.41). If the image of Spenser's ideal church is one where individuation is refused in favor of incorporation, then Error and Lust stand as the marked, and demarcated, flesh that is in obstruction to the spirit of Christian love.

Such a reading helps us to understand the fleshly materiality of Spenser's religious allegory. The body does not naturally surrender its prerogatives; it must be reformed in this image. But the properly tempered body is Christian by nature. Redcrosse must be prepared for the charity requisite to Christian communion. Medina must assuage the "bloud guiltinesse" (II.ii.30) of all three of the battling knights so that "louely concord," "most sacred peace," and "fast friendship" (II.ii.31) might occur among them. *Concord* herself negotiates the extremes of the passions and "well . . . temper[s] both" before the character of *Loue* can prevail (IV.x.33) in the Temple of Venus. We should not interpret Spenser's humoral language as a call to moderation: Redcrosse achieves the health of his body through a brutal regime. We should instead perceive in these moments the radical transformation that Spenser proposes as requisite to the building of a universal church.

That Lust feeds on chastity, the love held in temperate government that defines the actions of Charity in the house of Holiness, makes clear why "the heuens abhorre" his "vngodly trade" and why he is in (religious) Error. His dark cave is Hell on earth, where conduct of life guarantees that "both grace and gaine" are withheld (IV.vii.11). The specter of the living damned he conjures, as Sanchez has noted, is a combination of elements consistent with representations of "Irish, New World, Eastern, and African peoples."[73] A naked "saluage man" shirted in his own hair, Lust is girdled with ivy and armed (like Orgoglio) with an oak tree. His elephantine ears on either side of his gaping mouth invoke both female and foreign appetitive desires. Such depictions of wild men are familiar from Pliny's description of hairy humanoids in India. But while Spenser surely wants to set libidinous behavior on the other side of the moral spectrum—and outside of civilization—I want to underscore the extent to which Roman Catholics, religious others, and those assumed to have no religion are all arranged under the sign of pagan. The depiction of Lust, Sanchez observes,

> is neither the first nor the last time that Spenser will associate sexual excess and perversion with foreign locales, religions, and peoples. Duessa is the Catholic Whore of Babylon, and a prominent feature of her dress is a "Persian mitre" (I.ii.13). The . . . knights Sansfoy, Sansloy, and Sansjoy combine faithlessness and sexual excess . . . Acrasia is based on Tasso's Armida, a [Muslim] sorceress and enemy of Christian Crusaders. Ollyphant—an alternate spelling of "elephant"—engages in prenatal incest with his twin and embodies priapic sodomy. . . . The "saluage nation" that nearly devours Serena in Book VI resembles New World natives in their imputed cannibalism and the Irish in their nomadism and bagpipe playing. (VI.viii.35)[74]

These moments of conflation no doubt reflect the incarnate experience of the Roman Catholic Church. But they also reflect attachment to the law of man that is grounded in the flesh. In Paul's pronouncement, the law that resides in the ritual experience of the flesh is weak precisely because flesh is poor rock on which to build a church. Spenser's religious allegory dwells on this problem and persistently returns to the need to reform the flesh, even to its humoral complexion, before a life of the spirit is possible. For those who live outside of the spirit—Catholics, Muslims, and savages—their error resides in flesh itself.[75]

Benedict Robinson has written persuasively of how both the religious polemic and poetry of early modern England, including the *Faerie Queene*, represent Catholics "among the outcasts and infidels" in order to expose them as "Turks in disguise."[76] I would revise this claim: rather, at least in Spenser's poem, Catholics and infidels are imagined *in the same terms*—as all sharing the same somatic weakness that forbids the light of true religion and forecloses the possibility of Christian communion. Britton has observed how Luther's comparison of "Catholics to Jews, Turks, and ... heathens" is recycled even in Thomas More's refusal of it.[77] Robinson records examples of how "Judaism, Islam, Catholicism and Protestant sectarianism" were all counted as different "versions of the same error" in Protestant polemics.[78] An illustrative example of this is available in how Burton writes a world of religious affiliation in his *Anatomy of Melancholy*. Burton, like Christopher Brooke before him, casts religion in terms of humoral categories of human being. "At this present," he writes, "How small a part is truely religious? ... Diuide the World into six parts, and fiue are not so much as Christians."[79] He goes on to catalogue the four regions of the world controlled by "Idolaters," "Mahometans," and "Pagans." The eastern churches of Ethiopia, Greece, Syria, and Russia that make up the fifth piece suffer "such a mixture of Idolatry and paganisme" that they cannot be counted Christian.[80] And "That which remaines" of the Christian world "is the westerne Church with vs in *Europe*." But that too has been overtaken, for

> The Papists haue *Italy, Spaine, Savoy*, part of *Germany, France, Poland*, and a sprinckling in the rest of *Europe*. In *America* they hold all that which *Spaniards* inhabit ... in the East *Indies*, the *Philippins*, some small holdes about *Goa, Melacha, Zelen, Ormus*, [etc.] which the *Portugall* got not long since, and those land-leaping *Iesuits* haue assaid in *China* [and] *Iapan*. ... In *Africke* they haue *Melinda, Quiloa, Mombaza* ... and some few townes, they driue out one supe[r]stition with another.[81]

Just like "The Mahometans," the Catholics "extend themselues ouer ... dominions in *Europe, Africke* [and] *Asia*" and act as a conquering force over the Christian world.[82] Where their armies fail, they have Jesuit pirates to penetrate distant lands. Burton depicts a world captured by "*A people subiect to superstition* [and] *contrary to Religon*," where England is one of the last remaining strongholds.[83] But what is significant about the surrounding hostile forces that he depicts is their shared superstition and common disease. The delusion of all invading powers, the "Idolaters," "Mahometans," "Pagans," and "Papists," originates in the religious melancholy that afflicts them all, as Burton proceeds to demonstrate. "What shall we [do] with them," he asks, "but . . . [as] a good physitian?" He then abandons the study of their "Symptomes" and concentrates upon the "causes" of their collective illness.[84]

While not a contemporary of Spenser, Burton is instructive because of the religious controversies that his treatise is intended to address. As Gowland has detailed, Burton's principal objective was political in choosing to write a section on religious melancholy; indeed, he claims, "the most important function of the medical analytic framework was in fact to conceal (and so permit) the author's participation in theological and ecclesiastical controversy."[85] Burton writes about religious melancholy for the purpose of social and political commentary in contradistinction to other contemporary Christian physicians such as Bright, Platter, and Sassonia. We have seen how Bright entered the breach of polemics, but his intention was to counter opinion that undermined his doctrinal views, not to make a particular political point. Burton's was to counteract the political unrest that attended the religious disputes of his time. Hence, even "*Anabaptists, Brownists, Barrowists* [and] *Familists*" are all listed among the catalogue of those whose religion is suspect.[86] Burton depicts a small congregation of the elect surrounded on all sides by those afflicted with "monstrous melancholy" of unbelief. His account of religious melancholy should be understood as a polemical strategy whereby medical theory is used to support fantasies of human embodiment and human difference. For Burton, religious error is a fact of the body, and people with religious affiliation outside of those designated as elect are marked as physiologically corrupt.

Spenser is writing the *Faerie Queene* at a similarly fraught religio-political moment, surrounded by those whom he regards as religiously suspect.[87] That Spenser engages in similar strategies of racialization is only to show that Burton's procedure not unprecedented but perfected. The landscape of the *Faerie Queene* is overrun with "Paynims" and Muslims, Idolaters and Infidels, whose fantastic physical features set them outside of the Christian communion. As Jeffrey Jerome Cohen has observed, "The Christian body did not have a race (just as, ideally, it did not have a gender or a sexuality), because the body of the other always carried that burden on its behalf." The medieval *corpus Christianum* presented itself "as a universal body unmarked by such differentiations."[88] In reviving the convention of medieval crusade romance for a Protestant purpose, Spenser reanimates the figure of the unmarked Christian body in the androgyne and sets it against the exaggerated bodily features of its "Error" and its opposite.

Spenser's view from Ireland in 1596 reveals little hope for a unified church. The "naturall affection" (Proem, 2) that serves as adhesive in a Christian congregation is the promised topic of Book IV: Spenser eschews romantic love and instead focuses upon the love that grounds "[all] honor and . . . vertue," the full flowering of which "crowne[s] true louers with immortall blis" (Proem, 2). But the love that guarantees salvation is mostly absent from the book, and corruption or perversion of love occupies its place. Book IV depicts love melancholy: love is achieved by conquest, fidelity is never assured, and Lust is (literally) a central figure. Cambell and Triamond, the ostensible champions of the interlocking relationships of human love—kinship, friendship, and sexual love—that provide the foundation for charity, disappear quickly from the book, and there seems to be no defender of their cause. Florimell's girdle is treated as a "precious relicke" carried in "an arke" (IV.iv.15), hung up as a reward for purely physical virtues. Florimell is herself a false "Idole" (IV.v.15), and the competition for her belt reveals the sexual looseness of all but Amoret (IV.v.17–19). In the contests of strength and beauty, as Hamilton observes, force is not a means to right, and beauty is not an expression of virtue (IV.iv.16n). The knight of Chastity ultimately wins the Tournament of Love (IV.iv.48), but the trials of love persist throughout the book.

There are certainly reformed bodies in Book IV. When Placidas, the "true louer" of Amyas, who regards his friend as his own soul (IV.viii.55) and therefore shares his body, trades places with Amyas and accepts Poena as his wife, she reforms under his influence (IV.ix.16). Catholics in England, as I have noted, occupy a different category because of the potential for reform on English soil. But from the beginning of the revised 1596 *Faerie Queene*, we are faced with the prospect that the vision of the *corpus Christianum* that closed the former work might solely rely upon the individual bodies of a community of the elect. Artegall is forced to leave Ireland before he can "reforme it thoroughly" (V.xii.27), and the body of Christendom is left in ill health. The conclusion to Merlin's vision in Book III, which finally renders him speechless at a "ghastly spectacle dismayd" (III.iii.50), invokes an apocalyptic moment in the Gospel of Matthew: "Take hede that no man deceiue you. For manie shall come in my Name, saying, I am Christ, and shal deceiue manie. And ye shall heare of warres, and rumours of warres: se that ye be not troubled for all these things must come to passe, but the ende is not yet" (Matt. 24:4–6). Spenser sees a world at war, and his vision of a universal church is a deferred promise.

The cultural strategies of *The Faerie Queene* are intended to justify Spenser's remedy in Ireland, "by the sworde."[89] The "greate Contagion in [the] Soules" of the Irish have "bred in them [the] generall disease" of political unrest and insurrection, which "Cannot but onelye with verye strong purgacions be Clensed and Carryed awaie."[90] England is directed to act as "a good physitian" (or a good surgeon) in Spenser's *View of the Present State of Ireland*. The religious allegory of *The Faerie Queene*, particularly that of Book IV (published the same year that the *View* was written), lends insight into his lethal cure. His conviction that belief has material manifestations causes him to imagine a wholly humorous Irish nation that cannot be recuperated. As Keel notes, "Christian universalism entails a series of conceptual negotiations . . . that simultaneously 'other' specific populations and shore up the boundaries of Christian European identity." For Spenser, the Catholics of Ireland must be imagined as something other than Christian, or they cannot be purged from England or its Church.[91] The allegorical figures of his Faeryland depict Catholics as so committed to the flesh that they cannot be incorporated into the body of Christ. Spenser's final solution is to cut them away.

CHAPTER 5

Moral Husbandry

Cultivating Right Religion in New Worlds

> For if our virtues must in lines descend,
> The merit with the families would end,
> And intermixtures would most fatal grow;
> For vice would be hereditary too.
> —Daniel Defoe, "The True-Born Englishman"

In the early modern period, natural philosophy and medical theory underwrite ideas of the transmission of faith in the blood. Black melancholy served as both a source and an index of wrong religion, but colonial pressures and the economic interest in forced African labor move the meaning of complexion to the surface markings of the skin. With the emergence of a fixed quality of Blackness we also witness the emergence of Whiteness and White supremacy, premised upon notions of a superior religious constitution. Social hierarchies already naturalized through medical theory are revised in the Anglo New World as ideas of affirmed religious inheritance. Early moderns understood the body's physiology as crucially dependent upon the nature of the soul and belief as an adjunct of this condition. The instability of the humors obviously made Galenic materialism pliable to a range of ideas and convictions, but it was precisely this malleability that rendered it useful in political terms. As foreign lands became fertile ground on which to dismantle cultural narratives concerning lineage, essentialist notions of moral superiority that supported noble rule were transferred to White Christian subjects.

Daniel Defoe's "The True-Born Englishman" (1701) provides evidence that the idea that blood transmits virtue, respectability, and morality persists at least until the eighteenth century. Defoe's satire bears the history of racial thinking, a history obvious enough at the time to be ironically deployed. Defoe's language, Jennifer DeVere Brody has observed, suggests that "it is the viscous substance of blood itself that conveys both virtue and vice."[1] Defoe's description of "the well-extracted brood of Englishmen" also shows the extent to which ideologies attached to rank and lineage had conflated with fantasies of a national family by this time. These fantasies fused with older fictions of blood that appear to still be current at the start of the eighteenth century. Defoe's inverted pronouncement that "virtue gives nobility," not the other way around, tells us that "virtue" remains the concept upon which social authority is premised.[2] The language of Defoe's poem not only points to the crossover of the term "race" from family lines to national groups but also implies that both kinds of racial ideology—one that supports social hierarchy, another that affirms national superiority—rest upon the invisible qualities of blood.[3]

But essentialist notions of inherent—and heritable—moral *inferiority* also grounded the rationale of early English slave practices.[4] In 1667, Virginia's burgesses passed legislation declaring that no conferment of baptism upon a child born to a slave could secure its freedom because "baptisme doth not alter the condition of the person."[5] While the Virginia law simply assured that a baptized slave would remain in bondage, it subsequently permitted Anglo-Virginians to argue that Africans and Indigenous peoples were not capable of conversion at all—that "hereditary heathenism" guaranteed that they were obdurate to Christian faith.[6] The revised opinion of who should govern, and who would serve, turned upon who was counted as Christian. Spenser's strategy in Ireland was to disparage the integrity of the noble blood of Old English Lords as corrupted by both environment and wrong religion. But it is their religion that finally guarantees the decline in their moral constitution. The rearrangement of social hierarchy from privileging rank to religion draws a long arc, one that will be traced in this chapter chiefly through two dramatic works that stage a confrontation between residual notions of race as rank and emergent ones pertaining to religion and the surface markings of the skin: William Shakespeare's *Othello* (1602) and Thomas Southerne's stage adaptation of Aphra Behn's novella *Oroonoko* (1695).[7] These two works are written almost one hundred years apart, and one is indebted to the other for its dramatic appeal; the intervening history between the works traces much of the historical trajectory of this book.⁸ The benefit of this debt is to allow us to mark the difference in the racial episteme that Southerne stages, as religious essentialism is applied in a transatlantic New World context.

The crisis concerning noble blood is largely advanced by the displacement of nobles to foreign locations—where the ability to properly regulate their humoral constitution becomes suspect. Of course, this suspicion is aroused by the ambitions of common men who perceive an opportunity to land and power in dispossessing nobles of their heritage. The fiction that attended race as lineage—the essential nature that licensed rule—was rewritten to accommodate a new kind of man. Defoe's characterization of "The True-Born Englishman" suggests that as the race of family lines was in decline, the race of nations became ascendant. But this book has examined how notions of noble constitution informed ideas of moral and religious inheritance. The influence of faith upon colonial bodies shows these ideas most tested in foreign contexts. It is religion that emerges as the principal term of difference—and the black melancholy that marks wrong religion keeps the body resistant to reform.

In her analysis of Shakespeare's *Othello*, Jane Degenhardt sees it as a limit test of Christian universalism, arguing that Othello is a figure of difference that cannot be absorbed into the Christian communion.⁹ The play, she argues, "explicitly links conversion to embodiment by positing a conjunction between inner faith and outer difference."¹⁰ While I entirely agree with this reading, Othello's Black body is something more than obdurate: the melancholy that accounts for his surface marking assures that irreligion will also descend to his offspring. *Othello* indicates the liminal moment of one ideology of inheritance—one racial logic—beginning to disrupt, if not yet displace, another. In *Othello*, notions of inherited superior disposition, and evolving notions of foreign constitution as inferior, suspect, and unconvertible, come into combustive contact.¹¹

Indeed, one of the chief departures of Shakespeare's play from his source text in Cinthio is that Shakespeare includes rank as a key issue in the story. The oft-repeated claim that Iago lacks a motive for his hatred of Othello is undercut by the play's opening scene in which Iago clearly cites the cause:

> Three great ones of the city,
> In personal suit to make me his lieutenant,
> Off-capped to him, and by the faith of man
> I know my price, I am worth no worse a place.
> (I.i.7–10)¹²

But Othello refuses their suit in favor of "One Michael Cassio.... That never set a squadron in the field / Nor the division of a battle knows" (I.i.19–22). While Othello's disregard of Iago for promotion to officer has always been recognized as *a* reason for his revenge, his migration through a number of supposed offenses has caused critics to claim the absence of one. But Iago's assertions that it is rumored that Othello has performed his "office" with his wife "'twixt [his] sheets" (I.iii.386–87), that he loves Desdemona himself (II.i.289), or that Emilia has been sexually served by Cassio as well (II.i.305) are all adjuncts to his chief source of jealousy: his inferior rank.[13] Iago wants to live in a meritocracy, where his performance at Cyprus or at Rhodes has value. But the world that he inhabits inhibits his rise. He cannot earn a lieutenancy, even on the recommendation of "great ones"; instead, Cassio is advanced by family, education, and social affiliation. Cassio and Othello are friends—his experience in war or even his ability to serve in his military posting is made insignificant when rated with his rank. "Preferment" in the military might, as Iago claims, "[go] by letter and affection / And not by old gradation" (I.i.35–36), but Othello's affections are cast by social affiliation.

In the political environment of Venice, Othello and Cassio are social equals: Othello's "life and being" are derived "from men of royal siege" (I.ii.21–22), and his relationships reflect his own assumptions about rank. Exactly who in Venice is acquainted with his rank is unclear: Othello is recovered from slavery and restored to social advantage (I.iii.138–39). It seems clear that Iago knows him as a military superior, not a social one, from his assumption that Othello's marriage is a violation that puts him in reach of the law (I.ii.15–16).[14] Othello himself states that he has not "promulgate[d]" (I.ii.21) his heritage. But Iago certainly knows Cassio as a nobleman and understands that he has been passed over for promotion in favor of a man whose education has rendered him "a great arithmetician" (I.i.18), or a soldier of strategy, not experience.

Othello clearly forms his attachments—both platonic and conjugal—on a sense of shared identity. It is this identity that Iago seeks to eradicate with his "poison" (III.iii.328). The nature of his concoction matters:

> Dangerous conceits are in their natures poisons,
> Which at the first are scarce found to distaste,
> But with a little act upon the blood
> Burn like the mines of sulfur.
>
> (III.iii.329–32)

The "dangerous conceits" that Iago introduces "act upon [Othello's] blood"—
the passions to which Othello gives license transform both his mind and his
body.[15] They serve as solvent to sever the ties by which he perceives a social
connection. Othello understands his place in the world through rank—he
sees noble blood as a substance shared among his peers—and Iago's strategies
isolate him as a foreign body. Iago is able to use the emergent category of race
as nation, and as Blackness (because Blackness marks "outside" status), to
chart his intrepid revenge.

In strategy, Iago resembles the New English planters—using the insinuation of foreignness and degraded physiology to detach nobility from the authority it guarantees—but he differs in objective. He cannot achieve the meritocracy he wants and so will settle for revenge upon one noble in particular as compensation for all. But the very contest, between Othello's identity and Iago's attempt to dismantle it, shows the fluidity of race at this early modern moment. It affirms more than one racial logic that supports social hierarchies—and in their use of different discourses of race, Othello and Iago reveal the instrumental nature of race itself. Othello asserts the "parts . . . title and . . . perfect soul" (I.ii.31) that assure his social position while Iago resorts to racialized categories of "clime, complexion and degree" (III.iii.234) in order to set him outside of Venetian society.[16] The vertigo that this produces in Othello prompts his free fall from power—but it is made possible by the multiplicity of race at this time.

In *Othello* we see two kinds of racial logic put to combat: Othello defends his position, assured that his royal heritage entitles him to "as proud a fortune" as the one he has achieved (I.ii.23); his rank sanctions his marriage to a woman who is a social peer. Iago, the new man who covets his position, assails his confidence with "country forms," asserting that the principal category of racial identity is color and nation, not rank (III.iii.241). This dispute of racial identity is in evidence in the first image of the couple in copulation: "Even now, now, very now, an old black ram / Is tupping your white ewe!" (I.i.87–88). As Lara Bovilsky has pointed out, Othello and Desdemona are of the same kind in this imagining, "a sameness that complicates [Desdemona's] status as someone imperiled by the threat of exogamy."[17] But the depiction of their shared species is confounded by color difference. The concept of the superior blood of rank is derived from discourses on animal husbandry, and so depictions of animal breeding, invoking pedigree at the moment of sexual congress, would not necessarily shock the senses of an early modern audience.[18] But Iago's animal farm is quickly populated with creatures that are at first foreign and then grotesque: a "Barbary horse" becomes a "beast with two backs" (I.i.110–15). Notions of the similar heritage of the newly coupled (and coupling) pair yield to ideas of foreignness and demonic possession ("the devil will make a grandsire of you" [I.i.90]).

Brabantio is entirely responsive to this discourse: after declaring that his "house is not a grange" (I.i.104), he quickly resorts to bestial images that suggest the corruption of his family line. Othello is "a thing" (I.ii.71) in his estimation when held in comparison to "the wealthy, curled darlings" of his own "nation" (I.ii.68).[19] But this is a startling transformation from Brabantio's former love which caused him to have Othello as a frequent visitor to his home (I.iii.129). His charges of witchcraft do not sound very different from Egeus's claims that Lysander "bewitch'd the bosom of [his] child" (I.i.27) in redirecting Hermia's love.[20] What is different is the source of the magic: "Damned as thou art, thou hast enchanted her" (I.ii.63). Brabantio consistently yokes Othello's Blackness to damnation, dark magic, and paganism—insisting that if the marriage "have passage free / Bond-slaves and pagans shall our statesman be" (I.ii.98–99).

Brabantio perceives the demise of the nation in the insinuation of a Black foreigner into his bloodline: the consequence of Othello's trespass is that government will be given over to aliens to both nation and religion. The intrusion that he perceives upon his noble blood is a threat to the entire state, and Brabantio assumes that his brother senators will see the same danger.[21] That they do not—the Duke chides him that his virtuous "son-in-law is far more fair than black" (I.iii.291)—is cause for his despair. But it also points to a new racial ideology challenging the former one of rank, but not displacing it: for Brabantio, the inclusion of a Black foreigner into his family is "against all rules of nature" (I.iii.102) and assures the contamination of his noble line; for the Duke and other senators, Othello's virtue lies in his noble descent, and his African origin cannot corrupt it.[22]

Iago proffers, and Brabantio accepts, a revised racial logic in which the inherited qualities of nobility are corrupted by foreign agency.[23] The union of Othello and Desdemona is characterized as an abomination, and their offspring imagined as alien and degenerate. But significant in the construction of the new kind of heredity that he frames is that irreligion is an inbred trait. Iago need only suggest that "the devil will make a grandsire of [Brabantio]" for Brabantio to imagine a whole line of future statesmen who are pagan in nature. Since the law is ideally administered in accordance with Christian scripture, Brabantio's image is one of a state fallen to pagan influence. But aside from the hysteria of his imagining, one easily recognizable in other visions of a decline in noble blood (Elyot is one example), there are two crucial assumptions in his fantasy to consider: one is that Othello remains pagan in spite of all evidence that he is a practicing Christian; the other is that Othello will produce pagan offspring.[24] In the new essentialism that Iago and Brabantio describe, paganism is an inherited trait that is inured to the effects of baptism.

In spite of his conversion, Othello's religion remains uncertain. This suspicion of his religion is not simply rendered among certain characters of the play (Iago, Brabantio) but is structured into the play as a whole. Othello's demise is a cautionary tale of failing to counter Iago's "poison" with the strong tonic of Christian faith. But Othello is himself inherently vulnerable to moral and religious collapse. Dennis Britton has carefully picked through theological formations of race in the early modern period, particularly those of the Church of England. He argues that theological writings in the sixteenth century, particularly pertaining to baptismal theology, "transformed Christians and 'infidels' into distinctive races" in an effort to reassure Christians that their children were born into the faith and to guarantee their elect status.[25] The Protestant Reformation called all miracles into question, and so the miraculous transformation of religious identity through the powers of baptism was also rendered suspect. While Britton importantly accounts for a theology of race in which Christian identity—and that of the unbeliever—is confirmed by birth, theology mirrors what the medical theory of the period already affirmed: the moral inferiority of (religious) others as an essential fact.[26] Certainly, not all Christians were included in this formulation; but those who were denied Christian communion, such as Irish Catholics, were painted black.

Othello indicates an early alignment of "Christian" and "White," "pagan" and "Black"—an alignment that will increase under the pressure of New World contexts and early English slave practices. Even in the context of ideas of religious essentialism that developed throughout the sixteenth century and into the seventeenth, *Othello* marks an important departure: unlike the Ethiopian princesses of Jonson's *Masque of Blackness*, whose religious error can be revised and humoral constitution reformed, Othello's inclination to wrong religion seems secured by nature and obstinate to reform. Urvashi Chakravarty sees "Othello's redemption" as always "contingent upon and vulnerable to his 'weak function.'" Chakravarty argues that Othello's religion is a somatic fact, indicated by his (suggested) circumcision, that cannot be altered by baptism; rather "redemption [in *Othello*] signals not rebirth but (ever-present, clearly inevitable) revocability."[27]

This is not to claim that Shakespeare is unsympathetic to his titular character. Nor is it to claim that Othello is the devilish agent that Brabantio asserts. As Ayanna Thompson observes, Shakespeare divides his devil—gives his attributes to Iago and his face to Othello.[28] Iago is the true devil—but he ensnares Othello's soul (V.ii.298-99). Othello is easily gulled—or as Iago says, "led by th' nose / As asses are" (I.iii.400-401). But the ease with which he is captured seems to imply a weak rational instrument. His soul is seized because he is unable to see the truth (in spite of the dazzling white aspect of Desdemona). All of this suggests a man whose virtue is vulnerable, whose faith is weak, and whose religious capacity is limited. The play points to a natural defect in Othello, one that maps onto religious identity. It insinuates that Othello's soul might actually be "begrimed and black / As [his] own face" (3.3.390-91). The daughters of Niger in Jonson's masque might not be able to reform without the benefit of a temperate sun, but Othello appears unable to reform under any climate or Christian influence. The transactions between body and soul, and the correspondence between the color of the flesh and condition of the soul, have been the substance of this book. In *Othello* we perceive a different racial ideology from that contained in other cultural objects under consideration here: *in spite of* superior lineage and the evident virtue that it supplies, Othello is unable to overcome defects of nation and inherited paganism. The contest that Shakespeare constructs between two kinds of racial thinking is finally resolved in violent confrontation when one racial identity of Othello kills the other, quite literally, at the end of the play.

In spite of his demand for "ocular proof" (III.iii.363), Othello is not a man who can see. Iago foresees that "trifles light as air" will provide "confirmations strong / As proofs of holy writ" (III.iii.325-27). "The divine Desdemona" (II.i.73) is no match against a "demi-devil" (V.ii.298), but her truth would be evident to any man with eyes.[29] Like *The Tragedy of Mariam*, a play to which *Othello* is often compared, the purity of the woman accused is assured by her color: Desdemona's skin is "whiter . . . than snow / And smooth as monumental alabaster" (V.ii.4-5). Indeed, the whiteness that Desdemona either embodies or symbolizes within the play is so pronounced that it produces what Karen Newman has described as a "scopic economy" of moral difference color-coded in a "spectacular opposition of black and white."[30] But like Herod, Othello cannot perceive the innocence of his wife. Of course, Herod's moral vision is occluded because of low rank—because morally crooked, he cannot properly perceive moral rectitude in others. But this only underscores the distinction of *Othello* as a play that considers a man of high birth whose religious heritage obscures his judgment and overcasts his virtue.

In the context of the play, Othello is literally an unbeliever. While he has strong confirmation of Desdemona's love, he allows "trifles light as air" to refute it. Iago's prediction that he will transpose these "trifles" for "holy writ" is apt, for it is precisely the "faith, hope *and* loue" (1 Cor. 13:13) that Paul recommends as an earthly guide that Othello forfeits. Iago declares that "were't to renounce his baptism, / All seals and symbols of redeemed sin," Othello would yield to Desdemona out of love (II.iii.338–39); but this, in fact, indicates that his love is misdirected: Othello would love the creation before the creator, in violation of the Neoplatonic ideal.[31] He refuses the evidence of his wife's innocence in favor of unbelievable claims. He not only allows "perdition [to] catch [his] soul" (III.iii.90), he helps to spring the trap. Shakespeare appears to pity his predicament: he seems to understand the alienation effect that Iago imposes upon Othello's sense of shared identity. But it is also made clear that Othello easily surrenders the love of those upon whom he can rely: Cassio and Desdemona. He has no faith. Instead, he believes too easily that "thoughts unnatural" (III.iii.237) prompted his wife to choose to love him and commits himself to murdering her in their conjugal bed. The perversion of Christian love represented in this act is evident in the perversion of Christian rites that lead up to it. Othello's "sacred vow" that he takes before "marble heaven" (III.iii.463–64), very likely on the hilt of a sword, is one such instance: his swearing on a cross is depraved by the "capable and wide revenge" (III.iii.462) that is his intent. Likewise, his suggestion of charity in refusing to kill his wife's "unprepared spirit" (V.ii.31) is denied by the murder that he commits. The murder itself is construed as "sacrifice" (V.ii.65) in his distorted logic. But these corruptions of Christian rites serve to remind us of the sinister bend that Othello's professed religion has taken by the end of the play.

It is not as simple as the religious other of the play inclining home like a compass point: Shakespeare's treatment of Othello is considerably more complicated. Iago fashions himself as ambassador to an unknown world ("I know our country disposition well" [III.iii.204]), a strategy that puts Othello outside of it. But Othello easily complies with Iago's strategies of separation: he has other modes of contact that would allow him to cleave to those he loves. He understands his social connection through a racial identity that is too easily dissolved. Passion erodes his humoral constitution (passion is a non-natural that affects humoral equilibrium) until he is literally a melting man:

> [I am] one whose subdued eyes,
> Albeit unused to the melting mood,
> [Now] Drops tears as fast as the Arabian trees
> Their medicinable gum.
>   (V.ii.346–49)

But the adhesive of a human connection, a catholic faith, and the charity that attends both are refused by Othello. He has a remedy to the "dangerous conceits" that "act upon [his] blood": he could believe in love. The opposition of heaven and hell and the Christianized language that attends Othello's descent into dark places indicate other directions that he does not pursue. He could hold himself together by perceiving his own participation in an economy of love that is the foundation of Christian faith. Instead, he sacrifices love and chooses hell: "All my fond love thus do I blow to heaven: / 'Tis gone!" (III. iii.448–49).

Othello's noble constitution disintegrates because he is disposed to doubt. Brabantio's suspicions about him—that he is an unbeliever by nature—are confirmed by the play. As Iago reads the humoral instability that the introduction of his "medicine" (IV.i.45) to Othello produces ("I see this hath a little dashed your spirits . . . / . . . I do see you're moved" [III.iii.218–21]), we watch the decline of his noble equilibrium to distempered passion. The Othello at the beginning of the play is one whose balanced mind is evident in the metrical notes of his speech; this musicality gives way to a disordered reasoning that cannot form a sentence (IV.i.35–43). But the breakup of his mind is premised upon the "passion" that he insists must have "some instruction" (IV.i.40–41) beyond his own imagination. What the play makes clear, however, is that Othello allows himself to be controlled by his imagination rather than his reason. As we have seen in other representations of pagans—the Indigenous people of Brooke's poem, the Ethiopian nymphs of the *Masque of Blackness*, and "Paynims" of Spenser's *Faerie Queene*—the delusion of unbelief proceeds from imagination rather than reason, and the unbeliever is governed by the lower claims of the body rather than those of the higher self. Like the liquefied Arabian trees with which he associates himself, the fluid transactions of Othello's body are represented as both foreign and excessive. But while the noble daughters of Niger in Jonson's masque also have excited imaginations, they have "faithful" temperaments (125), and they seek a greater light (169). We are led to believe that they ultimately discover it under James's refining influence. But Othello's wrong belief seems to be an expression of his body's corrupted state—and reform, such as it is, comes in a horrible anagnorisis immediately before his end.

Othello reveals an early modern moment when two racial discourses—one regarding the superiority of rank and the other asserting the superiority of nation and religious affiliation—are challenging each other. Shakespeare puts both racial identities into contact within his protagonist, and each identity pulls in opposed direction until he is pulled apart. When Othello is restored to himself, and recognizes his error, his divided racial identity can only end in self-annihilation. The noble Venetian general who

> in Aleppo once,
> Where a malignant and a turbanned Turk
> Beat a Venetian and traduced the state,
> ... took by th' throat the circumcised dog
>
> Must once again perform the state's business
>
> And smote him—thus!   *He stabs himself.*
>   (V.ii.350–54)

It has been noticed before that Othello identifies himself with the Turk that must be killed. Whether Othello is himself circumcised, marked by a former religious practice, is unclear. But the implication that he is—and has been—is clear.[32] Also assured is the fact that he has (unlike Brabantio) "curse[d] his better angel from his side / And fall[en] to reprobance" (V.ii.206-07). He will not achieve heaven.

The play does not characterize Othello as evil: although his actions proceed from hell, they are the work of the European demi-devils that surround him. But he does seem animated by the melancholy of delusion and unbelief. In denying the love of Cassio and Desdemona, Othello refuses the communion that might have saved him. While the crypto-Catholic figures of Jonson's masque are also subject to delusion, they can be purged of their black melancholy—the purpose of the masque is precisely to signal their recuperation to the right faith. But Othello remains unrecuperated by the play's end, permanently reprobate, and his damnation seems secured by design.

Othello forecasts hereditary heathenism as one of the chief components of an emergent racial logic—one that will displace contemporary notions of noble virtue as an inherited trait. But if the play is a harbinger of a new social order, driven by New World contexts, the social hierarchy that it predicts remains contested for at least a century. *Oroonoko, or The Royal Slave* challenges these New World arrangements, as does the play based upon Behn's novella, Southerne's *Oroonoko: A Tragedy*. The position of either prose work or play is not ambivalent: in Behn's novella, the Lieutenant Governor of Surinam and his council, all of common extraction, were "such notorious villains as Newgate never transported . . . who understood neither the laws of God or man, and had no sort of principles to make them worthy the name of men."[33] Southerne's play characterizes them as those

> Whose bold Titanian Impiety
> Wou'd once again pollute their Mother Earth,
> Force her to teem with her old monstrous Brood
> Of Gyants, and forget the Race of Men.
> (V.iii.19–22)

Men who are natural governors, such as Oroonoko, whose reason and virtue are guaranteed by bloodline, are overthrown by rabble. That way be monsters. The social order of the New World puts authority in the hands of men who are "young, / Luxurious, passionate, and amorous" of "such . . . Complexion" as "to countenance all [they are] prone to do, / [and] Will know no bounds, no law" (III.ii.217–21).[34] But while those whose religion is suspect in these works are both European and Christian, the depiction of the world that they inhabit nonetheless shows how "White" and "Christian" evolve as inherited terms of difference that assure supremacy.

Questions of lineage are at the center of Oroonoko's story in both of the works bearing his name: the royal descent of the prince and the status of his child as a slave. The liminal position that he occupies—subject to a moment when his heritage will contest, but not eradicate, his servitude—is captured in the oxymoronic title of *Royal Slave*. Southerne's play also proclaims this central theme in the epigraph of its title page: *Virtus recludens immeritis mori / Cælum, negatâ tentat* [sic] *iter viâ*. Hor. Od. 2 lib. 3: "Virtue opening heaven to those undeserving of death, attempts the journey by the denied road" (my translation). But Behn's novella concentrates on the bad government of the low-born and the commercial economy that permits this travesty.[35] Southerne's play focuses on the other concern of lineage: sexual procreation and the status of children.

How the Irish Became White

Imoinda in Southerne's play is a White slave.[36] It was certainly not impossible for a White actress to portray a Black woman—the "mixed marriage" plot was popular and the Restoration stage populated by African and Indian queens.[37] Casting Imoinda as a White slave deliberately invokes *Othello* as Southerne's precedent and dramatic model, and the mixed marriage of Oroonoko and Imoinda, like that of Othello and Desdemona, will end in tragedy. The epilogue claims that audience's "different tastes divide our Poet's Cares: / One foot the Sock, t'other the Buskin wears" (Epilogue, 5–6). But the oddity of this tragi-comic play, in conventional terms, is emphasized by the structure of its marriage plot. Marriage and tragedy do not mix. And while *Othello* begins in the vein of comedy that gets redirected by Iago ("O, you are well tuned now: but I'll set down / The pegs that make this music, as honest / As I am." [II.i.198–200]), Southerne divides his plot.

Southerne dispenses with half of Behn's novella, beginning his story in the New World. The effect is to shift the emphasis from Oroonoko and to put focus on the world to which he is transported. As Thompson observes, "It is clear that Southerne constructs Surinam as a colony painfully aware of racial differences... everyone discusses the differences between the Europeans and Africans in terms of black and white."[38] In this New World, Oroonoko's status is irrelevant: the play "reads his blackness as more significant than his social position."[39] But Thompson also notices that the Surinam of the play is one of Southerne's imagination: the world of his play does not mirror the Surinam of Behn's story. The white laborers of Behn's novella are only "slaves for four years," terms too short for the carceral servants that populate Southerne's landscape. Instead, his dramatic world seems conveyed to the West Indies.[40]

The comic plot is also out of place for Surinam: Southerne's play is at least half of a New World adventure tale, and his two plotlines awkwardly abut, with little interaction. Sisters seeking husbands abroad—having ruined their chances at home—become the New World adventurers. The only women in Behn's story are those forced there by circumstance, not those seeking husbands. Surinam was long surrendered to the Dutch by the time of Southerne's writing, and he depicts the New World realities of his time. The comic plot of the play features two sisters: the cross-dressed Charlotte posing as "Welldone," the brother to her younger sister, Lucy; the two set to "Husband-hunting [in] *America*" about which they have heard stories of new world miracles:

> *Lucy*   I thought Husbands grew in
> these Plantations.
>
> *Welldone* Why so they do, as thick as Oranges, ripening one under
> another. Week after week they drop into some Woman's
> mouth.
>
> (I.i.4–8)

The comic plot is frankly bawdy. But in its bartering over sex, husbands, wives, and children, it self-consciously invokes the slave market that is the site of the sisters' first encounter with their new world.

> *Captain* I don't know whether your Sister will like me, or not
>   ... But I have Money enough: And if you are
> her Brother, as you seem to be a-kin to her, I know that will
> recommend me to you.
>
> *Welldone* This is your Market for Slaves; my Sister is a Free Woman,
> and must not be dispos'd of in publick.
>
> (I.ii.113–18)

Women as the adventurers of the play, rather than the more violent and venal men that surround them, set the brutality that it depicts at a remove. But they also underscore, as their situation in a market of human beings suggests, the play's focus upon female bodies in a slave economy.

Because Southerne chooses to invoke *Othello* through his mixed-marriage plot, he consequently forces a focus in the play upon the different legacy of laboring bodies based upon race. Imoinda's fortunes, and those of her unborn child, have to be explained. The obvious question becomes why she, the same chromatic race as the adventuring sisters, cannot inhabit a comic plot—why her marriage cannot end in the production of children. Jennifer Morgan has argued that the reproductive potential of African women was one of the chief economic engines of the New World slave economy and that "notions of African women's sexual identities" contributed to "the development of racialist ideology."[41] The process of determining the status of children of slaves and those of carceral servants in early English slave codes, particularly those of mixed race, expose the ground on which White privilege and White supremacy is constructed. Valerie Forman has written brilliantly on this topic, and my argument is deeply indebted to her analysis.[42] But my addition to the argument is in exposing how religion serves as the basis for heredity in early English slave practices.

Southerne's play exposes assumptions of inherited heathenism that secure the fate of Oroonoko and Imoinda's child, as it does their own status as slaves.[43] But in the split structure of its marriage plots—one tragic and one comic—it also reveals how in the production of people as commodities in the commercial traffic of the New World, phenotypical difference attaches to religion as a crucial term in determining the inherited status of a human being. The suspicion surrounding Catholics as Christians does not extend to the conversion of their children in this transatlantic traffic; the products of dark bodies, however, remain permanently pagan.

These divisions do not cleave neatly (although, for the purpose of argument, I am beginning at the end): the conclusion of phenotypical race as a principal category of distinction near the end of the seventeenth century is the result of a considerable negotiation of both custom and law over decades. As Ania Loomba hypothesized, and subsequent studies have now shown, the specter of conversion of African slaves becomes the ground for the construction of racial difference in chromatic terms.[44] But while this body of historical research shows the developments in law and custom that govern the separation of free and enslaved people based upon chromatic distinction, my research has shown that this distinction is premised upon the potential for recuperation of the soul—and that such potential resides in the nature of blood. Somatic thinking does not supply race with stability, as the shifting application of these somatic fantasies suggests. Scientific racism is only one mode of racial logic—but one that licenses the political force of law; it supplies the illusion of "proof" on which legal grounding rests. Historical research in this area is therefore reading the effect, not the cause—the historical documents and legal developments that are the products of this kind of race-thinking. Rebecca Goetz asserts that while notions of religion as heritable came to define Virginia law concerning slavery and servitude, "in England[,] ideas about lineage, blood, and religion were in large part uninterrogated."[45] But as we have seen, such discourses are derived from long discussion in England of religion as a somatic and heritable trait.

In the sustained negotiation concerning the status of the children of mixed relationships in the New World, we see the emergence of White supremacy through the conflation of "White" and "Christian."[46] The 1644 "Act Against Carnall Coppullation between Christian and Heathen" passed in Antigua, for example, centers upon religious identity in its prohibition, but the law also makes distinction between "white," "negro," and "Indian." While the category of Christian is not directly applied to White Europeans, "the language of the act nonetheless effectively created a universe in which only 'white' people could be Christian."[47] While there was no consistent policy across Barbados, the Leeward Islands, and the colonies about the status of mixed children, notions of hereditary heathenism are in evidence in England and throughout the transatlantic world before England *officially* enters the slave trade (considerably after its actual entrance).[48] In his treatise *The Birth Priviledge . . . of Beleevers and their Issue*, Thomas Blake writes in 1644 that "the *priviledges* or *burdens*, which in Family or Nation are hereditary, they are conveyed from parents to posterity. . . . As is the father, so is the child . . . the child of *a Free*-man . . . is *free* borne: The child of a *Noble man* is *noble*. The child of a *bond-man* . . . is a *bond-man* likewise." But by the same logic of lineage, he affirms that "so the child of a *Turke* is a *Turke*; The child of a *Pagan* is a *Pagan*; The child of a *Iew* is a *Iew*; The child of a *Christian* is a *Christian*."[49]

Questions of lineage and what is inherited are precisely at issue in *Oroonoko*. The categories that Blake lays out as clear and uncontested are challenged in the story—particularly in the growing body of Oroonoko's unborn child. But because Imoinda is a White slave in Southerne's play, the rationale for different categories of inheritance—and how these attach to religion, color, and gender in the human traffic of a slave economy—is thrown into relief in Southerne's *Oroonoko*. The play is forced to negotiate the categories of "White" and "Christian," "Negro" and "Indian," and this arbitration takes place in the drama, as it does in the New World context in which it is set, across women's raced bodies. The race of a subject in Southerne's play relies upon religious categories of difference that are then transferred to offspring. Southerne's drama reveals religious affiliation as the chief determinant of the status of a slave or the children that proceed from an enslaved female body.

Imoinda's status as a White slave has been a perplexing issue for critics of Southerne's play. She is the daughter of "a White" "Stranger" in the king of Angola's Court, who "chang'd his gods" for those of the African nation he joined (II.ii.76–79). That she is herself pagan is put beyond question in the epilogue, which, while not authored by Southerne, was written by his friend William Congreve:

> Forgive this *Indian's* fondness of her Spouse;
> Their Law no Christian Liberty allows:
> Alas! they make a Conscience of their Vows!
> If Virtue in a Heathen be a fault;
> Then Damn the Heathen School, where she was taught
> She might have learn'd to Cuckhold, Jilt, and Sham,
> Had *Covent-Garden* been in *Surinam*.
>   (Epilogue, 29–35)

Echoing Blanford's farewell to Oroonoko, we are assured of the virtue of the heathen and that "Pagan, or Unbeliever, yet he liv'd [virtuous] / To all he knew: And if he went astray, / There's Mercy still above to set him right" (V.v.353–5). Like the epigraph, the final words of the play affirm that Oroonoko and Imoinda have achieved heaven "by the denied road." But if the play follows the novella in casting low-born White Europeans as the villains of the piece, it adheres to the social hierarchy of the New World in the rationale given for Imoinda's slave status. Imoinda is a slave because she is pagan; her children will be slaves because she is pagan. It is telling that in putting a White slave at the center of his drama, Southerne is forced to account for it through her conversion to a pagan religion.[50] It is also telling that in writing about Southerne's alteration, critics sometimes construct Imoinda as African.[51] Joyce Green MacDonald was the first to notice—in refusing the erasure of Behn's African heroine in Southerne's play and "restor[ing] the black Imoinda to representational significance"—that Southerne's White female slave is constructed in identical relationship to White authority as her husband.[52] "Imoinda," Forman flatly declares, "is . . . not white."[53] Yes. And no. I would argue that Imoinda's blackness depends, as does that of her husband, upon her identity as a pagan.

It is Imoinda's "heathen" status that guarantees the perpetual enslavement of her offspring. But gradations of skin color come to signal religious distinctions, and so Forman is right to observe, as she does, that Imoinda is shaded in the play's epilogue for a reason. Which is to say that, from the vantage point of the play, Imoinda is Black—but Black because she is an "Unbeliever."[54]

As Matthias Fischer neatly puts it,

> When the first Africans arrived in Barbados in the 1630s, there were no "white" people there. That is, most Englishmen viewed themselves through the lens of religion, more than race or rank. White Europeans

were "Christians," not "whites," while black people were "heathens" or "infidels," and therefore generally slaves. They also connected their Protestant religion to a specific conception of Englishness and freedom under English common law. This differentiated them from less civilized Indians and Africans, but also from Catholics.[55]

English colonial activity had previously been directed against religious others. Plantation labor practices in the English colonies, even if practically administered in different ways in each colonial location (differences produced by terrain, surrounding populations, available laborers, and the potential for their control), largely made distinctions based upon religious affiliation.[56] The labor needs of the new English colonies, particularly those of Jamaica and Barbados, provided a means to deliver cheap punishment to tens of thousands of vagrants, criminals, and most especially prisoners of war. "Indenture" covers all manner of sins. Convict labor was considered indenture, but what distinguished it was the length of term—usually at least ten years. Even if the contract were written by magistrate or ship's captain, any servant covered by contract, however involuntary his or her labor, was counted an indentured servant. Frequent wars and rebellions in the seventeenth century provided large numbers of bound laborers to the colonies, and a great many of these prisoners came from Ireland to Barbados. Thousands were massacred by Oliver Cromwell in his military campaigns intended to bring Ireland to heel, a fate he was "persuaded [was] a righteous judgement of God upon these barbarous wretches," and so transportation to Barbados was counted as mercy.[57] Cromwell subsequently enacted a sweep of large numbers of the poor in Ireland, including women and children, who were sent as indentured servants to Barbados and Jamaica. It is impossible to reconstruct how many were sent to support the plantations of the West Indies, and the "distinction between voluntary, forced and judicial processes is almost impossible to discern."[58] This is because there is virtually no data for convicts transported out of Ireland from 1615 to 1717, when the Transportation Act was effected in England.[59] One contemporary estimate is of thirty-four thousand men sent from Ireland to America, and the majority were directed toward Barbados.[60] Most scholars agree that the largest percentage of bound laborers on the island were transported from Ireland and that they numbered at least ten thousand.

The trouble with the figures lies in the number of deaths.[61] Census numbers are unreliable. Poorly housed and fed, many did not survive the brutal work regime to which they were subject. Most recent histories of early seventeenth-century Barbados have revealed little difference in the treatment of indentured laborers and slaves in terms of living conditions, social lives, and labor performed.[62] Early plantation arrangements did not segregate slaves and servants, and they lived and worked alongside each other.[63] "In the English colonies, servants of all nationalities were subject to harsh working conditions," Kristen Block and Jenny Shaw have argued, "but Irish Catholic subjugation was magnified by English Protestants' sense of cultural and religious superiority."[64] Hilary Beckles has estimated that between the years of 1650 and 1690, 40 to 50 percent of the labor population in Barbados was Irish, who were regarded with special animosity. Beckles has argued that "it was the Irish who were perceived by English masters as a principal internal enemy—at times more dangerous and feared than the blacks."[65] Religiously suspect and subject to ill-treatment, the Irish prisoners raised the greatest fear of revolt among the Barbadian planters.[66] But if Irish bound laborers and African slaves were regarded as similarly irreligious, as natural allies in rebellion, and as comparable groups to be exploited, the chief distinction between them, at least through the mid-seventeenth century, lay not in how they were treated but in the length of their service and the status of their children.[67]

That the English government did not regard the Irish as Christian is evident in Henry Cromwell's correspondence with John Thurloe, secretary of state during the Protectorate. Regarding a shipment of boys, aged twelve to fourteen, to the West Indies, he expresses the belief that their time in bondage might be cause for their reform: "who knows, but that it may be a means to make them English-men, I mean rather, Christians."[68] Cromwell's suggestion is that they might be physiologically converted over time—that they might grow to be Christian under English influence.[69] (Certainly he does not perceive the possibility of their reform if they remain in Ireland.) He similarly sees heathenism as something that can be bred out of the Irish: in addressing the rape of Irish women, in a plan to send them to Jamaica to sexually service English soldiers, he writes that "although we must use force in takeing them up" it is justified in "beinge so much for their own good, and likely to be of... great advantage to the publique."[70] Cromwell's programs for reform show him imagining Irish bodies becoming English. But of course, the crucial feature of this racial fantasy is that they *might*.

While assuming their inherited heathenism, Cromwell allows for the recuperation of Catholics, even if the manner lies in mixing with English blood. Such assumptions inform the terms of bondage: whereas the Irish might, by means of enforced servitude, be made "English-men ... [or] Christians," there were no such fantasies about African bodies. Black Africans were permanently unfree because imagined as permanently resistant to Christian faith.[71] While Henry Whistler records that Indigenous people in Barbados were "borne to perpetuall slauery thay and thayer seed," some were technically "indentured": sold for terms of ninety-nine years.[72] This sets Indigenous people at a slightly intermediate status—mostly, but not entirely, irredeemable. But the production of children presents a more complicated issue. While early cases that sought to restrain fornication with non-Christians suggested that sex with an African or Indigenous people defiled a Christian (English) body, these cases nonetheless determined that the offspring of such unions would not be permanently enslaved. Illegitimate children who had English fathers were indentured servants until they reached majority under the 1644 act in Antigua "Against Carnall Coppullation between Christian and Heathen."[73] In Bermuda, similar actions were taken in case law in the 1640s and 1650s: children who were fathered by English indentured servants were indentured themselves until the age of thirty.[74]

While such laws and legal precedents indicate "the presence of a color line for religious affiliation," they also suggest that a "Christian" contribution to the bloodline alters the constitution of the offspring (in the redirection of the child's fortunes).[75] In 1662, Virginia attempted to codify this opinion and set a standard to govern fornication cases. The law stipulated that

> Whereas some doubts have arrisen whether children got by any Englishman upon a negro woman should be slave or ffree, *Be it therefore enacted and declared by this present grand assembly*, that all children borne in this country shalbe held bond or free only according to the condition of the mother, *And* that if any christian shall committ ffornication with a negro man or woman, hee or shee soe offending shall pay double the ffines imposed by the former act.[76]

As Goetz points out, the category of "negro" becomes aligned with non-Christian here, whether "slave or ffree," despite the fact that "many Africans arrived in Virginia already Christian" or converted shortly after.[77] But more importantly, this statute follows "the condition of the mother," guaranteeing that the children of enslaved African women would remain enslaved regardless of paternity.[78]

The reasons for this are made explicit in the comic plot of Southerne's play, when the Widow Lackitt complains about the very thing she lacks:

Widow Here have I six Slaves in my Lot, and not a Man among 'em; all Women and Children; what can I do with 'em, Captain? Pray consider, I am a Woman my self, and can't get my own Slaves, as some of my Neighbors do.

(I.ii.10–13)

Even the comic plot sounds notes of tragedy. But the candid sexual discussions of the plot afford more than a little insight into the production of people at the center of a slave economy. Given the habit of masters to produce more slaves through the rape of the women they presumed to own, the descent of Christianity through the paternal line was economically untenable. As Forman notes: "With just one exception, the slave codes of the colonies followed the matrilineal line even in the case of interracial children in which the mother was white. White women who gave birth to interracial children were punished and the children likely subject to a number of years of indentured service; but the children were not slaves and their children's children were not slaves."[79] But as the female adventurers of Southerne's comic plot make clear, women who came to the West Indies in search of husbands were in the market for money. They would contract with plantation owners or ship's captains who had made their fortunes. Due to the close quarters of slaves and servants, a White woman who gave birth to an interracial child would presumably be indentured. The slave codes of the West Indies pursue the policy of the Virginia statute in having the child follow the "condition of the mother"; such a policy continued the practice of indenture and allowed plantation owners to continue the practice of producing their own slaves without the risk of losing them.[80]

The same mercantile interest governs the codification of religion along racial lines. Richard Ligon records an incident where a Barbadian plantation owner refuses to allow his African slave to be baptized because "being once a Christian, he could no more account him a Slave."[81] But as Fischer has carefully reconstructed, there seems to have been no English law forbidding the holding of Christians as slaves—rather, it seems clear that there was an abiding *belief* throughout the colonies that the Christian status of their slaves compromised their ability to hold them in perpetuity.[82] The 1667 Virginia statute declaring that "baptisme [did] not alter the condition of the person" was intended precisely to address this. The fact that these statutes respond to commercial interests nicely underscores the extent to which racial discourses pursue economic agendas. But the attachment of chromatic race to distinctions of religious difference emerges through the negotiation of what categories of people could be held as property.

That these racial discourses align with earlier notions of the physiological consequences of belief, which read dark bodies as melancholy with wrong belief, naturalizes both the social hierarchy and the property rights that White English landholders wanted to secure for themselves. The end of this process of negotiation is that Christian and European became coterminous categories (even if not fully realized in practice)—as well as negro and slave. After having traveled from Virginia to Barbados, Morgan Godwyn asserted that by 1680, "these two words, *Negro* and *Slave*, [have] by custom grown Homogenous and Convertible; even as *Negro* and *Christian*, *Englishman* and *Heathen*, are by the like corrupt Custom and Partiality made *Opposites*." But if religious affiliation determined a person's status as property, or indeed, as human, Godwyn's assessment puts the stakes in Black and White: "one [group] could not be *Christians*, nor the other *Infidels*."[83]

Imoinda, heathen and White, confuses the issue. By the time of Southerne's writing, Imoinda, not Oroonoko, would determine the status of her child according to the slave codes of the West Indies. But Imoinda is a slave, not an indentured servant. She has no tenure, but an enduring status as a slave. Her body, pregnant throughout the play, is a persistent reminder that the hierarchy of the world we view is out of order: "the child of a *Noble* man is [not] *noble*"; "the child of *a free*-man . . . is [not] *free* borne." But "the child of a *Pagan* is a *Pagan*." The terms that do align in the play—in spite of its sympathies obviously allied to the romantic couple—are "Christian" and "White," "heathen" and "Black." If the epilogue to Southerne's play characterizes even members of its Christian audience in Covent Garden as beneath the virtue of the noble pair at its center, it still cannot imagine a slave as Christian—or White.

The language of chromatic race is developed over the course of a process by which people became legally codified as things.[84] If Othello's Blackness signals his outside status ("Haply for I am black / And have not those soft parts of conversation / That chamberers have" [III.iii.267–69]), renders him foreign and religiously suspect, there is much in the play to challenge this construction—not least the voice of Venetian authority. But in statutes and slave codes governing servant and slave, sex and the status of children, "Black" came to legally define a people as both permanently enslaved and obdurate to Christian faith.[85] The emergence of skin color as the principal category of difference—firmly anchored in ideas of permanent depravity—was not inevitable. Skin color becomes the settled term so that slaveholders could protect their human investments. Maintaining that Black Africans were incapable of Christianity, and writing this into law, guaranteed that slaveholders would not lose their human property to conversion. But privileging chromatic categories also allowed slaveholders to multiply their slave populations through a program of rape, and to profit from it. Cromwell's assertion that mixing English blood with those he regarded as pagan produced redeemable English subjects shows that theories of inherited heathenism indicated other lines of descent. But the law that oversaw a New World economy, which trafficked in people, firmly grappled the status of the soul to the surface markings of the skin.[86]

CODA

The One-Drop Rule

> Some view our sable race with scornful eye,
> "Their colour is a diabolic die."
> Remember, *Christians*, *Negros*, black as *Cain*,
> May be refin'd, and join th' angelic train.
> Phyllis Wheatley, "On Being Brought
from Africa to America"

Somatic markers, and *readings* of the humoral constitution that attend them, displace the fluid values that had previously appraised human worth. The consequences of the revaluation are evident in the one exception to the majority of colonial slave codes that followed the matrilineal line in determining the status of interracial children. In 1664, the Maryland council sought to address what "shall become of such weomen of the English or other Christian nacons being free that are now allready marryed to negros or other Slaves."[1] In this construction, the assumption is that Africans and Indigenous people are both non-Christians and slaves. But, as members of the legislature would have been fully aware, many Black Africans converted to Christianity on the passage over to the colonies. They are nonetheless regarded by legislators indifferently—Christian or non-Christian, their dark skin proclaims their irreligion and determines their status as slaves. The lower house originally proposed that the women of these marriages not serve with their husbands and that their children be indentured for thirty years. But the law that actually resulted from the debate in both houses was quite changed: it resolved that all African slaves were to serve life terms and that children born to slaves—male or female—would be enslaved. The free women who married slaves would surrender their status and serve the master of their husbands. This effectively assumed the pollution of Christian women through an African partner, whether Christian or not, in making the free Christian a servant through contact. But it assumed the pollution of the children as well: while slave status was derived from the mother in all other English colonies, the Maryland law determined that *all* offspring of slaves, regardless of the orientation of the union that produced them, would inherit a pagan, not a Christian, identity.[2]

One can perceive the origin of the one-drop rule in this construction: there is no longer the racial fantasy that the blood of Christians can produce subjects that are either Christian or English, indentured or free. The children of slaves are slaves. Urvashi Chakravarty has rightly pointed out that the "'one drop rule' precisely registered the heritability of slavery within a system which sought to resolve the instability of somatic markers alone."[3] Generations of mixed-race reproduction, largely conducted through programs of rape, meant that the legibility of racialized slavery became over time more opaque and, in many cases, erased. But the origins of the idea inhabit this moment when the skin, not baptism or conversion, served as proof of irreligion; the humoral constitution of Christians is overwhelmed by the black melancholy that marks pagans and slaves.[4] And dark skin proclaimed a partition from both God and human being.

"Our contemporary ideologies bear traces of older practices and thinking," Ania Loomba states, "ideologies are historical palimpsests."[5] In early modern England, dark skin becomes the signature of alienation from God. In the Anglo-Americas it serves as the mark of permanent servitude that eviction from Christian communion authorizes. The meanings that attach to black skin in the modern United States—of moral corruption, poverty, and criminality—are derived from its racist history. But that history is rooted in the assumptions that composed early modern slave codes in the English colonies. If there is no evolution between early modern and modern racial logic, there is much continuity between them precisely because the race concept recycles and revises prior stories about raced subjects. Moral depravity is one of these.

To end, then, where this book began: when my son walks abroad, meanings attach to his body—but they reside in his skin. His body is lean and powerful from sports; he is 5'8"; he is fourteen years old. He is a boy. Tamir Rice was 5'7"; he was twelve; he was a boy. But it was not his body that made him threatening, it was his skin. The skin of Black boys and men carries a moral code. To those inclined to read it as a moral message, it declares them cruel, impulsive, vicious, harmful, hurtful, dangerous.[6] The message of black skin to a White world is still one of being outside: community, communion, faith. If the complexion of belief in the early modern period was the premise for who was within Christian communion and who was without, of who was fully enfranchised as human and who was not, then complexion in the modern Anglo-American world still signals inclusion or exclusion within Christianity—which is still accounted as White.

NOTES

Preface

1. Ibram X. Kendi, *Stamped from the Beginning: The Definitive History of Racist Ideas in America* (New York: Bold Type Books, 2016), 3.

2. W. E. B. Du Bois famously declared, when campaigning for the use of *Negro*, rather than *negro*, that "eight million Americans are entitled to a capital letter." I capitalize White and Black in reference to groups of people not to confer dignity but in order to highlight the constructed nature of both races. These distinctions are created, as this research makes clear, only in reference to other racial distinctions. The production of a racial designation for Black people meant that Europeans *became* White.

3. In "Noble Dogs, noble blood: the invention of the concept of race in the late Middle Ages," in *The Origins of Racism in the West*, ed. Miriam Eliav-Feldon, Bejamin Isaac, and Joseph Ziegler (Cambridge: Cambridge University Press, 2009), 200–216, Charles de Miramon diverts the origin of the term *race* from the Spanish word *raza* and argues that it instead descends from fifteenth-century French breeding books.

4. See Kimberly Anne Coles, Ralph Bauer, Zita Nunes, and Carla L. Peterson, introduction to *The Cultural Politics of Blood, 1500–1900*, ed. Coles et al. (Basingstoke, Hampshire: Palgrave Macmillan, 2015), particularly 1–5 and 9–12.

5. Kimberly Anne Coles, "Moral Constitution: Elizabeth Carey's *Tragedy of Mariam* and the Color of Blood," in *Early Modern Studies: Gender, Race, and Sexuality*, ed. Ania Loomba and Melissa Sanchez (Abingdon, Oxon, UK: Routledge, 2016), 151. The introductions to a number of collections published in the 1990s importantly stressed the diversity of meanings in early modern race, as well as its cross-section with understandings of region, nationality, religion, and gender. Most of these, however, emphasized the cultural understanding of race rather than its embodied fantasies. See Margo Hendricks and Patricia Parker, eds., *Women, "Race," and Writing in the Early Modern Period* (New York: Routledge, 1994); Joyce Green MacDonald, ed., *Race, Ethnicity, and Power in the Renaissance* (Madison, NJ: Fairleigh Dickinson Press, 1997); and Michael McGiffert, ed., "Constructing Race: Differentiating Peoples in the Early Modern World," *William and Mary Quarterly*, special edition, 54:1 (1997).

6. In a recent article in the *Spenser Review*, Dennis Austin Britton and I claim that early modern English racial formation is invested in these three things: "Beyond the Pale," *Spenser Review* 50:1:5 (Winter 2020), https://www.english.cam.ac.uk/spenseronline/review/volume-50/501/beyond-the-pale/.

7. Janet Adelman, *Blood Relations: Christian and Jew in* The Merchant of Venice (Chicago: University of Chicago Press, 2008); Dennis Austin Britton, *Becoming Christian: Race, Reformation, and Early Modern English Romance* (New York: Fordham University Press, 2014); Urvashi Chakravarty, "Race, Natality, and the Biopolitics of Early Modern Political Theology," *Journal for*

Early Modern Cultural Studies 18 (2018), 140–66; Jane Hwang Degenhardt, *Islamic Conversion and Christian Resistance on the Early Modern Stage* (Edinburgh: Edinburgh University Press, 2010); Ania Loomba, "Periodization, Race, and Global Contact," *Journal of Medieval and Early Modern Studies* 37 (2007), 595–620; Ania Loomba, "Race and the Possibilities of Comparative Critique," *New Literary History* 40 (2009), 501–22; M. Lindsay Kaplan, "Jessica's Mother: Medieval Constructions of Jewish Race and Gender in *The Merchant of Venice*," *Shakespeare Quarterly* 58 (2007), 1–30; M. Lindsay Kaplan, "'His blood be on us and on our children': Medieval Theology and the Demise of Jewish Somatic Inferiority in Early Modern England," in *The Cultural Politics of Blood, 1500–1900*, ed. Coles et al., 107–26; and M. Lindsay Kaplan, *Figuring Racism in Medieval Christianity* (Oxford: Oxford University Press, 2019).

    8. See Suzanne Conklin Akbari, *Idols in the East: European Representations of Islam and the Orient* (Ithaca, NY: Cornell University Press, 2009), particularly chap. 4; Jonathan Boyarin, *The Unconverted Self: Jews, Indians, and the Identity of Christian Europe* (Chicago: University of Chicago Press, 2009); Jeffrey Jerome Cohen, "On Saracen Enjoyment: Some Fantasies of Race in Late Medieval France and England," *Journal of Medieval and Early Modern Studies* 31 (2001), 113–46; Jeffrey Jerome Cohen, "Race," in *A Handbook of Middle English Studies*, ed. Marion Turner (Chichester: Wiley-Blackwell, 2013), 109–22; John Block Friedman, *The Monstrous Races in Medieval Art and Thought* (Cambridge, MA: Harvard University Press, 1981); Geraldine Heng, *England and the Jews* (Cambridge: Cambridge University Press, 2019); Geraldine Heng, *The Invention of Race in the European Middle Ages* (Cambridge: Cambridge University Press, 2018); M. Lindsay Kaplan, "The Jewish Body in Black and White in Medieval and Early Modern England," *Philological Quarterly* 92 (2013), 41–65; M. Lindsay Kaplan, *Figuring Racism in Medieval Christianity*; Steven F. Kruger, *The Spectral Jew: Conversion and Embodiment in Medieval Europe* (Minneapolis: University of Minnesota Press, 2006); Dorothy Kim, "Reframing Race and Jewish/Christian Relations in the Middle Ages," *Transversal* 13 (2015), 52–64; Dorothy Kim, "Introduction to Literature Compass Special Cluster: Critical Race and the Middle Ages," *Literature Compass* 16 (2019), 1–16, https://doi.org/10.1111/lic3.12549; Lisa Lampert-Weissler, *Medieval Literature and Post-Colonial Studies* (Edinburgh: Edinburgh University Press, 2010), particularly 73–107; Sierra Lomuto, "The Mongol Princess of Tars: Global Relations and Racial Formation in *The King of Tars* (c. 1330)," *Exemplaria* 31 (2019), 171–92; Irven M. Resnick, *Marks of Distinction: Christian Perceptions of Jews in the High Middle Ages* (Washington, DC: Catholic University of America Press, 2012); and Cord J. Whitaker, *Black Metaphors: How Modern Racism Emerged from Medieval Race-Thinking* (Philadelphia: University of Pennsylvania Press, 2019).

    9. James Hankins, "Monstrous Melancholy: Ficino and the Physiological Causes of Atheism," in *Laus Platonici philosophi: Marsilio Ficino and His Influence*, ed. Stephen Clucas, Peter J. Forshaw, Valery Rees (Leiden: Brill, 2011), 29.

    10. In both "Periodization, Race, and Global Contact" and "Race and the Possibilities of Comparative Critique," Ania Loomba writes about how "Blackness was a condition of the lack of Christianity." Further, she observes that "although monogenesis *theoretically* facilitated the possibility of conversion, its actual possibility was severely limited by several prejudices and practices. One was the belief about the fixed moral being of non-Christians, especially Jews and Muslims, and their inability to change" ("Race and the Possibilities of Comparative Critique," 504).

    11. Britton, *Becoming Christian*, passim.

    12. Patricia Akhimie, *Shakespeare and the Cultivation of Difference: Race and Conduct in the Early Modern World* (New York: Routledge, 2018), 16. Akhimie looks at the numerous treatises and conduct books that describe the physiological superiority of the social elite and teach

them how to uphold it. More to the point, those *not* in power are "marked by a devastating lack" in the discourse of conduct, by "an inability to be better and even to know better—that is, to know that they *should* be better" (5). See also Urvashi Chakravarty, "More than Kin, Less than Kind: Similitude, Strangeness, and Early Modern English Homonationalisms," *Shakespeare Quarterly* 67 (2016), 14–29; and Urvashi Chakravarty, *Fictions of Consent: Slavery, Servitude and Free Service in Early Modern England* (Philadelphia: University of Pennsylvania Press, 2022).

13. For an examination of how notions of hereditary blood underwrite race-thinking in the French Atlantic World, see Guillaume Aubert, "'The Blood of France': Race and Purity of Blood in the French Atlantic World," *William and Mary Quarterly* 61 (2004), 439–78. For the French and Spanish context, see Noémie Ndiaye, "The African ambassador's travels: Playing black in late seventeenth-century France and Spain," in *Transnational connections in early modern theatre*, ed. M. A. Katritzky and Pavel Drábek (Manchester: Manchester University Press, 2019), 73–85.

14. Ficino writes: "Iudicium autem religioni favens reperitur in pluribus gravioribusque homnibus, in paucissimis vero levissimisque contrarium, quorum exemplo alii quoque nonnumquam inficiuntur. Atque in illis paucissimis non est hoc iudicium rationis, sed morbus animi formidolosaque suspicio a depravata complexione corporis proficiscens." *Platonic Theology* (14.10.7), ed. James Hankins and William Bowen, trans. Michael J. B. Allen, 6 vols. (Cambridge: Cambridge University Press, 2001–6), 4:310.

15. Angus Gowland, *The Worlds of Renaissance Melancholy: Robert Burton in Context* (Cambridge: Cambridge University Press, 2006), 160. Burton cites Philip Melanchthon, Levinus Lemnius (Levine Lemnie), Felix Platter, and Ercole Sassonia among dozens of authorities who discuss the physiological basis of unbelief and wrong religion.

16. Ficino, *Platonic Theology* (14.10.5–8), 4:307–13.

17. Jane Degenhardt also sees "the body's sway over the soul" in her analysis, although this "may seem to apply most clearly to involuntary converts. Of course . . . [there is] another category of apostates who willingly shed their Christian identities and embraced Islam. But even these converts are driven by an impulse that seems to originate in the body" (*Islamic Conversion and Christian Resistance on the Early Modern Stage*, 3).

18. Holly Brewer, "Subjects by Allegiance to the King?: Debating Status and Power for Subjects—and Slaves—Through the Religious Debates of the Early British Atlantic," in *State and Citizen: British America and the Early United States*, ed. Peter Thompson and Peter S. Onuf (Charlottesville: University of Virginia Press, 2013), 33. Brewer observes that Alberico Gentili argued this point in English law as early as 1590, while a professor at Oxford and a judge of the Admiralty Court in England.

19. Matthias Fischer, "A New Race of Christians: Slavery and the Cultural Politics of Conversion in the Atlantic World" (PhD diss., University of Maryland, 2020). I am grateful to Matthias for showing me portions of his dissertation in progress.

20. Brewer, "Subjects by Allegiance to the King?" 33.

21. *The Statutes at Large, being a Collection of all the laws of Virginia*, ed. William Walter Hening, 13 vols. (New York: R & W & G Barstow, 1819–23), 2:491, quoted in ibid., 34.

22. Dennis Austin Britton, "Race After the Reformation" (paper presented at "Race and Periodization: A Race B4 Race Symposium" sponsored by the Arizona Center for Medieval and Renaissance Studies and the Folger Shakespeare Library, September 6, 2019), my emphasis. My thanks to Dennis for generously sharing his talk so that I could cite it here specifically. A description of the symposium can be found here: https://acmrs.asu.edu/public-events/symposia/race-and-periodization (accessed March 1, 2020).

23. Ibid.

24. Atiya Husain, "Retrieving the Religion in Racialization: A Critical Review," *Sociology Compass* 11:9 (September 2017), https://doi.org./10.1111/soc4.12507 (accessed March 1, 2020). Of course, as I note throughout the Preface, there is no time when race is "born." Theories of race make use of existing discourses, changing tack and strategy depending upon shifting political agendas.

Introduction

1. In *The Invention of Race in the European Middle Ages*, Geraldine Heng exfoliates this process at various sites throughout Europe.

2. Heng, *England and the Jews*, 10. (While Heng repeats this phrase throughout the element, this is its first appearance in the book.) Cf. Heng, *The Invention of Race in the European Middle Ages*, 27–33.

3. In "Periodization, Race, and Global Contact," Ania Loomba has noticed the marking of converted Muslims and Jews in early modern drama and cast it in similar terms: "the conflation of color and religion in early modern drama," she writes, occurs "precisely because it was not possible to distinguish visually between Christians and converts to Christianity. To cast Muslims and Jews as literally black, or with other easily identifiable physical characteristics, was also to offer a reassurance that their difference could be easily identified" (613). While Loomba notices the occurrence, and similarly suggests that the need arises through the strategic marking of an unchanging inner state, I am discovering the medical discourse, and the convergence of science and religion, that rationalizes English colonial activities through the argument that certain peoples remain obdurate to Christianity. This, as I say in the Preface, draws from a long critical tradition; see, for example, Peter Biller, "Views of Jews from Paris Around 1300: Christian or 'Scientific'?" in *Christianity and Judaism: Studies in Church History*, vol. 29, ed. Diana Wood (Oxford: Blackwell, 1992); Peter Biller, "A 'Scientific' View of Jews from Paris Around 1300," *Micrologus* 9 (2001), 137–68; Jerome Friedman, "Jewish Conversion, the Spanish Pure Blood Laws, and Reformation: A Revisionist View of Racial and Religious Anti-Semitism," *Sixteenth Century Journal* 18 (1987), 3–29; Willis Johnson, "The Myth of Jewish Male Menses," *Journal of Medieval History* 24:3 (1998), 273–95; Kaplan, *Figuring Racism in Medieval Christianity*, chap. 2; Kruger, *The Spectral Jew*, 67–109; George Mariscal, "The Role of Spain in Contemporary Race Theory," *Arizona Journal of Hispanic Cultural Studies* 2 (1998), 7–23; Resnick, *Marks of Distinction*, passim; and Joseph Ziegler, "Physiognomy, science, and proto-racism, 1200–1500," in *The Origins of Racism in the West*, ed. Miriam Eliav-Feldon, Benjamin Isaac, and Joseph Ziegler (Cambridge: Cambridge University Press, 2009), 198.

4. I capitalize Black and White in reference to people in order to emphasize the artificial and constructed nature of both racial categories (see Preface, n. 2).

5. Quoted in Eckhard Kessler, "The Intellective Soul," in *The Cambridge History of Renaissance Philosophy*, ed. Charles B. Schmitt, Quentin Skinner, and Eckhard Kessler (Cambridge: Cambridge University Press, 1988), 503. The soul's essence therefore, Pomponazzi maintained, had to be situated in the material realm; it "was the highest material form, attaining in its most elevated operations something beyond materiality," but it was ultimately material in its terms (503). Pomponazzi was arguing against the Averroist position of a single and unified intellect informing the (Platonic) form of man. There was no way, he reasoned, of proving man an individual, rational animal, composed of body and soul, if serving as the subject of cognition—which is to say, subject to the higher faculties of the rational soul.

6. Gowland, *The Worlds of Renaissance Melancholy*, 96. See also Angus Gowland, "The Problem of Early Modern Melancholy," *Past and Present* 191 (2006), 77 –120; and Hankins, "Monstrous Melancholy."

7. Timothy Bright, *A Treatise of melancholie* (STC 3747), iii^r.

8. Ibid.

9. Ziegler, "Physiognomy, science, and proto-racism," 199. See also Valentin Groebner, "*Complexio*/Complexion: Categorizing Individual Natures, 1250-1600," in *The Moral Authority of Nature*, ed. Lorraine Daston and Fernando Vidal (Chicago: University of Chicago Press, 2003), 357–83.

10. See Preface, n. 8 for a list of works that are part of a new genealogy of medieval criticism that sees embodied terms underwriting religion.

11. See Kaplan, "The Jewish Body in Black and White in Medieval and Early Modern England"; Kaplan, *Figuring Racism in Medieval Christianity*, particularly chap. 5; Lampert-Weissig, *Medieval Literature and Post-Colonial Studies*; and Whitaker, *Black Metaphors*. While Kaplan looks at how medieval theological discussions of figural slavery inform later incarnations of the logic, she gestures toward but does not fully carry these constructions into the postcolonial situation.

12. Kim F. Hall, *Things of Darkness: Economies of Race and Gender in Early Modern England* (Ithaca, NY: Cornell University Press, 1995).

13. Dennis Britton provides a wonderful synopsis of the migration of racial formation from Catholic to Protestant theology, coming to the similar conclusion that stability, and the *inability* to convert, was what distinguished the Protestant influence upon the race concept. See Britton, *Becoming Christian*, 1–34, particularly 28–31.

14. Geraldine Heng, *Empire of Magic: Medieval Romance and the Politics of Cultural Fantasy* (New York: Columbia University Press, 2003), 231–32.

15. Ibid., 229.

16. Whitaker, *Black Metaphors*, 23.

17. Ibid., 27.

18. In *Things of Darkness*, Hall has rightly pointed out that "the easy association of race with modern [definitions of] science ignores the fact that language itself creates differences within social organization and that race was then (as it is now) a social construct that is fundamentally more about power and culture than biological difference" (6).

19. Ania Loomba and Jonathan Burton, eds., *Race in Early Modern England: A Documentary Companion* (Hampshire: Palgrave Macmillan, 2007), 27.

20. *The Works of John Jewel*, ed. John Ayre, 4 vols. (Cambridge: University Press for the Parker Society, 1845), 3:366, quoted in Britton, *Becoming Christian*, 46.

21. This is the title of the third chapter Rebecca Anne Goetz's book, *The Baptism of Early Virginia* (Baltimore: Johns Hopkins University Press, 2012), 61–85.

22. Kimberly Anne Coles, Kim F. Hall, and Ayanna Thompson, "BlacKKKShakespearean: A Call to Action for Medieval and Early Modern Studies," *Profession* (November 2019).

23. The list is extensive, but by way of example: Gail Kern Paster, *The Body Embarrassed: Drama and the Disciplines of Shame in Early Modern England* (Ithaca, NY: Cornell University Press, 1993); Gail Kern Paster, *Humoring the Body: Emotions and the Shakespearean Stage* (Chicago: University of Chicago Press, 2004); Carla Mazzio and David Hillman, eds., *The Body in Parts: Fantasies of Corporality in Early Modern Europe* (New York: Routledge, 1997); Carla Mazzio and Douglas Trevor, eds., *Historicism, Psychoanalysis, and Early Modern Culture* (New

York: Routledge, 2000); Mary Floyd-Wilson, Gail Kern Paster, and Katherine Rowe, eds., *Reading the Early Modern Passions: Essays in the Cultural History of Emotion* (Philadelphia: University of Pennsylvania Press, 2004); Douglas Trevor, *The Poetics of Melancholy in Early Modern England* (Cambridge: Cambridge University Press, 2004); and Mary Floyd-Wilson and Garrett A. Sullivan, eds., *Environment and Embodiment in Early Modern England* (Basingstoke, Hampshire: Palgrave Macmillan, 2007).

24. Sean McDowell makes this criticism in his assessment of the field: "The View from the Interior: The New Body Scholarship in Renaissance/Early Modern Studies," *Literature Compass* 3:4 (2006), 787. Garrett Sullivan registers a similar complaint when he writes the following: "Intellect is exclusive to man and ... is usually taken to comprise the immortal soul. However, the essentialist view isolates the operation of reason from other bodily processes ... [it] fails to account for the ways in which humoral physiology sutures cognition to embodiment, and thus the rational to the sensitive and vegetative powers. In sum, the view is anachronistic and conditioned by Cartesian dualism, which posits a profound separation between mind and body" (*Sleep, Romance and Human Embodiment: Vitality from Spenser to Milton* [Cambridge: Cambridge University Press, 2012], 6–7). Both critics argue that the Cartesian mind-body split still exerts pressure upon how early modern psychology (literally, for early moderns, the study of the soul) is perceived.

25. Nicholas Culpeper, *A New Method of Physick, or, A Short View of Paracelsus and Galen's Practice* (Wing P612), 15. My thanks to Katarzyna (Kat) Lecky for alerting me to this passage in Culpeper's treatise.

26. Dennis Des Chene has argued that this debate culminates in Cartesian separation of body and soul. In *Life's Form: Late Aristotelian Conceptions of the Soul* (Ithaca, NY: Cornell University Press, 2000), he writes, "The operations of the Cartesian soul have no intrinsic relation to nourishment, growth, or reproduction. Its sensations and passions are, Descartes believes, 'instituted' by God so as to provide a guide to life. But the institution of relations ... between modes of thought and modes of the body is required just because there is no other means by which the operations of the soul can be applied to the conservation of the body-machine" (5). In the development of what Des Chene terms "the science of the soul," Descartes separates the operations of soul from body in order to eliminate the corruption that the body might offer to the soul. Instead of the sensations and passions—previously the office of the sensitive soul—as an integral part of intellection, these are supplied by God for the direction of the body. But Descartes's situation of the contact point between body and soul in the pineal gland failed to settle the question of mind-body interaction; in fact, this became the particular point on which he was assailed, since other animals possessed a pineal gland but could not be said to be in possession of a soul. See also Dennis Des Chene, *Physiologia: Natural Philosophy in Late Aristotelian and Cartesian Thought* (Ithaca, NY: Cornell University Press, 1996); and Des Chene, *Spirits and Clocks: Machine and Organism in Descartes* (Ithaca, NY: Cornell University Press, 2001). But this further shows that the argument concerning the nature of soul is in no way confined to England: rather, the scope of my examination is to show how these ideas affected English colonial policy, practice, and culture.

27. Gowland, *The Worlds of Renaissance Melancholy*, 62–65; Gowland, "The Problem of Early Modern Melancholy," 97. See also Trevor, *The Poetics of Melancholy in Early Modern England*, 56.

28. For Kessler's elegant synopsis of the Pomponazzi affair, see Kessler, "The Intellective Soul," 500–7.

29. See n. 5, above.

30. Kessler, "The Intellective Soul," 502; 501–2.

31. Philip Melanchthon, *Liber de anima*, in *Opera quae supersunt omnia* (hereafter, *Corpus Reformatorum*), ed. Carol Gottlieb Bretschneider and H. E. Bindeil, 28 vols. (Braunschweig: C. A. Schwetschke and Son, 1834–60), vol. 13, col. 16: "Anima rationalis est spiritus intelligens, qui est altera pars substantiae hominis, nec extinguitur, cum a corpore discessit, sed immortalis est. Haec definitio non habet physicas rationes. Et quanquam nonnulli contra eam multa disputant, tamen nos quidem in his initiis doctrinae eam retinebimus, quia in Ecclesia propter haec dicta usitata est, videlicet quod Filius Dei inquit: Corpus possunt occidere, animam autem occidere non possunt" (The rational soul is the spirit of understanding, which is the other part of the essence of man, nor is extinguished, when it departs from the body, but is immortal. This definition does not have its ground in natural philosophy. And although not a few argue strongly against it, nevertheless we will retain it in these first principles of our doctrine, because in the Church at hand this has customarily been said, one may assume because the Son of God says: they are able to kill the body, but they are not able to kill the soul). Partially quoted in Kessler, "The Intellective Soul," 517n233 (my translation).

32. See Sachiko Kusukawa, *The transformation of natural philosophy: the case of Philip Melanchthon* (Oxford: Oxford University Press, 1995), 91–92.

33. This was the question that Pomponazzi had declared unresolved and possibly unresolvable through philosophical exposition. Almost immediately, in 1518, Pomponazzi published his *Apologia*; in 1519, his *Defensorium*. In the end, he argued (by proxy) that while the immortality of the soul was not provable by reason, its truth was accessible through revelation—a position closely paralleled by Melanchthon.

34. Melanchthon writes: "Ergo Galeno Anima, presertim sensitiva et vegetativa, aut temperamentum est, aut spiritus vitalis ac naturalis in animantibus: hoc est, aut temperamentum, aut spiritus vitalis est principium vitae ac motus in animantibus, seu est res movens corpus. Ita rem aliquam moventem Galenus digito monstrare conatus est, ut quae res esset anima, suspicari possemus" (Therefore for Galen the soul, particularly the sensitive and vegetable soul, is either the constitution, or the vital natural breath in living things; this is, either the temperament, or the vital breath is the origin of life and also [of] motion in living things, or else is the thing moving the body. And so Galen has tried to point to something moving, so that we would be able to apprehend what the soul is). *Commentarius de anima* (Lyon, 1542), 20 (b2v), quoted in Kusukawa, *The Transformation of Natural Philosophy*, 90n73 (my translation).

35. Franciscus Toletus [Francisco de Toledo], for example, also simply concedes the argument to Pomponazzi: "Unde erravit Pomponatuis dicens animam mortalem secundum philosophiam, et quamvis non esset fortasse error dicere, quod non potest demonstrari naturaliter animae immortalitas, hoc enim dicit Scotus" (Hence, Pomponazzi has gone astray saying that the soul is mortal according to [natural] philosophy; but maybe he was not wrong to say that the immortality of the soul cannot be proved by natural reason, for Duns Scotus says this). Toletus, *Commentaria una cum quaestionibus in tres libros Aristotelis* De anima (Cologne, 1576), fol. 152^v, quoted in Kessler, "The Intellective Soul," 511n194 (my translation).

36. See Kusukawa, *The Transformation of Natural Philosophy*, 91.

37. Sullivan, *Sleep, Romance and Human Embodiment*, 162n9.

38. Kessler, "The Intellective Soul," 507.

39. Ibid.

40. See Ittzés Gábor, "'The Breath Returns to God Who Gave It': The Doctrine of the Soul's Immortality in Sixteenth-Century German Lutheran Theology" (PhD diss., Harvard Divinity School, 2009), 87–89.

41. See Gowland, *The Worlds of Renaissance Melancholy*; Gowland, "The Problem of Early Modern Melancholy"; and Hankins, "Monstrous Melancholy."

42. Gowland, "The Problem of Early Modern Melancholy," 105–6.

43. Hankins, "Monstrous Melancholy," 25. In "Cultural Revolution in the Renaissance?" *Quillette* (July 29, 2020), https://quillette.com/2020/07/29/cultural-revolution-in-the-renaissance (accessed August 19, 2020), James Hankins seems to argue against the implications of his own work. While he quite brilliantly exposes the physiological grounds for atheism from Ficino forward, he cannot acknowledge the potential for violence, intolerance, or suppression that might attend such an attitude. He argues that "young people" will lose interest in the Renaissance as a "period of Western civilization if their teachers constantly hammer away at its culpability in establishing 'white supremacy.' . . . Do we really think the modern world can learn nothing of value from the past?" He concludes with the question: "If we don't, why are we teaching about the Renaissance at all?" Setting aside the false choice of the either/or proposition that Hankins lays out, he demonstrates the position of studied innocence in his formulation.

44. Miramon, "Noble Dogs, noble blood."

45. See Akhimie, *Shakespeare and the Cultivation of Difference*; Chakravarty, "More than Kin, Less than Kind; Chakravarty, *Fictions of Consent*; and Jean E. Feerick, *Strangers in Blood: Relocating Race in the Renaissance* (Toronto: University of Toronto Press, 2010). For the Spanish entanglements of rank and religion, and the importation of *limpieza de sangre* to the Iberian Americas, see Ruth Hill, "The Blood of Others: Breeding Plants, Animals, and White People in the Spanish Atlantic," in *The Cultural Politics of Blood, 1500–1900*, ed. Coles et al., 45–64; and María Elena Martínez's excellent study, *Genealogical Fictions: Limpieza de Sangre, Religion, and Gender in Colonial Mexico* (Stanford, CA: Stanford University Press, 2008).

46. Miramon, "Noble Dogs, noble blood," 208. See also Aubert, "'The Blood of France.'"

47. Jonathan Burton, "Race," in *A Cultural History of Western Empires in the Renaissance (1450–1650)*, vol. 3, ed. Ania Loomba (London: Bloomsbury, 2018), 220.

48. Levinus Lemnius [Levine Lemnie], *The touchstone of complexions generallye appliable, expedient and profitable for all such, as be desirous & carefull of their bodylye health*, trans. Thomas Newton (STC 15456), 62.

49. Ibid. For an explanation of the contemporary Aristotelian arguments, see Des Chene, *Life's Form*, 67–102.

50. Lemnius, *The touchstone of complexions*, 63. Two recent studies in intellectual history have explored this phenomenon in detail: see Gowland, *The Worlds of Renaissance Melancholy*; and Jeremy Schmidt, *Melancholy and the Care of the Soul: Religion, Moral Philosophy and Madness in Early Modern England* (Aldershot, Hampshire: Ashgate, 2007).

51. Lemnie justifies the composition of his treatise in terms of the operation of the soul: the soul is unable to fulfill its office and effect its will in an impaired body (*The touchstone of complexions*, A1v). But the distinction that he draws between body and soul at the start quickly disappears, and the soul and rational mind are treated almost interchangeably. This is precisely because the compromised mind can misdirect the human subject to vice, and ultimately, the soul to damnation.

52. Ibid., 4r–v, 63r–65v, 146r, 149v. See also Juan Huarte, *The examination of mens witts* (STC 13891), 147–48; Thomas Wright, *The passions of the minde* (STC 26039), 61–63; and Edward Reynolds, *A treatise of the passions and faculties of the soule of man* (STC 20938), 291–92.

53. Lemnius, *The touchstone of complexions*, 63r–v. We can see in Lemnie's logic the progress of the term "complexion" from an internal distribution of humors to an external expression of humoral balance. Both senses of the word are in current use, although "complexion" more often refers to temperament at this time. But we can also perceive in this migration of the term a progress of racial logic from interpreting inner disposition in moral terms to reading outward hue as a set of inward characteristics.

54. Akhimie, *Shakespeare and the Cultivation of Difference*, 5.

55. Ibid., 6.

56. Ibid., 5.

57. Lemnius, *The touchstone of complexions*, 16v.

58. Peter Erickson and Kim Hall, "'A New Scholarly Song': Rereading Early Modern Race," *Shakespeare Quarterly* 67:1 (2016), 10–11..

59. Burton, "Race," 3:222.

60. Ficino, *Platonic Theology* (14.10.7), 310: "Neque solum contracta vel a parentibus vel a sideribus iniqua complexio, sed usu inducta qualitas, ut significavimus ab initio, a religione humanum genus abducit."

61. Akhimie, *Shakespeare and the Cultivation of Difference*, 5.

62. See Goetz, *The Baptism of Early Virginia*, passim.

63. Heng, *England and the Jews*, 12.

64. Leerom Medovoi, "Dogma-Line Racism: Islamophobia and the Second Axis of Race," *Social Text* 30:2 (2012), 44. This formulation differs from the Balibarian concept of neoracism. Rather, Balibar proposes a "racism which does not have the pseudo-biological concept of race as its driving force," and claims that such racism "has always existed, and it has existed at exactly [the] level of secondary theoretical elaborations. Its prototype is anti-Semitism." See Étienne Balibar, "Is There Neo-Racism?" in *Race, Nation, Class: Ambiguous Identities*, ed. Étienne Balibar and Immanuel Wallerstein, trans. Chris Turner (New York: Verso, 1991), 23.

65. See Cheryl I. Harris, "Whiteness as Property," *Harvard Law Review* 106:8 (1993), 1715–44, "The Construction of Race and the Emergence of Whiteness as Property." Harris argues that "the hyper-exploitation of Black labor was accomplished by treating Black people themselves as objects of property. Race and property were thus conflated by establishing a form of property contingent on race—only Blacks were subjugated as slaves and treated as property. Similarly, the conquest, removal, and extermination of Native American life and culture were ratified by conferring and acknowledging the property rights of whites in Native American land. Only white possession and occupation of land was validated and therefore privileged as a basis for property rights. These distinct forms of exploitation each contributed in varying ways to the construction of whiteness as property" (1716). It is the case that Indigenous people could be enslaved as well after 1622 and are written into early English slave codes as enslaved property. I examine how these categories of human (or nonhuman) are constructed at length in Chapter 5—when the treatment of Irish Catholic labor, and particularly offspring, in the Caribbean plays a crucial role in the creation of White supremacy.

66. John Donne, *Letters to severall persons of honour written by John Donne* (Wing D1864), 101–2.

67. Kasey Evans, "Temperate Revenge: Religion, Profit, and Retaliation in 1622 Jamestown," *Texas Studies in Literature and Language* 54 (2012), 159.

68. Christopher Brooke, *A Poem on the Late Massacre in Virginia* (London, 1622), A4r. All citations are from the facsimile in the *Virginia Magazine of History and Biography*, 72:3 (1964), 259–92.

69. See Mary Floyd-Wilson, *English Ethnicity and Race in Early Modern Drama* (Cambridge: Cambridge University Press, 2003).

70. Molly Murray, "Performing Devotion in *The Masque of Blacknesse*," *Studies in English Literature* 47 (2007), 427–49. Ben Jonson was also a Catholic convert at the time of this masque composition.

71. Gowland, *The Worlds of Renaissance Melancholy*, 160.

72. *Mary Wroth's Poetry: An Electronic Edition*, ed. Paul Salzman, wroth.latrobe.edu.au. All citations are from this edition.

73. Sharon Patricia Holland, *The Erotic Life of Racism* (Durham, NC: Duke University Press, 2012), 46.

74. John Temple, *The Irish Rebellion* (Wing T627), 10.

75. *The Geneva Bible: A Facsimile of the 1560 Edition*, Introduction by Lloyd E. Berry (Madison: University of Wisconsin Press, 1969). All biblical citations are from this edition.

76. See Chapter 5, n. 8.

77. Thomas Southerne, *Oroonoko: Adaptations and Offshoots*, ed. Susan B. Iwanisziw, Early Modern Englishwoman series (Aldershot, Hampshire: Ashgate, 2006). All citations are from this facsimile edition.

78. Since Restoration stage conventions did not compel this choice on the part of Southerne, it is likely that he created a White Imoinda in order to draw the comparison to Shakespeare's *Othello*.

79. As Ania Loomba reminds us: "Our own tools of recovery, to the extent that they are necessarily our own, are necessarily incommensurate with the objects of our analysis, especially if such objects lie in the past or within social formations very different from our own. But they are necessary starting points, if only because our contemporary ideologies bear traces of older practices and thinking, of historical transformation as well as of movements of peoples." "In other words," she writes, "ideologies are historical palimpsests, as Gramsci taught us." Ania Loomba, "Identities and Bodies in Early Modern Studies," in *The Oxford Handbook of Shakespeare and Embodiment: Gender, Sexuality and Race*, ed. Valerie Traub (Oxford: Oxford University Press, 2016), 235.

80. Insofar as the process that this book describes is one of an interior humoral disposition moving to the surface as an expression of this complexion, my research rests heavily upon two important studies: Roxann Wheeler, *The Complexion of Race: Categories of Difference in Eighteenth-Century British Culture* (Philadelphia: University of Pennsylvania Press, 2000); and Sujata Iyengar, *Shades of Difference: Mythologies of Skin Color in Early Modern England* (Philadelphia: University of Pennsylvania Press, 2005).

Chapter 1

1. John Donne, *Letters to severall persons of honour written by John Donne*, 13, 16. In the 1651 edition of the *Letters*, this one is directed to T[homas] Lucey (11), but modern editors of the letters have reached consensus that it is actually addressed to Goodyer. See P. M. Oliver, ed., *John Donne: Selected Letters* (New York: Carcanet Press, 2002), 27–30. The dating of the letters is uncertain: in the facsimile edition of the *Letters*, edited by M. Thomas Hester (New York: Georg

Olms Verlag, 1977), both of the letters under interrogation in the opening section of this chapter are assigned a date of spring of 1608. However, P. M. Oliver sets the composition of the first at October 1607 and the second at March 1608. I have tried to preserve the uncertain date of the letters under interrogation, while assigning them collectively to a particular period.

2. Donne, *Letters to severall persons*, 13. Donne compares this "lazie weariness" to "Princes [who having] travailed with long and wastfull war, descend to such conditions of peace, as they are soon after ashamed to have embraced" (12).

3. Kessler, "The Intellective Soul," 503. Cf. Introduction, n. 5.

4. Bright, *A Treatise of melancholie*, iiiv.

5. In *The Poetics of Melancholy*, Douglas Trevor observes this problem in relation to Spenser, arguing that "Neoplatonic tenets like the immateriality of forms and a universal hierarchy of spiritual transcendence were far more accommodating" to Spenser's own sense of election and apparent predestinarianism (56).

6. Bright, *A Treatise of melancholie*, iii^r.

7. Robin Robbins, ed., *The Complete Poems of John Donne* (Harlow: Pearson Education Limited, 2008); all citations of Donne's poetry are from this 2008 edition. In her book *John Donne: Body and Soul* (Chicago: University of Chicago Press, 2008), Ramie Targoff writes that "for Donne, the relationship between body and soul—a relationship that he regarded as one of mutual necessity—was the defining bond of his life" (1). This is undeniably true. But it is also a relationship that, due to the developments in both natural philosophy and medical treatment, captured the sustained and vexed attention of physicians, philosophers, theologians, and laypeople both in England and on the Continent. I am locating Donne's particular anxieties concerning the body's ability to affect the state of the soul within the context of a cultural anxiety and a particular set of cultural arguments. My interest is how Donne comprehends the cooperative relationship of the material and immaterial in the human soul.

8. Robin Robbins dates this verse epistle to roughly the same time, 1607, as Donne's exchange with Goodyer (*The Complete Poems of John Donne*, 665).

9. Donne, *Letters to severall persons*, 18.

10. Ibid., 17.

11. Ibid.

12. Ibid., 16.

13. Des Chene, *Life's Form*, cites both of these points of opposition as contemporary Aristotelian arguments against the respective positions of Galenic materialism and Platonism (70). What I am noticing here is that the grounds on which Donne rejects these claims are also the terms on which a corporal view of the soul or the belief that the soul was purely spiritual in substance could be rejected. Of course, the religious doctrines themselves should not be understood to have derived from the philosophy of either Galen or Plato. Traducianism is advocated, in its material view of the soul, by Tertullian and accepted in its spiritual sense by Augustine, Luther, and some Calvinists (for whom this view coheres with the doctrine of innate depravity); creationism is advanced by Jerome and Aquinas: see Robbins, *The Complete Poems of John Donne*, 179, 62n.

14. The particularity of the human soul, advanced by Avicenna in contradistinction to Averroes (see Introduction, n. 5), was a sustained conviction of Donne's. Avicenna argued that the intellective soul does not exist before the body but rather has its beginning with a specific body. It is individuated by its particular disposition and attributes, which guarantee that it will not become part of a collective after the death of the body (see Dag Nikolaus Hasse, *Avicenna's*

De Anima *in the Latin West: The Formation of a Peripatetic Philosophy of the Soul, 1160–1300* [London: Warburg Institute, 2000], 175). Donne's argument against creationism is precisely that such an infusion does not understand the soul as coming "into the body of her own disposition" (*Letters to severall persons*, 17).

15. "A sermon preached at St. Paul's" (Easter day, March 28, 1623), in *The Sermons of John Donne*, ed. George R. Potter and Evelyn M. Simpson, 10 vols. (Berkeley: University of California Press, 1953–62), 4:358.

16. All italics within quotations are found in the original.

17. Donne frequently takes momentary comfort in this association: "so at the Resurrection of this body, I shall be able to say to the Angel of the great Councell, the Son of God, Christ Jesus himselfe, I am of the same stuffe as you, Body and body, Flesh and flesh." *The Sermons of John Donne*, 4:46 (sermon preached at Whitehall, March 8, 1622).

18. John Carey and John Stachniewski are the most commonly invoked proponents of a religious despair in the Holy Sonnets that draws from Calvinist doctrine; see Carey, *John Donne: Life, Mind, Art* (London: Faber and Faber, 1990); Stachniewski, "John Donne: The Despair of the 'Holy Sonnets,'" *ELH* 48 (1981), 677–705; and Stachniewski, *The Persecutory Imagination: English Puritanism and the Literature of Religious Despair* (Oxford: Oxford University Press, 1991), 254–91. Trevor has tracked the melancholy humor of the sonnets that he sees as an integral part of Donne's religious devotion in *The Poetics of Melancholy*, 87–115. Richard Strier has argued against Donne as a convinced Calvinist and reads the poems as the text of a struggle to accept the prevailing faith of the Church of England in "John Donne, Awry and Squint: The 'Holy Sonnets,' 1608–1610," *Modern Philology* 86 (1989), 357–84. Molly Murray does not treat the Holy Sonnets specifically but argues that the pressure of conversion shapes much of Donne's poetry; see *The Poetics of Conversion in Early Modern English Literature* (Cambridge: Cambridge University Press, 2009), 69–104.

19. Strier's article "John Donne, Awry and Squint" is appropriately recognized as perhaps the best exposition of how conversion impacts the formal structures of the sonnets themselves. Strier takes his title from Donne's description concerning the lingering marks upon a person who alters their religion. But Strier understands the remark as a metaphor. Michael Schoenfeldt is the only critic that I know of to have studied the "complex continua between body and soul" evident in Donne's love lyrics; see Schoenfeldt, *Bodies and Selves in Early Modern England: Physiology and Inwardness in Spenser, Shakespeare, Herbert, and Milton* (Cambridge: Cambridge University Press, 1999), 158.

20. Donne, *Letters to severall persons*, 101–2.

21. Ibid., 70 [March 1608?].

22. Donne writes: "Of all these ['Soul, and Body and Minde'] the diseases are cures, if they be known. Of our souls sicknesses, which are sinnes, the knowledge is, to acknowledge, and that is her Physique.... Of our bodies infirmities though our knowledge be ... from the opinion of the Physician, and that the subject and matter be flexible, and various; yet their rules are certain, and if the matter be rightly applyed to the rule, our knowledge thereof is also certain. But of the diseases of the minde, there is no *Criterium*, no Canon, no rule; for, our own taste and apprehension and interpretation should be the Judge, and that is the disease it selfe." Ibid., 70–71.

23. Ibid., 72. Donne can only be referring to reason here, since the choice of the soul's direction at death is determined by the "naturall guide" of the "minde."

24. *The essayes or morall, politike and millitarie discourses of Lo[rd] Michaell de Montaigne*, trans. John Florio (STC 18041), 44.

25. Heinrich von Stadan, "Body, Soul, and Nerves: Epicurus, Herophilus, Erasistratus, the Stoics, and Galen," in *Psyche and Soma: Physicians and Metaphysicians on the Mind-Body Problem from Antiquity to Enlightenment*, ed. John P. Wright and Paul Potter (Oxford: Oxford University Press, 2000), 106.

26. *The Sermons of John Donne*, 9:136 (a sermon preached at St. Paul's, Christmas Day, 1629).

27. Donne, *Letters to seuerall persons*, 71.

28. See Kusukawa, *The Transformation of Natural Philosophy*, passim.

29. Ibid., 91.

30. The *OED* cites *geographer* as the commonly accepted meaning of *cosmographer* in sixteenth- and seventeenth-century England.

31. Stachnewski argues for a "Calvinist pressure on [Donne's] imagination," but not for Calvinism as his religious identity per se (*The Persecutory Imagination*, 254–91). Stachniewski's position has since been challenged by numerous critics, and most directly by Strier. However, Strier is still persuaded that "evidence for Calvinism" is "present" in the Holy Sonnets ("John Donne, Awry and Squint," 366). For an account of the history of critical attempts to unmask Donne's religious identity, see Murray, *The Poetics of Conversion*, 69–71.

32. See Lori Anne Ferrell, "Transfiguring Theology: William Perkins and Calvinist Aesthetics," in *John Foxe and His World*, ed. Christopher Highley and John N. King (Aldershot, Hampshire: Ashgate, 2002), 164–65; and Kimberly Anne Coles, *Religion, Reform, and Women's Writing in Early Modern England* (Cambridge: Cambridge University Press, 2008) 114, 113–48.

33. Peter Lake, *Moderate Puritans and the Elizabethan Church* (Cambridge: Cambridge University Press, 1982), 99, 219.

34. Robbins, *The Complete Poems of John Donne*, 520.

35. Donne, *Letters to seuerall persons*, 102, 35.

36. Douglas Trevor provides a sketch of the competing Galenic and Platonic positions and points out the religious implications of these arguments in *The Poetics of Melancholy*, 51–56.

37. Gowland, "The Problem of Early Modern Melancholy," 105–6. While Melanchthon was far more charitable toward Catholics than either of his contemporaries, he assailed atheism as a monstrosity of humoral distemper; see Hankins, "Monstrous Melancholy," 26n4. As I trace throughout this book, Catholics are characterized as irreligious, pagan, and atheist in Protestant polemic—and this becomes increasingly racialized in its terms as Catholics, particularly in Ireland, become colonial targets.

38. Cf. *A commentarie vpon the Epistle of Saint Paul to the Romanes, written in Latine by M. Iohn Caluin, and newely translated into Englishe by Christopher Rosdell preacher* (STC 4399), ¶¶¶r.

39. Robert Burton, *The anatomy of melancholy What it is, with all the kinds causes, symptomes, prognostickes, & seuerall cures of it* (STC 4161), 3.4.1.1, 580, quoted in Gowland, *The Worlds of Renaissance Melancholy*, 161. All citations from Burton are drawn from the 1628 edition.

40. In her dedication of Calvin's printed sermons on Hezekiah to Katherine Bertie, the dowager duchess of Suffolk, Anne Vaughan Lok writes of the sad case of those "overwhelmed with grosse faithlesse and papisticall humors," writing the very formulation that Bright deplores into the preface to Calvin's text. See *Sermons of Iohn Caluin, vpon the songe that Ezechias made after he had bene sicke* (STC 4450), A4v.

41. Stachniewski, *The Persecutory Imagination*, 227.

42. Bright's associations with Sir Francis Walsingham and Laurence Chaderton put him in the ranks of the hotter sort of Protestant in late sixteenth-century England; see Lori Anne

Ferrell, "Method as Knowledge: Scribal Theology, Protestantism, and the Reinvention of Shorthand in Sixteenth-Century England," in *Making Knowledge in Early Modern Europe: Practices, Objects and Texts, 1400–1800*, ed. Pamela H. Smith and Benjamin Schmidt (Chicago: University of Chicago Press, 2007), 170.

43. Bright, *A Treatise of melancholie*, 48.

44. Ibid., 45.

45. Ibid.

46. G. Blakemore Evans makes a persuasive case for Donne's acquaintance with the *Treatise of melancholie*; see "Donne's 'Subtile Knot,'" *Notes and Queries*, n.s., 34 (1987), 228–30.

47. *The Sermons of John Donne*, 2:261 (a sermon preached to the prince and princess Palatine, June 16, 1619).

48. Ibid., 2:261–62.

49. Hardin Craig, ed., *A Treatise of Melancholie by Timothy Bright* (New York: Columbia University Press, 1940), xi.

50. *The Sermons of John Donne*, 4:358 (a sermon preached at St. Paul's, Easter day, March 28, 1623).

51. Ibid., 6:128 [Whitsun, 1624?].

52. Bright uses *spirit* and *spirits* interchangeably in his treatise because natural, vital, and animal spirits are, for him, all one spirit: "I know commonly there are accompted three spirits: animall, vitall, and natural: but these are in deede, rather distinctions of diuerse office of one spirit" (*A Treatise of melancholie*, 46–47).

53. Pierre Charron, *Of Wisdom*, trans. Samson Lennard (STC 5051), 29. Charron's treatise was popular in England: it was reprinted eight times in the forty years after its 1608 translation.

54. Ibid. Sullivan, *Sleep, Romance and Human Embodiment*, 32, cites another passage, just previous to this one, in which Charron sounds remarkably like Bright in his terms: "The . . . Soule is alwaies well, because for it there is no need of the bodie, though whilst it is within it, it make vse thereof to exercise it selfe" (Charron, *Of Wisdom*, 27). But the subsequent passage makes clear that Charron's construction is similar to Aquinas, in that the soul is affected by bodily disorder but not fundamentally disturbed in its essence. For the time that the immortal soul inhabits the body, however, it can be misdirected by the illness or delusion that the body offers.

55. Bright, *A Treatise of melancholie*, 45.

56. Ibid., 46.

57. William Perkins, *A treatise tending vnto a declaration whether a man be in the estate of damnation or in the estate of grace* (STC 19752), 42–43.

58. Ibid., 87.

59. John Abernethy, *A Christian and heauenly treatise. Containing physicke for the soule* (STC 75), A3ʳ.

60. When Thomas Adams, for example, juxtaposes humoral conditions and their cures against spiritual ones in his 1616 *Diseases of the soule* (STC 109), he is emphasizing the impotence of medical remedies for spiritual concerns.

61. Kusukawa, *The Transformation of Natural Philosophy*, 99.

62. Bright, *A Treatise of melancholie*, 52.

63. Ibid., 60, 66.

64. Ibid., 72.

65. Ibid., 52–53.

66. Donne, *Letters to severall persons* (1651), 134–35.

67. Lemnius, *The touchstone of complexions*, Alv.

68. While this sonnet is given the number 19 in John Carey's edition of Donne's poems (*John Donne: A Critical Edition of the Major Works* [Oxford: Oxford University Press, 1990], 288–89), Robin Robbins sets it chronologically outside of the composition of the other Holy Sonnets and titles it simply "Sonnet: 'Oh, to vex me'" (*The Complete Poems of John Donne*, 494–95). It is one of three sonnets (identified as *HSW* 1, 2, and 3) that can only be found in the Westmoreland MS. The sonnet is dated by Robbins to around 1608, in part because of verbal echoes in Donne's letters to Henry Goodyer that introduced the discussion at the start of this chapter.

69. Carey, *John Donne: Life, Mind, Art*; Brian Cummings, *The Literary Culture of the Reformation: Grammar and Grace* (Oxford: Oxford University Press, 2002), 365–77; Stachniewski, *The Persecutory Imagination*, 251–91; Strier, "John Donne, Awry and Squint"; Targoff, *John Donne: Body and Soul*; Trevor, *The Poetics of Melancholy*, 87–115.

70. Cummings, *The Literary Culture of the Reformation*, 385.

71. Trevor, *The Poetics of Melancholy*, 87.

72. Robbins, *The Complete Poems of John Donne*, 494.

73. Stachniewski, "John Donne: The Despair of the 'Holy Sonnets,'" 684.

74. Donne, *Letters to severall persons*, 100.

75. Ibid., 102.

76. Ibid., 101.

77. Trevor, *The Poetics of Melancholy*, 87–115.

78. Of course, this is not to exclude the wonderful article by Elaine Scarry, "Donne: But Yet the Body Is His Booke," in *Literature and the Body: Essays on Populations and Persons*, ed. Elaine Scarry (Baltimore: Johns Hopkins University Press, 1988), 70–105. As the title suggests, however, Scarry sees Donne reading both the material and spiritual world(s) through the materials of his own body.

79. Murray, *The Poetics of Conversion*, 69.

80. Donne, *Letters to severall persons*, 101–2.

81. Wright, *The passions of the minde*, 6. There is little question that Wright's treatise relates a common apprehension of the body's operations. A popular tract, it was reprinted five times between 1601 and 1630.

82. Stachniewski, *The Persecutory Imagination*, 284.

83. Thanks is due to dear Marshall Grossman for pointing this out to me.

84. *The Sermons of John Donne*, 5:267 (a sermon preached to the Earl of Carlisle [1622?]).

85. Ibid.

86. Robin Robbins assigns this poem to a collection of "Divine Meditations" that he calls "A different version of 'Holy Sonnets'" (*The Complete Poems of John Donne*, 520–42). Four of these poems, "Thou hast made me," "Oh might those sighs and tears," "I am a little world," and "If faithful souls," are not included among the twelve sonnets that he terms Holy Sonnets, and the three Holy Sonnets taken from the Westmoreland MS (*HSW* 1, 2, and 3). Cf. n. 69.

87. Obviously, Donne is using the word *sprite* in terms of the soul here. For a similar construction of the spirit, see *The Sermons of John Donne*, 4:46 (a sermon preached at Whitehall, March 8, 1622): "as soon as my soul enters into heaven, I shall be able to say to the angels, I am of the same stuff as you, spirit and spirit." For the manifold definitions of the word that Donne employs, see Robbins, *The Complete Poems of John Donne*, 178–79; much of the discussion that follows is indebted to Robbins's note on lines 61–64 of "The Ecstasy."

88. *The Sermons of John Donne*, 2:261 (a sermon preached to the prince and princess Palatine, June 16, 1619).

89. Ibid., 5:65 (an undated sermon), quoted in Robbins, *The Complete Poems of John Donne*, 179.

90. Ibid.

91. Cf. *The Sermons of John Donne*, 3:368 (a sermon preached at St. Paul's, Christmas Day, 1621).

92. Murray, *The Poetics of Conversion*, 69.

93. William Perkins, *A discourse of conscience wherein is set downe the nature, properties, and differences thereof* (STC 19696), 140.

94. In a verse letter, "To Mr. Tilman after he had Taken Orders," Donne also invokes the impression made on the substance of the body: "Art thou the same materials as before, / Only the stamp is changed, but no more . . . as new-crowned kings alter the face / But not the money's substance." Robbins, *The Complete Poems of John Donne*, 114 (lines 13–16). This would seem to undercut my argument but for the fact that Donne was (however obliquely) responding to Tilman's own feeling that his humoral temperament—which rendered him "inconstant, lustful, hot-tempered, and ambitious"—also rendered him unfit for an office in the church (113). The poem is reassuring, in that Donne is saying that he has traded God's image (or old Adam's) for Christ's.

95. *The Sermons of John Donne*, 6:57 (a sermon preached on the penitential Psalms, April, May, or June 1623), quoted in Robbins, *The Complete Poems of John Donne*, 530.

96. *The Sermons of John Donne*, 4:358 (a sermon preached at St. Paul's, Easter day, March 28, 1623). That this is Tertullian's formulation is noteworthy in that Tertullian advocated a material view of the soul (cf. n. 13 above).

97. Ibid., 9:64 (a sermon preached to the king at court, April 1629).

98. Wright, *The passions of the minde*, 6.

99. Trevor notices this in *The Poetics of Melancholy*. He responds to the connection between Donne's turbulent mind and the turbulent images of the body to which he repeatedly returns. But he reads the earthbound images of this sermon as a symptom of Donne's melancholy mind—an obsession with death: "Donne's descriptive tendencies themselves," he writes, "reflect his melancholy: he builds up . . . earthly images, only to allow such images to decompose" (101).

100. *The Sermons of John Donne*, 6:214 (a sermon preached at St. Paul's the Sunday after the conversion of Saint Paul, 1624).

101. Ibid., 6:213.

102. King James translation. Robin Robbins points to the correspondence: see *The Complete Poems of John Donne*, 522, ll. 7–8n.

103. Cf. *Satyre 3*: "and shall thy father's spirit / Meet blind philosophers in Heav'n, whose merit / Of strict life may be imputed faith[?]" Ibid., 387–88 (ll. 11–13).

104. Robin Robbins notes that while this is a medieval Scholastic debate, it was debated as recently as 1605 at University Church, Oxford, in front of King James (ibid., 539, ll. 1–7n.).

105. Cf. "Turne over all the folds, and plaits of thine own heart, and finde there the infirmities, and waverings of thine *owne faith*, and an ability to say, *Lord, I beleeve, help mine unbeleefe*." *The Sermons of John Donne*, 3:367 (a sermon preached at St. Paul's, Christmas Day 1621).

106. Michelle O'Callaghan, "Christopher Brooke (c. 1570–1628)," *Oxford Dictionary of National Biography*.

107. Kasey Evans provides the most sustained, side-by-side analysis of the two responses, Donne's "Sermon to the Virginia Company" (November 13, 1622) and Brooke's *A Poem on the*

Late Massacre in Virginia, published in September 1622; see Evans, "John Donne, Christopher Brooke, and Temperate Revenge in 1622 Jamestown," in *Colonial Virtue: The Mobility of Temperance in Renaissance England* (Toronto: University of Toronto Press, 2012), 127–59. Donne's "Sermon" appeared in *Four Sermons Vpon Speciall Occasions* in 1625 (STC 7042), and Brooke's poem was printed in 1622 for Robert Mylbourne for sale at Paul's churchyard. Only one copy (STC 3830.5) is known to have survived and is reproduced with an introduction by Robert C. Johnson in the *Virginia Magazine of History and Biography*.

108. In n. 43 of the Introduction, I recount an episode where James Hankins, writing in *Quillette* (July 29, 2020), abhors teaching the Renaissance as a period that is "[culpable] in establishing 'white supremacy.'" But it is his avoidance of this very culpability that best explains why he fails to see the "Monstrous Melancholy" that produces atheism as a potential racial marker.

109. Justin E. H. Smith, *Nature, Human Nature, and Human Difference: Race in Early Modern Philosophy* (Princeton, NJ: Princeton University Press, 2015), 56.

110. See McDowell, "The View from the Interior."

111. Smith, *Nature, Human Nature, and Human Difference*, 2.

112. Joyce E. Chaplin, *Subject Matter: Technology, the Body, and Science on the Anglo-American Frontier, 1500–1676* (Cambridge, MA: Harvard University Press, 2001), 9.

113. The most well-known example of this is Thomas Harriot's 1590 *A briefe and true report of the new found land of Virginia* (STC 12786), which includes the engravings of Theodor de Bry. Since he had not visited the colonies, de Bry relied on the watercolor illustrations of the English colonist John White; but both visually linked the "New World" natives and ancient Britons.

114. Chaplin, *Subject Matter*, 9.

115. Gregory Ablavsky, "Making Indians 'White': The Judicial Abolition of Native Slavery in Revolutionary Virginia and Its Racial Legacy," *University of Pennsylvania Law Review* 159:5 (2011), 1465.

116. O'Callaghan, "Christopher Brooke."

117. Brooke, *A Poem on the Late Massacre in Virginia*.

118. William Shakespeare, *The Tempest*, ed. Frank Kermode (New York: Routledge, 1989). All citations are from this edition.

119. [Anon.], *A True and Sincere Declaration of the Purpose and Ends of the Plantation Begun in Virginia* (STC 24832), 2, quoted in Evans, *Colonial Virtue*, 127. Evans spends some time analyzing the shift in colonial intention that occurs with the Powhatan attack.

120. Floyd-Wilson, *English Ethnicity and Race in Early Modern Drama*.

121. Precisely how right religion is cultivated in New World contexts—and what bodies are permanently resistant to reform—is explored at length in Chapter 5.

122. Samuel Purchas, *Hakluytus Posthumus, or, Purchas his Pilgrimes*, 20 vols. (Glasgow: Glasgow University Press, 1905–7; rpt., Cambridge University Press, 2014), 19:220, 221.

123. Ibid., 224.

124. Ibid., 225.

125. Loomba and Burton, *Race in Early Modern England*, 27–28.

126. Purchas, *Hakluytus Posthumus*, 237–38.

127. Ibid., 230.

128. Ablavsky, "Making Indians 'White,'" 1465.

129. See, in particular, Goetz, *The Baptism of Early Virginia*.

130. Ablavsky, "Making Indians 'White,'" 1474.

131. Goetz, *The Baptism of Early Virginia*, chaps. 3 and 4.

132. Quoted in ibid., 86. I revisit these questions and explore the issues of lineage, blood, and religion at length in Chapter 5.

Chapter 2

1. Murray, "Performing Devotion in *The Masque of Blacknesse.*"
2. *The Masque of Blackness*, in *Ben Jonson: The Complete Masques*, ed. Stephen Orgel (New Haven, CT: Yale University Press, 1969). All citations are from this edition.
3. *Ben Jonson*, ed. C. H. Hereford Percy and Evelyn Simpson, 11 vols. (Oxford: Clarendon Press, 1925–52), 10:448.
4. Drew Daniel, *The Melancholy Assemblage: Affect and Epistemology in the English Renaissance* (New York: Fordham University Press, 2013), 15.
5. Burton, *The anatomy of melancholy*, 1.2.3.1, 82. This particular citation is quoted in Michael Schoenfeldt, "Eloquent Blood and Deliberative Bodies: The Physiology of Metaphysical Poetry," in *Renaissance Transformations: The Making of English Writing, 1500–1650*, ed. Thomas Healy and Margaret Healy (Edinburgh: Edinburgh University Press, 2009), 146. Cf. Thomas Wright's 1601 *The passions of the minde*: Wright situates the soul in the seat of the heart but additionally asserts that "the passions inhabite, not onely the heart, but also are stirred vp in euery parte of the bodie" (63) and "that there are Passions in the reasonable soule" (56–59).
6. This loosely paraphrases Angus Gowland, "Melancholy, Passion and Identity in the Renaissance," in *Passions and Subjectivity in Early Modern Culture*, ed. Brian Cummings and Freya Sierhuis (Farnham, Surrey: Ashgate, 2013), 76. See André Du Laurens, *A discourse of the preservation of the sight: of melancholike diseases; of rheumes, and of old age* (STC 7304), 72–140; Burton, *The anatomy of melancholy*, 1.1.1.4, 8–11.
7. Britton, *Becoming Christian*, 15.
8. Miles P. Grier brilliantly argues that the marking of the Ethiopian nymphs in the *The Masque of Blacknesse* indicates them as failed readers of the Word in "Inkface: The Slave Stigma in England's Early Imperial Imagination," in *Scripturalizing the Human: The Written as the Political*, ed. Vincent L. Wimbush (New York: Routledge, 2015), 195.
9. Clare McManus, *Women on the Renaissance Stage: Anna of Denmark and Female Masquing in the Stuart Court (1590–1619)* (Manchester: Manchester University Press, 2002), 4.
10. Ibid., 72–90 in particular.
11. Ibid., 75.
12. Ibid.
13. Ibid., 80.
14. The entertainments on both occasions at which the queen was present were arranged by Anne's secretary, William Fowler—a fervent Protestant and former employee of Walsingham. For Fowler's sometimes strained relationship with his mistress, see *The Works of William Fowler: Secretary to Queen Anne, Wife of James VI*, ed. Henry Meikle, James Craigie, and John Purves, 3 vols. (Edinburgh: Scottish Text Society, 1914–40), 3:ix–xlii.
15. Ibid., 2:190, 174.
16. Mara R. Wade, "Duke Ulrik (1578–1624) as Agent, Patron, Artist: Reframing Danish Court Culture in the International Perspective c. 1600," in *Reframing the Danish Renaissance: Problems and Prospects in a European Perspective*, ed. Michael Andersen, Birgitte B. Johannsen, and Hugo Johannsen (Copenhagen: National Museum, 2011), 248.
17. Mara R. Wade, "The Coronation of King Christian IV 1596," in *Europa Triumphans: Court and Civic Festivals in Early Modern Europe*, ed. J. R. Mulryne, Helen Watanabe-O'Kelly,

and Margaret Shewring, 2 vols. (Basingstoke: Palgrave Macmillan, 2004), 2:253. For a translation of the original festival account, see 248–67.

18. Since the Turks invaded Iran in 1037, and the empire of the Turkish Seljuks ruled in Iran until 1197 CE, these could sometimes be interchangeable.

19. Wade, "Duke Ulrik," 252–53. For the possible transmission of details of these court festivities to Inigo Jones through the court musician John Dowland when he was on embassy to Denmark in 1603, the year before he entered the service of Queen Anne, see ibid., 250.

20. McManus, *Women on the Renaissance Stage*, 92.

21. Peter Davidson and Thomas M. McCoog, "Father Robert's Convert: The Private Catholicism of Anne of Denmark," *Times Literary Supplement* 24 (November 2000), 16–17.

22. This incident was recorded—as well as the argument that preceded it—by the Venetian Secretary at the English court, Scaramelli. See McManus, *Women on the Renaissance Stage*, 92.

23. Hall, *Things of Darkness*, 6–7.

24. See Grier, "Inkface," 195.

25. Eric Griffin has begun some of the work of understanding how Protestant biblicists and propagandists effectively reconstructed Spanish Catholics as no longer Christian at all: "More than simply identifying the presence of the propagandistic discourse and observing its pervasiveness, I am concerned with *how* the 'white' proponents of this discourse were so successful in fashioning an opponent that is so manifestly their 'black' opposite" (*English Renaissance Drama and the Specter of Spain: Ethnopoetics and Empire* [Philadelphia: University of Pennsylvania Press, 2009], 15).

26. John Florio, *A world of wordes, or Most copious, and exact dictionarie in Italian and English* (STC 11098), 219, quoted in Griffin, *English Renaissance Drama and the Specter of Spain*, 97.

27. While Moor was originally the term applied to the nomadic Berber people of North Africa (the name itself comes from the Roman province of Mauritania), it was eventually extended to African populations more generally. As such, this list is slightly repetitive, depending upon time and location. However, with forced migration across the Atlantic, Black Africans lost their associations with Moors and are more commonly ascribed Ethiopians. See Walter D. Mignolo, "What Does the Black Legend Have to Do with Race?" in *Rereading the Black Legend: The Discourses of Religious and Racial Difference in the Renaissance Empires*, ed. Margaret R. Greer, Walter D. Mignolo, and Maureen Quilligan (Chicago: University of Chicago Press, 2007), 318.

28. Griffin, *English Renaissance Drama and the Specter of Spain*, 88.

29. These distinctions are extremely hard to draw. But a potent example might be found in John Minsheu's (revised from Richard Perceval) 1599 *A dictionarie in Spanish and English* (STC 19620), which designates "an Ethnicke" as a "heathen," "gentile," or "pagan" (133). "Pagan" is enlarged as: "one that knoweth not God" (295). The conflation of terms, then, speaks volumes.

30. Eric Griffin, "Nationalism, the Black Legend, and the Revised *Spanish Tragedy*," ELR 39 (2009), 368.

31. See, in particular, Barbara Fuchs, "Spanish Lessons: Spenser and the Irish Moriscos," *Studies in English Literature, 1500–1900* 42:1 (2002), 43–62.

32. As I note in the Introduction: in Aquinas, bodily disease, such as melancholy, can impair, but not obstruct, the faculties of the rational soul such as reason, will, and moral judgment.

33. "Ac Medicis necessariam esse considerationem harum dissimilitudinum, constat. Prodest autem et communi vita ad tuendam valetudinem, ad regendos mores, ad circumspectionem in familiaritatibus. Omnino necessaria diligenia est vitare monstrosas, superbas, malevolas et perfidiosas naturas" (*Corpus Reformatorum*, vol. 13, col. 87). This sense is further reinforced

by the commentary source from which Burton read *De Anima*, which has the written marginalia: "mores plerunq, imitantur tempermenta humorum." *Ioannis Magiri, doctoris medici et philosophi . . . commentarivs . . . In aureum Philippi Melanchthonis libellum* de Anima (Frankfurt, 1603), 359. In the Clarendon edition of *The Anatomy of Melancholy*, ed. J. B. Bamborough and Martin Dodsworth, 6 vols. (Oxford: Clarendon Press, 1989–2000), Bamborough cites this edition as Burton's source (6:261).

34. "Ex humorum enim cognitione de naturae inclinationibus, affectibus, Studiis, virtutibus & vitiis hominum iudicum sumere possumus. Denique ab humorum proprietate sumunt Medici prognostica de morbis. Ob has ergo & alias rationes haec doctrina nobis admodum commendata erit." *In aureum Philippi Melanchthonis libellum de Anima*, 361.

35. Gowland, "Melancholy, Passion and Identity in the Renaissance," 75.

36. Bright, *A Treatise of melancholie*, iii^r.

37. Gowland, *The Worlds of Renaissance Melancholy*, 42. See also Kusukawa, *The Transformation of Natural Philosophy*, 89; and Emily Michael, "Renaissance Theories of Body, Soul, and Mind," in *Psyche and Soma: Physicians and Metaphysicians on the Mind-Body Problem from Antiquity to Enlightenment*, ed. John P. Wright and Paul Potter, 163–65. Melanchthon declares not only that the nature of the soul can be known by the operations of the body but that knowledge of God himself is achieved through the same means: "Itaque sapientissime Galenus inquit, doctrinam anatomicam initium esse Theologiae, et aditum ad agnitionem Dei" ("Therefore Galen said most wisely that the anatomical teaching is the beginning of Theology and the path to the knowledge of God"); quoted and translated in Kusukawa, *The Transformation of Natural Philosophy*, 103.

38. Burton, *The anatomy of melancholy*, 3.4.2.1, 614. In the *Corpus Reformatorum*, which I have been citing, Melanchthon's assertion appears in vol. 13, col. 87.

39. See *In aureum Philippi Melanchthonis libellum* de Anima, 359–60. Cf. n. 33, above.

40. See Gábor, "The Breath Returns to God Who Gave It," 87–89.

41. Bright, *A Treatise of melancholie*, iiir.

42. In Burton, "Papists" and "Turkes" suffer from the same disease, and are equally defective, and he sets both within the "company of Pagans, Jewes" and "Infidels" (see *The anatomy of melancholy*, 3.4.1.4, 611).

43. See Iyengar, *Shades of Difference*, 11, 47, and 67–70 for a fuller description. See also her excellent discussion of *The Masque of Blackness*, 80–93.

44. Gowland, *The Worlds of Renaissance Melancholy*, 63.

45. Ibid., 62. Some theorists, Burton among them, went as far as isolating particular areas of the brain that were affected; in Burton, this is the anterior ventricle of the brain, but a similar account is found in André Du Laurens. See Burton, *The anatomy of melancholy*, 1.2.3.2, 32–33; Du Laurens, *A discourse of the preservation of the sight*, 87.

46. See, for example, Du Laurens, *A discourse of the preservation of the sight*, 74, 82.

47. Melanchthon, in describing various melancholic states, claims that adust melancholy guarantees frenzy and madness: "Nam adust a efficit furores et amentias" (*Corpus Reformatorum*, vol. 13, col. 85).

48. Ian Smith, "The Textile Black Body: Race and 'Shadowed Livery,' in *The Merchant of Venice*," in *The Oxford Handbook of Shakespeare and Embodiment: Gender, Sexuality, and Race*, ed. Valerie Traub (Oxford: Oxford University Press, 2016), 179.

49. Ovid, *Metamorphoses: The Arthur Golding Translation, 1567*, ed. John Frederick Nims (Philadelphia: Paul Dry Books, 2000), 2:300–301, quoted in ibid.

50. *Mary Wroth's Poetry*, ed. Salzman.
51. Hall, *Things of Darkness*, 105–7.
52. Holland, *The Erotic Life of Racism*, 47.
53. Kim F. Hall, "'These bastard signs of fair': Literary whiteness in shakespeare's sonnets," in *Post-Colonial Shakespeares*, ed. Ania Loomba and Martin Orkin (New York: Routledge, 1998), 80.
54. David M. Halperin, "Is There a History of Sexuality?" *History and Theory* 28 (1989), 257–74.
55. Kimberly Anne Coles and Eve Keller, eds. "Introduction: Sex Education," in *The Routledge Companion to Women, Sex, and Gender in the Early British Colonial World* (New York: Routledge, 2019), 1.
56. Holland, *The Erotic Life of Racism*, 51.
57. Melissa E. Sanchez, "The Politics of Masochism in Mary Wroth's 'Urania,'" *ELH* 74 (2007), 449–78. Of course, Sanchez's analysis is of *Urania* but captures some of the sonnet sequence as part of the critique.
58. Coles and Keller, "Introduction: Sex Education," 2.
59. This would be Michel Foucault's formulation; see "Right of Death and Power over Life," in *The History of Sexuality, Volume I, An Introduction*, trans. Robert Hurley (New York: Vintage, 1980).
60. Romans 2:28-29, *The Geneva Bible*.
61. In Luther, Jews are committed to the Law, and "no one will be justified by fulfilling the requirements of the law, because the law was given only to show the nature of sin." "Preface to the Epistle of St. Paul to the Romans," [1522], in *Martin Luther: Selections from His Writings*, trans. John Dillenberger (New York: Anchor, 1962), 27.
62. Holland, *The Erotic Life of Racism*, 47.
63. Paster, *The Body Embarrassed*, 16.
64. Gowland, *The Worlds of Renaissance Melancholy*, 160.
65. Burton, *The anatomy of melancholy*, 3.4.1.1, 577. The discussion that follows is greatly indebted to Gowland, Ibid.
66. Ficino, *Platonic Theology* (14.9.1), 4:292: "Nullum enim bruta prae se ferunt religionis indicium, ut propria nobis sit mentis in deum caeli regem erecto sicut corporis in caelum erectio propia."
67. Ibid., 4:295: "If man is the most perfect of all mortal animals because of what makes him man, then he is the most perfect chiefly because of the gift among all the gifts which he . . . does not share with the animals. This gift is religion" ("Rursus si homo animalium mortalium perfectissimus est, qua ratione est homo, ex ea praecipue dote est omnium perfectissimus, quam inter haec ipse propriam, animalibus non commune. Ea religio est").
68. Ibid. (14.10.5–8), 4:307–13.
69. Burton, *The anatomy of melancholy*, 3.4.1.1, 577. The marginalia cites: "*Liber de anima*. Ad hoc objectum amandum & fruendum nati sumus, & hunc expetisset unicum, hunc amasset humana voluntas, ut summum bonum & ceteras res omnes eo ordine."
70. This is Dennis Britton's central claim in *Becoming Christian*.
71. Ficino, *Platonic Theology* (14.10.6), 4:308: "Ceterum meminisse oportet eam opinionem sive affectionem non satis habere fidei, quae sequitur aut ingenium melancholicum, aegrum et quodammodo vitae contrarium . . . quae etiam complexionem pervertit humanam ac defectum

affert secum, non modo quantum spectat ad vitae fiduciam, sed etiam quantum ad humanarum rerum gubernationem."

72. Ibid.: "Qui dum insania propter atram bilem concitaretur."

73. Gowland, *The Worlds of Renaissance Melancholy*, 160.

74. As Burton writes: "[Clement of Alexandria] calls *amoris & amicitiæ impletionem & extentionem*, the extent and complement of loue; And that not for feare or worldly respects, but *ordine ad Deum*, for loue of God himselfe. This we shall doe if wee be truely enamored" (*The anatomy of melancholy*, 3.4.1.1, 579).

75. Ibid.

Chapter 3

1. Feerick, *Strangers in Blood*, 5.
2. See Coles et al., introduction to *The Cultural Politics of Blood*, for a fuller discussion.
3. Ibid.
4. See, in particular, Feerick, *Strangers in Blood*, 55–77.
5. For a revealing analysis of how notions of hereditary blood become racialized in France and Spain, see Ndiaye, "The African ambassador's travels."
6. Akhimie, *Shakespeare and the Cultivation of Difference*, 5.
7. Akhimie writes that "the body markers that indicate membership in [the] hierarchically inferior group are associated with innate moral attributes and capacities (or lack thereof) that are inherited and thus indelible" (ibid., 25).
8. While we do not know exactly when Cary wrote *The Tragedy of Mariam*, it was probably between 1602, when she married Henry Cary, and 1609 when she gave birth to the couple's first child. It was certainly after the circulation of Thomas Lodge's translation of *The famous and memorable vvorkes of Iosephus* (STC 14809) in print or manuscript, since the play is obviously indebted to this translation. This would place the composition of the play after 1598 when Lodge's translation was licensed. But a passage in *The Lady Falkland: Her Life*, written by one of her daughters, refers to a time when Cary wrote "many things for her private recreation, on severall subiects . . . all in verse" (see *Elizabeth Cary, Lady Falkland: Life and Letters*, ed. Heather Wolfe [Cambridge: RTM Publications, 2001], 110). Heather Wolfe assigns this period to around 1605 and assumes that the play was written during this prolific time. In the most recent edition of the play, Ramona Wray sets the period of composition to between 1603 and 1606, with 1605 as the most likely date. See *The Tragedy of Mariam*, ed. Ramona Wray, Arden Early Modern Drama Series (London: Bloomsbury, 2012), 10–11.
9. Dympna Callaghan, "Re-reading Elizabeth Cary's *The Tragedie of Mariam, Faire Queene of Jewry*," in *Women, "Race," and Writing in the Early Modern Period*, ed. Hendricks and Parker (New York: Routledge, 1994), 164.
10. Callaghan's analysis does not overlook the fact that the power relations in the play are a function of rank: she perceives the "differences of power and morality" presented in the drama as determined "not only by gender, but also by 'race,' and class" (172). Her critique recognizes that the transgressive natures of Herod and Salome have their "origins in . . . inferior heritage," but the heritage upon which she most often focuses is that of nation and not family relation (ibid., 173).
11. Margaret Ferguson, *Dido's Daughters: Literacy, Gender, and Empire in Early Modern England and France* (Chicago: University of Chicago Press, 2003), 266.
12. Particularly when I have been advised not to do so in relation to the play by scholars such as Callaghan, Ferguson, Kim Hall, and Ania Loomba: see Ferguson, *Dido's Daughters*,

chap. 6, particularly 316–29; Hall, *Things of Darkness*, 2–7, 184–85; and Ania Loomba, "The Color of Patriarchy: Critical Difference, Cultural Difference, and Renaissance Drama," in *Women, "Race," and Writing in the Early Modern Period*, ed. Hendricks and Parker, 17–34.

13. Kaplan, "The Jewish Body in Black and White in Medieval and Early Modern England," 42. See also Kaplan, "Jessica's Mother."
14. Thomas Elyot, *The boke named the governour* (STC 7635), 16v.
15. See Feerick, *Strangers in Blood*, 60.
16. Elyot, *The boke named the governour*, 17r.
17. Ibid.
18. William Shakespeare, *II Henry IV*, ed. A. R. Humphreys, The Arden Shakespeare (New York: Bloomsbury, 1967).
19. Thomas Elyot, *The castel of helthe* (STC 7642.7), 11.
20. Flavius Josephus, *The famous and memorable vvorkes of Iosephus*, 384.
21. All quotations are from Elizabeth Cary, *The Tragedy of Mariam: The Fair Queen of Jewry*, ed. Barry Weller and Margaret W. Ferguson (Berkeley: University of California Press, 1994).
22. For the examination of a historically later development of this phenomenon, where the logic and language of veterinary handbooks and farmer's manuals become a source for a New World essentialism linking blood and skin color, see Hill, "The Blood of Others." Since Charles de Miramon and others have traced the emergence of ideas of hereditary blood to these same manuals, these arguments show the influence of Aristotelianism and natural histories in the production of the race concept in pre- and early modern periods. See Miramon, "Noble Dogs, noble blood." See also Aubert, "'The Blood of France.'"
23. Josephus, *The famous and memorable vvorkes of Iosephus*, 349.
24. Ibid., 350.
25. Ibid.
26. Ibid., 355–56. It is important to bear in mind that Antipater ruled as "gouernour of Iudea by the commaundement of Hircanus" (359) and gave the governorship of Jerusalem to his eldest son, Phasaelus, and that of Galilee to Herod (361). After his assassination, Herod and Phasaelus ruled as Tetrarchs with Hircanus (370).
27. Ibid., 387.
28. Ibid., 388.
29. Ibid., 398.
30. Hall, *Things of Darkness*, 185.
31. See, in particular, Akhimie, *Shakespeare and the Cultivation of Difference*. See also Coles et al., introduction to *The Cultural Politics of Blood, 1500–1900*.
32. (Elizabeth Cary), *The History of the Life, Reign, and Death of Edward II, King of England* (Wing F313), 2. Most critics have followed Donald A. Stauffer's convincing appraisal that Elizabeth Cary wrote *The History . . . of Edward II* (see "A Deep and Sad Passion," in *Essays in Dramatic Literature*, ed. Hardin Craig [Princeton, NJ: Princeton University Press, 1935], 289–314). The confidence in this argument, however, has been undermined by the presence of a related, much shorter, octavo text, *The History of the Most Unfortunate Prince King Edward II* (Wing F314). Margaret Ferguson and Barry Weller declared themselves "agnostic on the question of who wrote either" history (*The Tragedy of Mariam*, 16). However, the discovery of the manuscript sources for both printed texts in the 1990s by the late Jeremy Maule has led to subsequent analysis that, to my mind, positively establishes Cary as the author of both works: see Margaret Reeves, "From Manuscript to Printed Text: Telling and Retelling the *History of Edward II*," in

The Literary Career and Legacy of Elizabeth Cary, 1613–1680, ed. Heather Wolfe (Basingstoke, Hampshire: Palgrave Macmillan, 2007), 125–44.

33. (Cary), *The History . . . of Edward II*, 2..
34. Ibid., 4.
35. Ibid., 9.
36. Ibid., 20–21.
37. Ibid., 39. When the king's favors transfer to Hugh Despenser, whose father was a newly created baron who rose by Edward, Despenser is dubbed a "false Imposter" (62), and even turns to piracy (a suggestion of his theft of a title) when he is banished from England (64–65).
38. Ibid., 44.
39. Josephus, *The famous and memorable vvorkes of Iosephus*, 400.
40. When Salome claims that she "uprear[ed]" him from a "low estate" (I.vi.397), she means that she rescued him when he was laid low due to his plots against Herod (*The famous and memorable vvorkes of Iosephus*, 400).
41. As the notes to Weller and Ferguson's edition make clear, Graphina originates in a passing mention in Josephus's *Jewish War* (1.24.5), but she is Cary's invention (*The Tragedy of Mariam*, 160).
42. Dympna Callaghan has raised appropriate objection to reading the play in allegorical terms in relation to Cary's life ("Re-reading Elizabeth Cary's *The Tragedie of Mariam*," 167). I am rather trying to read a set of values as they are represented in Cary's play and in *Her Life*.
43. See *Elizabeth Cary, Lady Falkland: Life and Letters*, ed. Heather Wolfe (Cambridge: RTM Publications, 2001), 115.
44. Ibid., 117 (my emphasis).
45. Alison Shell, "Elizabeth Cary's Historical Conscience: *The Tragedy of Mariam* and Thomas Lodge's Josephus," in *The Literary Career and Legacy of Elizabeth Cary, 1613–1680*, ed. Wolfe, 57.
46. Hall, *Things of Darkness*, 7.
47. Ferguson, *Dido's Daughters*, 317.
48. Temple, *The Irish Rebellion*, 9–10.
49. *Spenser's Prose Works*, ed. Rudolf Gottfried, in *The Works of Edmund Spenser: A Variorum Edition*, ed. Edwin Greenlaw, Ray Heffner, Charles Grosvenor Osgood, and Frederick Morgan Padelford, 11 vols. (Baltimore: Johns Hopkins University Press, 1932–58), vol. 10 (1949), 43.
50. "The Supplication of the Blood of the English Most Lamentably Murdered in Ireland . . . etc. (1598)," ed. Willy Maley, *Analecta Hibernica* 36 (1995), 33, quoted in David J. Baker, "'Men to Monsters': Civility, Barbarism, and 'Race' in Early Modern Ireland," in *Writing Race Across the Atlantic World Medieval to Modern*, ed. Phillip Beidler and Gary Taylor (Basingstoke, Hampshire: Palgrave Macmillan, 2005), 161.
51. Ibid. "The Supplication" is a tract composed between November and December 1598, most likely by an English cleric, for the purpose of persuading the queen to a more violent policy (9).
52. For this reason, Jean Feerick spends a full chapter on "uncouth milk and the Irish wet nurse," in *Strangers in Blood*, 55–77.
53. Burton, *The anatomy of melancholy*, 3.4.2.1, 614.
54. "The Supplication of the Blood of the English," ed. Maley, 33.
55. Ibid., 35.
56. Ibid., 37.

57. Reared in the royal nursery of Henry VIII when the education of the children was overseen by Katherine Parr, Thomas Butler, 10th Earl of Ormond, was taught by Protestant tutors alongside Henry's two children, Edward and Elizabeth.

58. "The Supplication of the Blood of the English," ed. Maley, 51.

59. Iyengar, *Shades of Difference*, 92.

60. I have written about this literature elsewhere, and in a different context; see "West of England: The Irish Specter in *Tamburlaine*," in *The Blackwell Companion to Tudor Literature*, ed. Kent Cartwright (Oxford: Wiley-Blackwell, 2010), 459–74.

61. Iyengar, *Shades of Difference*, 90.

62. New English tracts that advanced the project of conquest and colonization of Ireland include: John Davies, *A discovery of the true causes why Ireland was never entirely subdued* (STC 6348); John Derricke, *The image of Irelande with a discoverie of woodkarne* (STC 6734); Edmund Spenser, *View of the Present State of Ireland* (1596); Barnabe Riche, "Anothomy of Ireland" (c. 1591)," and *A new description of Irelande* (STC 20992). There are also many anonymous New English manuscript texts that struck a tone of racial and cultural intolerance and circulated 1590–1600 (see "The Supplication of the Blood of the English," ed. Maley, 4n1, for an extensive list).

63. The following section closely paraphrases observations that I have previously made in "West of England," 459.

64. Richard Beacon, *Solon his Follie* (STC 1653), A3r.

65. PRO SP 63/178/28, 28v; quoted in *Richard Beacon, Solon His Follie (1594)*, ed. Clare Carroll and Vincent Carey (Binghamton, NY: MRTS, 1996), xxviii.

66. N.L.I, MS 669, fol. 55; quoted in David Beers Quinn, "Edward Walshes's 'Conjectures' Concerning the State of Ireland (1552)," *Irish Historical Studies* 5 (1947), 303.

67. Ibid.; see also David Beers Quinn, *The Elizabethans and the Irish* (Ithaca, NY: Cornell University Press, 1966). Old English tracts include: "Edward Walshes's 'Conjectures' Concerning the State of Ireland (1552)"; Nicholas Canny, ed., "Rowland White's 'Discors touching Ireland' (c. 1569)," *Irish Historical Studies* 20 (1977), 439–63; Nicholas Canny, ed., "Rowland White's 'The Dysorders of the Irisshery' (1571)," *Studia Hibernica* 19 (1979), 147–60; and Richard Stanyhurst, "Description of Ireland," in *Chronicles of England, Scotlande, and Irelande*, ed. Raphel Holinshed (STC 13568). See *Richard Beacon, Solon His Follie (1594)*, xxvi.

68. The Nine Years' War began as a series of rebellions. While its inception is usually dated 1594, the conflict became a serious contest in 1595 when Hugh O'Neill, the second Earl of Tyrone, joined the rebellion.

69. David Beers Quinn, "'A Discourse of Ireland' (*Circa* 1599): A Sidelight on English Colonial Policy," *Proceedings of the Royal Irish Academy*, 47 (1942), 164.

70. Ibid.

71. Temple, *The Irish Rebellion*, 7.

72. Ibid., 5.

Chapter 4

1. Toni Morrison, *Playing in the Dark: Whiteness and the Literary Imagination* (New York: Vintage Books, 1993), 46.

2. This is the term applied by Karen E. Fields and Barbara J. Fields to the sociocultural process that constructs race: see *Racecraft: The Soul of Inequality in American Life* (New York: Verso, 2012). See also Ayanna Thompson, "Me, *The Faerie Queene*, and Critical Race Theory," in "Spenser and Race," ed. Dennis Britton and Kimberly Anne Coles, *Spenser Studies* 35 (2021), 285–390.

3. As Peter Erickson and Kim Hall have put it: "Initial opposition to early modern race studies ... was encapsulated in the single word 'anachronism' and informally deployed as a scare tactic and conversation stopper"; see "A New Scholarly Song," 4.

4. Dennis Austin Britton and Kimberly Anne Coles, introduction to "Spenser and Race," 4. Indeed, that this is the first volume of *Spenser Studies* devoted to the investigation of race in Spenser's poetry underscores the dearth of material written on Spenser and race.

5. Some will argue that, as a secretary to Lord Grey of Wilton, Spenser could not have had much influence at all. But his influence upon the Lord Deputy of Ireland, and the political elite of Ireland, is described in Ludowick Bryskett, *A discourse of ciuill life containing the ethike part of morall philosophie* (STC 3958); see n. 32 in this chapter. For the argument concerning Spenser as an early draftsman of English race-thinking, see Britton and Coles, Introduction.

6. As Britton observes in *Becoming Christian*: "Conspicuously absent from Spenser's poem are moments of infidel conversion" (61).

7. Terence Keel, *Divine Variations: How Christian Thought Became Racial Science* (Stanford, CA: Stanford University Press, 2018), 9.

8. Boyarin, *The Unconverted Self*. See also Kaplan, "The Jewish Body in Black and White in Medieval and Early Modern England"; Kaplan, *Figuring Racism in Medieval Christianity*; Kruger, *The Spectral Jew*; and Resnick, *Marks of Distinction*.

9. Gregory Kneidel, *Rethinking the Turn to Religion in Early Modern English Literature: The Poetics of All Believers* (Basingstoke, Hampshire: Palgrave Macmillan, 2008), 147.

10. Julia Reinhard Lupton, *Citizen-Saints: Shakespeare and Political Theology* (Chicago: University of Chicago Press, 2005), 21–22.

11. Daniel Boyarin, *A Radical Jew: Paul and the Politics of Identity* (Berkeley: University of California Press, 1994), 7–8. See also Britton, *Becoming Christian*, 13–14.

12. Degenhardt, *Islamic Conversion and Christian Resistance on the Early Modern Stage*, particularly chap. 1. "In the decades surrounding the start of the seventeenth century," Degenhardt writes, "the popular stage participated in testing the limits of Pauline universalism" (73). See Lisa Lampert, *Gender and Jewish Difference from Paul to Shakespeare* (Philadelphia: University of Pennsylvania Press, 2004): while Lampert explores the construction of Jewishness and gender, she also examines the legitimating function these figurations performed for White European Christian identity—particularly sixteenth-century English Christian identity.

13. Edmund Spenser, *The Faerie Queene*, ed. A. C. Hamilton (New York: Longman Group, 1977; revised, 1980), II.ix.argument. All citations are from this edition.

14. See Trevor, *The Poetics of Melancholy*, 56. See also Chapter 1, n. 5.

15. Angus Gowland, "Religious Melancholy and the Afflicted Conscience" (unpublished paper); Beth Quitslund, "Despair and the Composition of the Self," *Spenser Studies* 17 (2003), 91–106.

16. Quitslund, "Despair and the Composition of the Self," 91.

17. In *Praxeos medicae* (Basel, 1602–3), first translated into English as *A golden practice of physick* (Wing P2395), Felix Platter writes that a melancholy attended by religious systems is the most persistent, intense, and obdurate form: "As when [patients] perswade themselves that they *are damned, that God takes no care of them, that they are not predestinated*, although in the interim they be godly and religious, and they fear the last judgement, and external punishment, which *horrible melancholly* (and oft times driving men to despair) is the most frequent species,

in the curing of which I have oftentimes been much hindrered" (27); quoted in Gowland, "Religious Melancholy and the Afflicted Conscience."

18. Bryskett, *A discourse of ciuill life*, 274.

19. Donne, *Letters to severall persons*, 18.

20. *A View of the Present State of Ireland*, in *Spenser's Prose Works*, 119. This parrots the title of Galen's treatise, *Quod animi more corporis temperamenta sequantur* (That psychic behavior follows bodily temperaments).

21. Michael Schoenfeldt is the chief proponent of Maleger as a figure of melancholy (see *Bodies and Selves in Early Modern England*, 51–52).

22. Daniel T. Lochman has pointed out in "*Energeia* in Melanchthon's *Liber de Anima* and Philip Sidney's *Apology*" (paper presented at the Sixteenth Century Society Conference, New Orleans, October 2014) that Melanchthon also affirms the view of philosophers who situate the rational soul in the heart. "Others prefer the heart as the seat of the soul," Melanchthon writes, "because the heart is the source of life and seat of all affects that result from cognition" ("Alli malunt cor sedem esse animae, quia cor vitae fons est et sedes omnium adfectuum, qui cognitionem sequuntur"; *Corpus Reformatorum*, vol. 13, col. 19). I am indebted to Daniel's translation here and grateful to him for sharing his work with me.

23. Benedict Robinson's "'Swarth' Phantastes: Race, Body and Soul in *The Faerie Queene*" brilliantly considers the racializing term of "black melancholy" in our encounter with "swarth" Phantastes at the top of Alma's castle (II.ix.52); see *Spenser Studies* 35, 133–52.

24. Edmund Spenser, *Edmund Spenser: The Shorter Poems*, ed. Richard McCabe (London: Penguin, 1999), 466.

25. That the soul itself remains untouched by the body—associated, but not united, with it—is an idea frequently attributed to Plato. It is not, of course, Plato's idea. Plato's description of the soul "plunged into the turbulent streams of the body" in the *Timeaus* (43a–d) recalls that there is plenty in Plato to underwrite the material interactions of body and soul. Nonetheless, Plato had been assigned, in the early modern period, the role of chief opponent to more materialist accounts of psychosomatic relations.

26. Robert L. Reid, "Spenserian Psychology and the Structure of Allegory in Books 1 and 2 of *The Faerie Queene*," *Modern Philology* 79 (1982), 364.

27. Cf. II.iv.6 note: "the psychological and physical nature of temperance is expressed through the power of the hand in contrast to holiness which depends upon spiritual armour."

28. A. S. P. Woodhouse, "Nature and Grace in the *Faerie Queene*," *ELH* 16 (1949), 194–228.

29. Elizabeth Spiller, *Reading and the History of Race in the Renaissance* (Cambridge: Cambridge University Press, 2011), 24. See Huarte, *The examination of mens witts* (1594); Du Laurens, "The Diseases of Melancholy," in *A discourse of the preservation of the sight*; Lemnius, *The touchstone of complexions*; Platter, *Praxeos medicae* (Basel, 1602–3); Ercole Sassonia, "De Melancholia," in *Opera practica* (Padua, 1607); and Wright, *The passions of the minde*.

30. Von Stadan, "Body, Soul, and Nerves," 106.

31. Burton, *The anatomy of melancholy*, 3.4.2.1, 614; cf. *Corpus Reformatorum*, vol. 13, col. 87.

32. The others include: Sir Robert Dillon, William Dormer (Queen's Solicitor), Thomas Smith, and Captains Carlyle, Dawtrey, Norris, and Warham St. Leger.

33. Bryskett, *A discourse of ciuill life*, 260–61, my emphasis.

34. Schoenfeldt, *Bodies and Selves in Early Modern England*, 41, 40.

35. "Some will say," Bryskett declares, "that *Aristotle* . . . [thought] that the soule of man, euen concerning the vunderstanding, was not immortall; because . . . when the soule hath no more the senses of the bodie to serue her as instruments whereby she vunderstandeth and knoweth, she should no longer liue" (*A discourse of ciuill life*, 261).

36. Ibid., 273.

37. Cf. Chapter 1, n. 14 concerning Avicenna's position in opposition to Averroes.

38. In his claim the character of Spenser seems to contradict Walter Ralegh, in his *Treatise of the Soul*, as well: Ralegh flatly claims that the "soul is neither body, nor proceedeth from a body. And to be short, the matter of the soul can be no bodily thing" (quoted in Trevor, *The Poetics of Melancholy*, 52).

39. Lochman, "*Energeia* in Melanchthon's *Liber de Anima* and Philip Sidney's *Apology*."

40. John Calvin, *The Institutes of the Christian Religion*, ed. John T. McNeill and trans. Ford Lewis Battles, 2 vols. (Philadelphia: The Westminster Press, 1960), I.3.1, 44.

41. "Et sermo propheticus ac apostilicus saepe nominat cor, cum loquitur non de fonte adfectuum, sed de parte cognoscente." *Corpus Reformatorum*, vol. 13, col. 19.

42. "Ut cum ait Paulus: Homines habere legem scriptam in cordibus" (ibid.). I borrow all of these observations from Daniel Lochman's argument.

43. Cf. Wright's *The passions of the minde*: "No philosopher can denie, but that our passions are certain accidents and qualities, whose immediate subiect, house, and lodging is the very facultie and power of the soule, because all vitall operations (of which sorte Passions are) challenge, by right, that mother which hatched them, should also sustaine them, and harbour them in her own house. But a question may bee demaunded, and not easily resolued, whether the facultie of our sensitive appetite hath allotted vnto it some peculiar part of the body. . . . To which question I answer, that the very seate of all Passions, is the heart" (60–61).

44. *The booke of common prayer* (STC 16293), S6v.

45. Spenser, *Edmund Spenser: The Shorter Poems*, ed. McCabe, 443.

46. The positive readings of the image, by Thomas P. Roche (*The Kindly Flame* [Princeton, NJ: Princeton University Press, 1964], 134–36), C. S. Lewis (*Spenser's Images of Life*, ed. Alastair Fowler [Cambridge: Cambridge University Press, 1967], 38), and A. R. Cirillo ("The Fair Hermaphrodite: Love-Union in the Poetry of Donne and Spenser," *Studies in English Literature, 1500–1900* 9 [1969], 81–95), have been largely replaced by Donald Cheney's skeptical interpretation, citing the "conflicting meanings . . . [in] the image of marriage" ("Spenser's Hermaphrodite and the 1590 *Faerie Queene*," *PMLA* 87 [1972], 199).

47. Jonathan Goldberg, *The Seeds of Things: Theorizing Sexuality and Materiality in Renaissance Representations* (New York: Fordham University Press, 2009), 75.

48. Much of my discussion on the subject of the Spenserian hermaphrodite has been informed by two key articles: Dana Luciano, "Unrealized: The Queer Time of *The Hermaphrodite*," in *Philosophies of Sex: Critical Essays on* The Hermaphrodite, ed. Renée Bergland and Gary Williams (Columbus: Ohio State University Press, 2012), 215–41; and Melissa E. Sanchez, "'What Hath Night to Do with Sleep?' Biopolitics in Milton's *Mask*," *Early Modern Culture: An Electronic Seminar* 10 (2014).

49. Luciano, "Unrealized," 228.

50. Alain Badiou, *Saint Paul: The Foundation of Universalism*, trans. Ray Brassier (Stanford: Stanford University Press, 2003), 14. My own exposition of Saint Paul's philosophy is deeply indebted to Badiou's interpretation. I am grateful to Gail Kern Paster for drawing my attention to this study—and for perceiving its relevance to my argument.

51. Ibid., 22.
52. Ibid.
53. Goldberg, *Seeds of Things*; Joseph Campana, *The Pain of Reformation: Spenser, Vulnerability, and the Ethics of Masculinity* (New York: Fordham University Press, 2012).
54. Spenser, *The Faerie Queene*, ed. Hamilton, 163.
55. Badiou, *Saint Paul*, 86.
56. Ibid, 15.
57. Spenser, *The Faerie Queene*, ed. Hamilton, 738.
58. Badiou, *Saint Paul*, 92.
59. Kimberly Anne Coles, "'Perfect Hole': Elizabeth I, Spenser, and Chaste Productions," *ELR* 32 (2002), 31–61.
60. Colin Burrow, "Spenser and Classical Traditions," in *The Cambridge Companion to Spenser*, ed. Andrew Hadfield (Cambridge: Cambridge University Press, 2001), 222–24.
61. As Linda Gregerson observes, both the story of Amoret and the quest of Britomart "expose the boundaries and ideologies of gender to considerable strain" ("Sexual Politics," in *The Cambridge Companion to Spenser*, ed. Hadfield, 187). Indeed, she notes, the "surest possessions" of Amoret "are her absences—the absence of sexual experience . . . and the anatomical 'absence' that signifies subordinate gender" (186–87).
62. Melissa E. Sanchez, "Sex and Eroticism in the Renaissance," in *Edmund Spenser in Context*, ed. Andrew Escobado (Cambridge: Cambridge University Press, 2017), 349.
63. Badiou, *Saint Paul*, 79.
64. Janet Adelman, "Hugh Maclean Memorial Lecture: Revaluing the Body in *The Faerie Queene* I," *Spenser Review* 36 (2005), 20.
65. Badiou, *Saint Paul*, 55.
66. These descriptions are taken from Hamilton's note on Cymochles (Spenser, *The Faerie Queene*, II.iv.41n). It is worth observing that many contemporary descriptions understand a phlegmatic nature as dull-witted, gloomy, and without passion. However, the phlegmatic characters that populate Spenser's second book, such as Cymochles and Acrasia, make clear that Spenser is apprehending a moist humoral constitution in the unstable terms employed by Chapman.
67. Spenser, *The Faerie Queene*, ed. Hamilton, II.ii.21, 5n.
68. As Burton writes: "loue of God is a *habit infused* of God . . . *by which a man is inclined to loue God aboue all, and his neighbor as himself*" (*The anatomy of melancholy*, 3.4.1.1, 578).
69. Burton, for example, writes that "loue presupposeth . . . faith [and] hope and vnites vs to God himself." Those that cannot love God properly are divided into "two extremes of *Excesse* and *Defect* . . . idolatry and Athisme" (ibid., 578–79). I am not suggesting, of course, that Spenser read Burton in 1621; but I hope that I have shown how available this discourse was, spanning over a century prior to Burton. The discussion that takes place at the end of Bryskett's *Discourse of civill life* imagines the terms of these arguments as part of the evening conversation of educated men.
70. William Oram, "Elizabethan Fact and Spenserian Fiction," *Spenser Studies* 4 (1984), 42.
71. Ibid.
72. William Oram makes this observation (ibid).
73. Sanchez, "Sex and Eroticism in the Renaissance," 342.
74. Ibid., 342–43.
75. In "The Depoliticized Saracen and Muslim Erasure," *Literature Compass* 16 (2019); https://doi.org/10.1111/lic3.12548 (accessed August 15, 2020), Shokoofeh Rajabzadeh argues "that

we depoliticize and delegitimize the violent and painful Islamophobia and racism of objects of study concerning Muslim representation when we choose to use the offensive label Saracen over Muslim." As Rajabzadeh points out, embedded in the term is a history of shame and expulsion: ashamed of their descent from Hagar, "Saracens" pretended an alternate genealogy from Sara; as such, they were maligned as both wanderers and liars, undeserving of Christian communion.

76. Benedict Robinson, *Islam and Early Modern English Literature: The Politics of Romance from Spenser to Milton* (Basingstoke, Hampshire: Palgrave Macmillan, 2007), 46.

77. Britton, *Becoming Christian*, 56. See also Benedict Robinson, "Returning to Egypt: 'The Jew,' 'the Turk,' and the English Republic," in *Milton and the Jews*, ed. Douglas A. Brooks (Cambridge: Cambridge University Press, 2008), 178–99.

78. Robinson, *Islam and Early Modern English Literature*, 47.

79. Burton, *The anatomy of melancholy*, 3.4.1.1, 582.

80. Ibid.

81. Ibid.

82. Ibid.

83. Ibid., 583.

84. Ibid. Channeling Erasmus, Burton asks: "*Quid quæso . . . hisce Theologis faciamus aut quid preceris, nisi forte fidelem medicum, qui cerebro medeatur*" (What, I ask . . . what is to be done with these theologians, or else what do you pray for [on their behalf], if not, perchance, a trustworthy doctor, who would cure [their] brain? [my translation]).

85. Gowland, *The Worlds of Renaissance Melancholy*, 140.

86. Burton, *The anatomy of melancholy*, 3.4.1.1, 583.

87. I am not suggesting that Spenser wrote the books of the *Faerie Queene* chronologically; to the contrary, it seems entirely likely that he wrote episodes out of order. In Gabriel Harvey and Edmund Spenser, *Three Proper, and wittie, familiar Letters* (STC 23095), printed in 1580, Spenser writes of his intention to shortly compose a book that he will "entitle, *Epithalamion Thamesis*," and proceeds to give some detail to his conception of "the marriage of the Thames" (A4r). Whether Spenser did write the episode of the marriage of Thames and Medway (IV.xi) shortly after is unknown. But it has caused some to speculate that portions of Book IV were completed early in the process of writing the *Faerie Queene*. But what is certain is that Spenser revised his work before publication, so that the orientation of Book IV was decided after his publication of the 1590 version of the work.

88. Cohen, "On Saracen Enjoyment," 116.

89. *Spenser's Prose Works*, 10:148.

90. Ibid., 137–38. See Eamon Grennan, "Language and Politics: A Note on Some Metaphors in Spenser's *A View of the Present State of Ireland*," *Spenser Studies* 3 (1982), 103–9.

91. Regarding Irish religion, Spenser says: "The faulte that I finde in religion is but one but the *same vniversall throughe all that Countrye*, that is that they are all Papistes by theire profession but in the same so blindelye and brutishly enformed for the moste parte as that ye woulde rather thinke them *Atheists* or infidles" (*Spenser's Prose Works*, 136; my emphasis).

Chapter 5

1. Jennifer DeVere Brody, *Impossible Purities: Blackness, Femininity, and Victorian Culture* (Durham, NC: Duke University Press, 1998), 3.

2. Daniel Defoe, *A True Collection of the Writings of the Author of the True-Born Englishman* (London, 1703), 195–96.

3. I have made this argument (with my coeditors) in another context: see *The Cultural Politics of Blood, 1500–1900*, 9, 14–15.

4. This argument forms the backbone of Patricia Akhimie's *Shakespeare and the Cultivation of Difference*. My work is heavily indebted to her invaluable study.

5. Goetz, *The Baptism of Early Virginia*, 86.

6. Goetz coins this phrase, which I will use more than once throughout my consideration here. See Chapters 3 and 4.

7. E. A. J. Honigmann sets the performance date of *Othello* to "winter-spring of 1601–2." William Shakespeare, *Othello*, revised edition, with editorial matter by E. A. J. Honigmann and introduction by Ayanna Thompson (London and New York: Bloomsbury, 1997, 2016), 355; Southerne's *Oroonoko* was first performed in 1695, and published in 1696.

8. While the works of natural philosophy and medical theory that this book explores precede (for obvious reasons) the appearance of black bile as a way of marking Christian subjects as outside the faith, the earliest literary work explored is Spenser's 1590 *Faerie Queene* and the latest polemical work is Temple's 1646 *Irish Rebellion*. Southerne's *Oroonoko* brings us to the end of the seventeenth century—but I am arguing that it stages the developments of early English slave practices, in the West Indies in particular, that bridge Temple's work and the slave codes that fully invest Black and brown skin with the melancholy that guarantees their permanent paganism.

9. See Chapter 4, n. 12.

10. Degenhardt, *Islamic Conversion and Christian Resistance on the Early Modern Stage*, 49.

11. Ambereen Dadabhoy has also argued for the unconvertible nature of Othello, signaled through his Blackness—she further argues that ideas of the Black body that is obdurate to Christian faith transfer to America's first Black president, Barack Obama. See Dadabhoy, "The Moor of America: Approaching the Crisis of Race and Religion in the Renaissance and in the Twenty-First Century," in *Teaching Medieval and Early Modern Cross-Cultural Encounters*, ed. Lynn Shutters and Karina Attar (New York: Palgrave, 2014), 123–40.

12. Shakespeare, *Othello* (see n. 7). All citations are from this edition.

13. Some of these motivations are culled from Shakespeare's source in Cinthio's *Gli Hecatommithi*, where the Ensign of the story is driven by unrequited love for Disdemona.

14. There is some slippage here: it is clear from Cinthio's tale that the Venitian army represents something of the meritocracy that Iago envisions. The unnamed Moor rises because he is "personally valiant and had given proof in warfare of great prudence and skilful energy" (Geoffrey Bullough, ed., *Narrative and Dramatic Sources of Shakespeare*, 8 vols. [London: Routledge and Kegan Paul, 1957–75], 7:242). However, while Disdemona's relatives "did all they could to make her take another husband," they seem to have no recourse to the law. So, while Shakespeare is imagining a military system of promotion that copies Venice, he is applying the English legal standard to marriage, whereby those who marry outside of their rank without parental permission can be subject to incarceration.

15. While Jean Feerick claims that Othello's humors are undermined by allowing "his blood to rise to passion and distemperance" (*Strangers in Blood*, 11), and while this is almost certainly true, I see the play conveying different information: Othello is unable to inoculate himself against Iago's "poison," or to remedy it with the antidote of Christian faith. Othello refuses to see himself as fully participant in Christian love and communion—and this leaves him vulnerable. But I will also suggest that the play presents Othello's inclination to unbelief as natural—as a feature of his humoral constitution.

16. Jonathan Burton makes this point in "Race," 3:223.

17. Lara Bovilsky, *Barbarous Play: Race on the English Renaissance Stage* (Minneapolis: University of Minnesota Press, 2008), 41.

18. See, in particular, Miramon, "Noble Dogs, noble blood." For a reading of how animal husbandry is adapted to race in New World contexts, see Hill, "The Blood of Others."

19. See Matthew Vernon, "Unkynde Monstrous Races and 'Curled Darlings of Our Nation,'" in *A Cultural History of Race in the Renaissance and Early Modern Age (1350–1550)*, ed. Kimberly Anne Coles and Dorothy Kim (London: Bloomsbury, 2021).

20. William Shakespeare, *A Midsummer Night's Dream*, ed. Harold F. Brooks (New York: Routledge, 1996).

21. Lara Bovilsky notices this in *Barbarous Play*, 47.

22. Feerick makes the case for the double nature of rank in the early modern period in *Strangers in Blood*, but she specifically makes this point regarding Othello.

23. See Elizabeth Spiller, "From Imagination to Miscegenation: Race and Romance in Shakespeare's 'The Merchant of Venice,'" *Renaissance Drama*, n.s., 29 (1998), 137–64. Spiller also traces "how an old impulse to maintain the purity of the family line is reconfigured through narratives of racial difference" (143).

24. While he is a suspect source, Iago claims that Othello has been baptized—and is able to "renounce" it (II.iii.338).

25. Britton, *Becoming Christian*, 4.

26. As I have exfoliated throughout this book, the terms and relations of inherited difference—such as those that Patricia Akhimie tracks in *Shakespeare and the Cultivation of Difference*—get used for different service in the English colonial enterprise. But as Akhimie points out, the terminology for essential difference, inherited and ineradicable, was already in place and ready for use.

27. Chakravarty, "Race, Natality, and the Biopolitics of Early Modern Political Theology," 145.

28. Shakespeare, *Othello*, 20. As E. A. J. Honigmann notes several times in his editorial material, devils were thought to be black—hence, the characterizations of Othello as the devil and references to his damnation. Medieval religious iconography represented the devil with a black face; for a discussion of the tradition (and its consequences), see Anthony Gerard Barthelemy, *Black Face, Maligned Race: The Representation of Blacks in English Drama from Shakespeare to Southerne* (Baton Rouge: Louisiana State University Press, 1987), 2–6.

29. I take the point of Will Stockton that the truth of her chastity is simply withheld in the play—unknown and unknowable (see "Chasing Chastity: The Case of Desdemona," in *Rethinking Feminism in Early Modern Studies*, ed. Ania Loomba and Melissa Sanchez, 195–211). But I am trying to notice how her truth is *represented* in the play, not what conclusions we can draw from it.

30. Karen Newman, *Fashioning Femininity and English Renaissance Drama* (Chicago: University of Chicago Press, 1991), 86.

31. As Chakravarty observes, "Othello's soul, Iago suggests, is 'enfettered.' His love for Desdemona thus *returns* him to a state of slavery" ("Race, Natality, and the Biopolitics of Early Modern Political Theology," 144).

32. Chakravarty notices that "in the final moments of the play . . . Othello signals his initiations into multiple faiths" and argues that "the act of stabbing or of cutting through the flesh evokes the image—or in this case the memory—of circumcision" (ibid., 146).

33. Aphra Behn, *Oroonoko, The Rover and Other Works*, ed. Janet Todd (London: Penguin, 1992; rpt., 2003), 133–34.

34. Such declarations do not sound different from Thomas Tryon's *Friendly Advice to the Gentlemen Planters of the East and West Indies* (Wing T3179): "luxurious Masters stretch themselves on their soft Beds and Couches, they drink Wine in overflowing Bowls, and set their Brains a-float without either Rudder or Compass, in an Ocean of other strong and various Drinks, and vomit up their Shame and Filthiness . . . their chief *Study* and *Philosophy* being to gratifie their liquorish Palates . . . they make frequent and solemn *Feasts*, (that is, offer Sacrifices, and celebrate Festivals to their Idol *Belly-God-Paunch*, the Divinity which they chiefly adore)" (122–24).

35. The brutal government of those who are not born to rule, and the commercial traffic that licenses their power, is perfectly captured in the figure of Banister, who carries out the ultimate barbarity in executing Oroonoko on behalf of the Lieutenant Governor. Banister is "a wild Irishman, and one of the [Lieutenant Governor's] council, a fellow of absolute barbarity, and fit to execute any villainy, *but . . . rich*" (Behn, *Oroonoko*, 139–40, my emphasis).

36. While the Restoration period describes the restoration of the monarchy under Charles II, "Restoration comedy" captures works as late as 1710.

37. Aphra Behn's *The Widow Ranter*, with its female heroine Semernia, the Indian queen, was first performed in 1689.

38. Ayanna Thompson, *Performing Race and Torture on the Early Modern Stage* (Abingdon, Oxon, UK: Routledge, 2008), 65.

39. Ibid., 66.

40. Behn, *Oroonoko*, 125. At a moment of insurrection in Southerne's drama, the Governor makes a distinction between the danger offered by the "White Slaves" (who will "not stir") and the "Black Slaves" (II.iv.44–46). The implication is that the White laborers of Southerne's imagined world were not a labor pool indentured by election but by force. Cromwell (as the rest of the chapter will outline) began the practice of shipping Irish prisoners of war to the West Indies. According to a contemporary account, these "Irish" are frequently "derided by the negroes as white slaves" (see W. N. Sainsbury, ed., *Calendar of State Papers, Colonial Series, 1574–1715*, 10 vols. [London: Longman, 1860–1928], 5:529). This is precisely because they are carceral servants.

41. Jennifer L. Morgan, *Laboring Women: Reproduction and Gender in New World Slavery* (Philadelphia: University of Pennsylvania Press, 2004), 7.

42. Valerie Forman, "Constructing White Privilege: Transatlantic slavery, reproduction and the segregation of the marriage plot in the late seventeenth century," in *The Routledge Companion to Women, Sex, and Gender in the Early British Colonial World*, ed. Kimberly Anne Coles and Eve Keller (New York: Routledge, 2019), 304–21.

43. Imoinda is not, for example, one of the "White Slaves" that the Lieutenant Governor declares will "not stir" when the surrounding Indigenous tribes plunder neighboring plantations (II.iv.44). Imoinda is pagan and is therefore a permanent slave.

44. See Loomba, "Race and the Possibilities of Comparative Critique," 507–8. For historical studies, see Holly Brewer, *By Birth or Consent: Children, Law, and the Anglo-American Revolution in Authority* (Chapel Hill: University of North Carolina Press, 2005), chap. 2; Brewer, "Subjects by Allegiance to the King?"; Goetz, *The Baptism of Early Virginia*, passim; and Fischer, "A New Race of Christians."

45. Goetz, *The Baptism of Early Virginia*, 62.

46. In discussing the descent of race-thinking in France through ideas of hereditary blood, Noémie Ndiaye writes that a "revealing detail" lies in the fact that the children born of the "mixed" marriages of members of the emergent bourgeois class with those of noble rank "were

called *métis*—a term that is still commonly used today to refer to people of mixed heritage" ("The African Ambassador's Travels," 75).

47. Jenny Shaw, *Everyday Life in the Early English Caribbean: Irish, Africans, and the Construction of Difference* (Athens: University of Georgia Press, 2013), 35. Shaw sees this language as laying "bare a continuing problem for English authorities who were struggling with a worldview formerly dominated by their ideas about religious difference but increasingly becoming inflicted with theories about more biologically based distinctions among and between groups" (35). It is this apparent conflict that I have tried to resolve: many English authorities already understood religion as both somatic and heritable. What changed over time was how this notion anchored particular national identities—and eventually chromatic difference.

48. While it seems clear that most of the African slaves in Barbados were supplied by English shippers—whose operation along the Gold Coast is noted in Dutch records—England did not technically enter the slave trade until Charles II granted a royal charter to "Adventurers into Africa" in 1660. See Larry Gragg, *Englishmen Transplanted: The English Colonization of Barbados, 1627–1660* (Oxford: Oxford University Press, 2003), 122.

49. Thomas Blake, *The birth-priviledge, or, Covenant-Holinesse of beleevers and their issue in the time of the Gospel together with the right of infants to baptisme* (Wing B3143), 6, quoted in Goetz, *The Baptism of Early Virginia*, 63. It should be noted that "Blake's pamphlet launched him into a sustained controversy over the inclusiveness or exclusiveness of admission to the church's sacraments" (*DNB* article by William Lamont).

50. Since Imoinda was brought to Angola as an infant, there is no suggestion that her heathenism is inherited from her father—only that her rearing in the faith of her adopted nation was due to her father.

51. As Forman observes, Southerne's change of Imoinda's chromatic racial category displaces the Black female body and therefore avoids the specter of the rape of a Black female slave by a White master ("Constructing White Privilege," 314).

52. Joyce Green MacDonald, "Race, Women, and the Sentimental in Thomas Southerne's *Oroonoko*," *Criticism* 40 (1998), 556, 564.

53. Forman, "Constructing White Privilege," 315.

54. Joyce MacDonald concludes that "the Africans [of the play] are fated to remain in the control of others, a bondage from which they can be freed only by death" ("Race, Women, and the Sentimental in Thomas Southerne's *Oroonoko*," 564). In this claim, she is constructing Imoinda as African. But as Forman also observes, MacDonald is not wrong to construct Imoinda's relationship to political authority in terms that are identical to Oroonoko's ("Constructing White Privilege," 314).

55. Fischer, "A New Race of Christians," 130–31.

56. For the purposes of this argument, I will focus on the labor practices of plantations in Barbados. The historical record, particularly governing the period of 1615 (when the practice of transportation begins) to 1660 in the British colonies, is thin on the ground everywhere, but it is thickest in Barbados where some wills and local accounts survive.

57. *Oliver Cromwell's Letters and Speeches*, ed. Thomas Carlyle, 5 vols. (New York: John Wiley, 1845), 1:461 (To John Bradshaw, Secretary to Council of State to William Lenthall, September 17, 1649). Famously, Cromwell is said to have ordered the killing of every tenth soldier taken at Drogheda and to have transported the rest to Barbados.

58. Gwenda Morgan, *Banishment in the Early Atlantic World: Convicts, Rebels and Slaves* (London: Bloomsbury, 2013), 61.

59. Peter Wilson Coldham has recovered the names of over six thousand individuals sentenced to transportation from England proper during this period (see *British Emigrants in Bondage, 1614–1788* [Baltimore: Genealogical Publishing, 2005], CD Rom). But the bombing of the Public Records Office in Dublin in 1922 has meant the data from Ireland concerning the number of convicts and prisoners of war, as well as the terms of their involuntary servitude, is largely unrecoverable. See Hamish Maxwell Stewart, "Convict Transportation from Britain and Ireland, 1615–1870," *History Compass* 8 (2010), 1224. See also Christopher Tomlins, "Reconsidering Indentured Servitude: European Migration and the Early American Labor Force, 1600–1775," *Labor History* 42 (2001), 5–43; Gragg, *Englishmen Transplanted*, 113–31; Carla Gardina Pestana, *The English Atlantic World in the Age of Revolution, 1640-61* (Cambridge, MA: Harvard University Press, 2004), 189–93; and Simon P. Newman, *A New World of Labor: The Development of Plantation Slavery in the British Atlantic* (Philadelphia: University of Pennsylvania Press, 2013), 71–88.

60. Newman, *A New World of Labor*, 81.

61. Of one transportation of 1,300 prisoners of war to Barbados, one prisoner records that "As far as I know no one returned except myself" (Alexander Gunkel and Jerome S. Handler, eds. and trans., "A German Indentured Servant in Barbados in 1652: The Account of Heinrich Von Uchteritz," *Journal of the Barbados Museum and Historical Society* 33 [1970], 92).

62. See, in particular, Gragg, *Englishmen Transplanted*; Newman, *A New World of Labor*; and Michael Guasco, *Slaves and Englishmen: Human Bondage in the Early Modern Atlantic World* (Philadelphia: University of Pennsylvania Press, 2014), chap. 5.

63. Gragg, *Englishmen Transplanted*; Shaw, *Everyday Life in the Early English Caribbean*; Douglas V. Armstrong and Matthew C. Reilly, "The Archeology of Settler Farms and Early Plantation Life in Seventeenth-Century Barbados," *Slavery and Abolition* 35 (2014), 399–417.

64. Kristen Block and Jenny Shaw, "Subjects Without an Empire: The Irish in the Early Modern Caribbean," *Past and Present* 210 (2011), 35, quoted in Jerome Handler and Matthew C. Reilly, "Father Antoine Beit's Account Revisited: Irish Catholics in Mid-Seventeenth Century Barbados," in *Caribbean Irish Connections*, ed. Alison Donnell, Maria McGarrity, and Evelyn O'Callaghan (Kingston: University of the West Indies Press, 2015), 41.

65. Hilary McD. Beckles, "A 'Riotous and Unruly Lot': Irish Indentured Servants and Freeman in the English West Indies, 1644–1713," *William and Mary Quarterly* 47 (1990), 504, quoted in Handler and Reilly, "Father Antoine Beit's Account Revisited," 40–41.

66. Indeed, this fear was not unfounded. Richard Ligon records one such plot discovered in 1649. But throughout the seventeenth century, the majority of rebellions, both enacted and quashed, were instigated by Irish bound laborers. See Newman, *A New World of Labor*, 82–83.

67. The petition of Marcellus Rivers and Oxenbridge Foyle makes clear that in a number of cases—and it is impossible to determine how many—no contracts were written, even for captured Englishmen who were transported. See *England's slavery, or Barbados merchandize; represented in a petition to the high court of Parliament* (Wing R1553), 6.

68. *A Collection of the State Papers of John Thurloe*, ed. Thomas Birch, 7 vols. (London, 1742), 4:40 (September 18, 1655).

69. This is not very different from suggested solutions to the Irish problem at the end of the sixteenth century that recommended the Irish be moved to England (as servants) until the change in climate and religion altered them over generations. See Quinn, "'A Discourse of Ireland' (*Circa* 1599)," 164–65.

70. *A Collection of the State Papers of John Thurloe*, 4:23 (September 11, 1655).

71. I am certainly not suggesting that this is the position of all Christians or all Englishmen. To someone like Morgan Godwyn, for example, or to Thomas Tryon, such a suggestion would be absurd. But I am arguing that laws governing servants and slaves from the New English colonies to the West Indies betray these ideas as underlying assumptions.

72. "Extracts from Henry Whistler's Journal of the West Indian Expedition," in *The Narrative of General Venebles with an appendix of papers relating to the expedition to the West Indies and the conquest of Jamaica, 1654–1655*, ed. C. H. Firth (London: Longmans, Green, 1900), 146. Richard Ligon also refers to Indigenous people "fecht" from other places, and those brought to the island "we make slaves" (*A true & exact history of the island of Barbados* [Wing L2075], 54); both quotations are cited in Gragg, *Englishmen Transplanted*, 114. Carolyn Arena has discovered archival evidence of considerable exploitation of captives from Guiana pressed into slave labor in Barbados; see "Indian Slaves from Guiana in Seventeenth-Century Barbados," *Ethnohistory* 64 (2017), 65–90. Recorded contracts for Indigenous people in Bermuda, however, have them in service for "fourscore & nineteen years" (*Bermuda Colonial Records*, 2:99, cited in Guasco, *Slaves and Englishmen*, 188). Guasco notes that the *BCR* contains deeds and bills of sale for 131 lifetime servants, and 26 of these were Indigenous slaves (*Slaves and Englishmen*, 283n91).

73. Goetz, *The Baptism of Early Virginia*, 74.

74. Ibid. In some cases, the age of freedom for the offspring was twenty-eight years.

75. Ibid., 73.

76. *The Statutes at Large, being a Collection of all the laws of Virginia*, 2:170, quoted in ibid., 78.

77. Goetz, *The Baptism of Early Virginia*, 79.

78. Unlike Barbados or Jamaica, there were many African indentured servants in the North American colonies, serving for fixed periods after which they would live among the English. This led to what was for English colonial authorities an alarming problem: the mixing of Christian and "heathen" bodies (ibid., 72).

79. Forman, "Constructing White Privilege," 314.

80. In *Laboring Women*, Jennifer Morgan explores how gender and reproduction were central to the development of racial ideologies in the New World. Morgan argues that the forced labor of black women operated legally in two senses—work and procreation. In both senses, the black female body is treated in legal terms as an instrument of production.

81. Ligon, *A true & exact history of the island of Barbados*, 50.

82. Fischer, "A New Race of Christians," passim.

83. Morgan Godwyn, *The Negro's & Indians advocate, suing for their admission into the church* (Wing G971), 36.

84. See Edward B. Rugemer, "The Development of Mastery and Race in the Comprehensive Slave Codes of the Greater Caribbean During the Seventeenth Century," *William and Mary Quarterly* 70 (2013), 446–7.

85. Goetz, *The Baptism of Early Virginia*, 137.

86. Indeed, it did not take long for laws to refuse to recognize any condition, on behalf of either parent, that would redeem the child of a Black African slave. The first such law was passed in Maryland in 1664 (ibid., 80–81).

Coda

1. Goetz, *The Baptism of Early Virginia*, 80. The discussion in the Maryland legislature, carried on between the council and the lower house, specifically concerns free White women

who marry slaves. See William Hand Browne, ed., *Archives of Maryland* (Annapolis: Maryland Historical Society), 1 (1883), 527, 533–34 (September 1664).

2. Goetz, *The Baptism of Early Virginia*, 81.

3. Chakravarty, *Fictions of Consent*, 214..

4. For a discussion of marking bodies with ink to indicate slave status, and how this stigmata is transferred to Indigenous peoples of North America and Africans, see Grier, "Inkface," 196.

5. Loomba, "Identities and Bodies in Early Modern Studies," 235; cf. Introduction, n. 79.

6. See in particular, Whitaker, introduction to *Black Metaphors*, for analysis of how black skin is overwritten with metaphors of moral depravity that derive from pre- and early modern readings of Black bodies.

BIBLIOGRAPHY

Primary

John Abernethy, *A Christian and heauenly treatise. Containing physicke for the soule* (London, 1630).

Thomas Adams, *Diseases of the soule* (London, 1616).

[Anon.], *A True and Sincere Declaration of the Purpose and Ends of the Plantation Begun in Virginia* (London, 1610).

Richard Beacon, *Solon his Follie* (London, 1594).

Thomas Blake, *The birth-priviledge, or, Covenant-Holinesse of beleevers and their issue in the time of the Gospel together with the right of infants to baptisme* (London, 1644).

The booke of common prayer (London, 1559).

Timothy Bright, *A Treatise of melancholie* (London, 1586).

Ludowick Bryskett, *A discourse of ciuill life containing the ethike part of morall philosophie* (London, 1606).

Robert Burton, *The anatomy of melancholy: What it is, with all the kinds causes, symptomes, prognostickes, & seuerall cures of it. In three partitions, with their seuerall sections, members & subsections. Philosophically, medicinally, historically, opened & cut up. By. Democritus Iunior* (London, 1628).

John Calvin, *Sermons of Iohn Caluin, vpon the songe that Ezechias made after he had bene sicke* (London, 1560).

——, *A commentarie vpon the Epistle of Saint Paul to the Romanes, written in Latine by M. Iohn Caluin, and newely translated into Englishe by Christopher Rosdell preacher* (London, 1583).

(Elizabeth Cary), *The History of the Life, Reign, and Death of Edward II, King of England* (London, 1680).

Henry Cary, Viscount Falkland [Elizabeth Cary], *The History of the Most Unfortunate Prince King Edward II* (London, 1633).

Pierre Charron, *Of Wisdom*, trans. Samson Lennard (London, 1608).

Nicholas Culpeper, *A New Method of Physick, or, A Short View of Paracelsus and Galen's Practice* (London, 1654).

John Davies, *A discovery of the true causes why Ireland was never entirely subdued* (London, 1612).

Daniel Defoe, *A True Collection of the Writings of the Author of the True-Born Englishman* (London, 1703).

John Derricke, *The Image of Irelande with a discoverie of woodkarne* (London, 1581).

John Donne, *Letters to seuerall persons of honour written by John Donne* (London, 1651).

André Du Laurens, *A discourse of the preservation of the sight: of melancholike diseases; of rheumes, and of old age* (London, 1599).
Thomas Elyot, *The boke named the governour* (London, 1531).
———, *The castel of helthe* (London, 1539).
Marsilio Ficino, *Platonic Theology*, ed. James Hankins and William Bowen, trans. Michael J. B. Allen, 6 vols. (Cambridge: Cambridge University Press, 2001–6).
John Florio, *A world of wordes, or Most copious, and exact dictionarie in Italian and English* (London, 1598).
The Geneva Bible: A facsimile of the 1560 edition, intro. Lloyd E. Berry (Madison: University of Wisconsin Press, 1969).
Morgan Godwyn, *The Negro's & Indians advocate, suing for their admission into the church* (London, 1680).
Thomas Harriot, *A briefe and true report of the new found land of Virginia* (London, 1590).
Gabriel Harvey and Edmund Spenser, *Three Proper, and wittie, familiar Letters* (London, 1580).
Raphel Holinshed, ed., *Chronicles of England, Scotlande, and Irelande* (London, 1577).
Juan Huarte, *The examination of mens witts*, trans. R[ichard] C[arew] (London, 1594).
Flavius Josephus, *The famous and memorable vvorkes of Iosepus*, trans. Thomas Lodge (London, 1602).
Levinus Lemnius [Levine Lemnie], *The touchstone of complexions generallye appliable, expedient and profitable for all such, as be desirous & carefull of their bodylye health*, trans. Thomas Newton (London, 1576).
Richard Ligon, *A true & exact history of the island of Barbados* (London, 1657).
Ioannis Magiri, doctoris medici et philosophi . . . commentarivs . . . In aureum Philippi Melanchthonis libellum de Anima (Frankfurt, 1603).
Philip Melanchthon, *Commentarius de anima* (Lyon, 1542).
The essayes or morall, politike and millitarie discourses of Lo[rd] Michaell de Montaigne, trans. John Florio (London, 1603).
Richard Perceval, *A dictionarie in Spanish and English*, edited and enlarged by John Minsheu (London, 1599).
William Perkins, *A treatise tending vnto a declaration whether a man be in the estate of damnation or in the estate of grace* (London, 1590).
———, *A discourse of conscience wherein is set downe the nature, properties, and differences thereof* (London, 1596).
Felix Platter, *A golden practice of physick* (London, 1662).
Edward Reynolds, *A treatise of the passions and faculties of the soule of man* (London, 1640).
Barnabe Riche, *A new description of Irelande* (London, 1610).
Marcellus Rivers and Oxenbridge Foyle, *England's slavery, or Barbados merchandize; represented in a petition to the high court of Parliament* (London, 1659).
Ercole Sassonia, *Opera practica* (Padua, 1607).
John Temple, *The Irish Rebellion* (London, 1646).
A Collection of the State Papers of John Thurloe, ed. Thomas Birch, 7 vols. (London, 1742).
Franciscus Toletus [Francisco de Toledo], *Commentaria vna cum quaestionibus in tres libros Aristotelis* De anima (Cologne, 1576).
Thomas Tryon, *Friendly Advice to the Gentlemen Planters of the East and West Indies* (London, 1684).
Thomas Wright, *The passions of the minde* (London, 1601).

Secondary

Gregory Ablavsky, "Making Indians 'White': The Judicial Abolition of Native Slavery in Revolutionary Virginia and Its Racial Legacy," *University of Pennsylvania Law Review* 159:5 (2011), 1457–1532.

Janet Adelman, "Hugh Maclean Memorial Lecture: Revaluing the Body in *The Faerie Queene* I," *Spenser Review* 36 (2005), 15–25.

———, *Blood Relations: Christian and Jew in* The Merchant of Venice (Chicago: University of Chicago Press, 2008).

Suzanne Conklin Akbari, *Idols in the East: European Representations of Islam and the Orient* (Ithaca, NY: Cornell University Press, 2009).

Patricia Akhimie, *Shakespeare and the Cultivation of Difference: Race and Conduct in the Early Modern World* (New York: Routledge, 2018).

Carolyn Arena, "Indian Slaves from Guiana in Seventeenth-Century Barbados," *Ethnohistory* 64 (2017), 65–90.

Douglas V. Armstrong and Matthew C. Reilly, "The Archeology of Settler Farms and Early Plantation Life in Seventeenth-Century Barbados," *Slavery and Abolition* 35 (2014), 399–417.

Guillaume Aubert, "'The Blood of France': Race and Purity of Blood in the French Atlantic World," *William and Mary Quarterly* 61 (2004), 439–78.

John Ayre, ed., *The Works of John Jewel*, 4 vols. (Cambridge: University Press for the Parker Society, 1845).

Alain Badiou, *Saint Paul: The Foundation of Universalism*, trans. Ray Brassier (Stanford, CA: Stanford University Press, 2003).

David J. Baker, "'Men to Monsters': Civility, Barbarism, and 'Race' in Early Modern Ireland," *Writing Race Across the Atlantic World Medieval to Modern*, ed. Phillip Beidler and Gary Taylor (Basingstoke, Hampshire: Palgrave Macmillan, 2005), 153–70.

Étienne Balibar, "Is There Neo-Racism?" in *Race, Nation, Class: Ambiguous Identities*, ed. Étienne Balibar and Immanuel Wallerstein, trans. Chris Turner (New York: Verso, 1991), 17–28.

Anthony Gerard Barthelemy, *Black Face, Maligned Race: The Representation of Blacks in English Drama from Shakespeare to Southerne* (Baton Rouge: Louisiana State University Press, 1987).

Richard Beacon, Solon His Follie (1594), ed. Clare Carroll and Vincent Carey (Binghamton, NY: MRTS, 1996).

Hilary McD. Beckles, "A 'Riotous and Unruly Lot': Irish Indentured Servants and Freeman in the English West Indies, 1644–1713," *William and Mary Quarterly* 47 (1990), 503–22.

Aphra Behn, *Oroonoko, The Rover and Other Works*, ed. Janet Todd (London: Penguin, 1992; rpt. 2003).

Peter Biller, "Views of Jews from Paris Around 1300: Christian or 'Scientific'?" in *Christianity and Judaism: Studies in Church History*, vol. 29, ed. Diana Wood (Cambridge: Blackwell, 1992).

———, "A 'Scientific' View of Jews from Paris Around 1300," *Micrologus* 9 (2001), 137–68.

Kristen Block and Jenny Shaw, "Subjects Without an Empire: The Irish in the Early Modern Caribbean," *Past and Present* 210 (2011), 33–60.

Lara Bovilsky, *Barbarous Play: Race on the English Renaissance Stage* (Minneapolis: University of Minnesota Press, 2008).

Daniel Boyarin, *A Radical Jew: Paul and the Politics of Identity* (Berkeley: University of California Press, 1994).

Jonathan Boyarin, *The Unconverted Self: Jews, Indians, and the Identity of Christian Europe* (Chicago: University of Chicago Press, 2009).

Holly Brewer, *By Birth or Consent: Children, Law, and the Anglo-American Revolution in Authority* (Chapel Hill: University of North Carolina Press, 2005).

———, "Subjects by Allegiance to the King?: Debating Status and Power for Subjects—and Slaves—Through the Religious Debates of the Early British Atlantic," in *State and Citizen: British America and the Early United States*, ed. Peter Thompson and Peter S. Onuf (Charlottesville: University of Virginia Press, 2013), 25–51.

Dennis Austin Britton, *Becoming Christian: Race, Reformation, and Early Modern English Romance* (New York: Fordham University Press, 2014).

———, "Race After the Reformation," paper presented at "Race and Periodization: A Race B4 Race Symposium," Arizona Center for Medieval and Renaissance Studies and the Folger Shakespeare Library, September 6, 2019.

Dennis Austin Britton and Kimberly Anne Coles, "Beyond the Pale," *Spenser Review* 50:1:5 (Winter 2020), http://eee.english.cam.ac.uk/spenseronline/review/item/50.1.5.

———, eds., "Spenser and Race," *Spenser Studies* 35 (2021).

Jennifer DeVere Brody, *Impossible Purities: Blackness, Femininity, and Victorian Culture* (Durham, NC: Duke University Press, 1998).

Christopher Brooke, *A Poem on the Late Massacre in Virginia* (London, 1622), *Virginia Magazine of History and Biography* 72:3 (1964), 259–92.

William Hand Browne et al., eds., *Archives of Maryland* (Annapolis: Maryland Historical Society, 1883–1972).

Geoffrey Bullough, ed., *Narrative and Dramatic Sources of Shakespeare*, 8 vols. (London: Routledge and Kegan Paul, 1957–75).

Colin Burrow, "Spenser and Classical Traditions," in *The Cambridge Companion to Spenser*, ed. Andrew Hadfield, 217–36.

Jonathan Burton, "Race," in *A Cultural History of Western Empires in the Renaissance (1450–1650)*, ed. Ania Loomba (London: Bloomsbury, 2018), 3:203–23.

Robert Burton, *The Anatomy of Melancholy*, ed. J. B. Bamborough and Martin Dodsworth, 6 vols. (Oxford: Clarendon Press, 1989–2000).

Dympna Callaghan, "Re-reading Elizabeth Cary's *The Tragedie of Mariam, Faire Queene of Jewry*," in *Women, "Race," and Writing in the Early Modern Period*, ed. Margo Hendricks and Patricia Parker, 163–77.

John Calvin, *The Institutes of the Christian Religion*, ed. John T. McNeill and trans. Ford Lewis Battles, 2 vols. (Philadelphia: Westminster Press, 1960).

Joseph Campana, *The Pain of Reformation: Spenser, Vulnerability, and the Ethics of Masculinity* (New York: Fordham University Press, 2012).

Nicholas Canny, ed., "Rowland White's 'Discors touching Ireland' (c. 1569)," *Irish Historical Studies* 20 (1977), 439–63.

———, ed. "Rowland White's 'The Dysorders of the Irisshery' (1571)," *Studia Hibernica* 19 (1979), 147–60.

John Carey, *John Donne: Life, Mind, Art* (London: Faber and Faber, 1990).

———, *John Donne: A Critical Edition of the Major Works* (Oxford: Oxford University Press, 1990).

Elizabeth Cary, *The Tragedy of Mariam: The Fair Queen of Jewry*, ed. Barry Weller and Margaret W. Ferguson (Berkeley: University of California Press, 1994).

———, *Elizabeth Cary, Lady Falkland: Life and Letters*, ed. Heather Wolfe (Cambridge: RTM Publications, 2001).

———, *The Tragedy of Mariam*, ed. Ramona Wray, Arden Early Modern Drama Series (London: Bloomsbury, 2012).

Urvashi Chakravarty, "More than Kin, Less than Kind: Similitude, Strangeness, and Early Modern English Homonationalisms," *Shakespeare Quarterly* 67 (2016), 14–29.

———, "Race, Natality, and the Biopolitics of Early Modern Political Theology," *Journal for Early Modern Cultural Studies* 18 (2018), 140–66.

———, *Fictions of Consent: Slavery, Servitude and Free Service in Early Modern England* (Philadelphia: University of Pennsylvania Press, 2022).

Joyce E. Chaplin, *Subject Matter: Technology, the Body, and Science on the Anglo-American Frontier, 1500-1676* (Cambridge, MA: Harvard University Press, 2001).

Donald Cheney, "Spenser's Hermaphrodite and the 1590 *Faerie Queene*," *PMLA* 87 (1972), 192–200.

A. R. Cirillo, "The Fair Hermaphrodite: Love-Union in the Poetry of Donne and Spenser," *Studies in English Literature, 1500-1900* 9 (1969), 81–95.

Jeffrey Jerome Cohen, "On Saracen Enjoyment: Some Fantasies of Race in Late Medieval France and England," *Journal of Medieval and Early Modern Studies* 31 (2001), 113–46.

———, "Race," in *A Handbook of Middle English Studies*, ed. Marion Turner (Chichester: Wiley-Blackwell, 2013), 109–22.

Peter Wilson Coldham, *British Emigrants in Bondage, 1614-1788* (Baltimore: Genealogical Publishing, 2005), CD Rom.

Kimberly Anne Coles, "'Perfect Hole': Elizabeth I, Spenser, and Chaste Productions," *ELR* 32 (2002), 31–61.

———, *Religion, Reform, and Women's Writing in Early Modern England* (Cambridge: Cambridge University Press, 2008).

———, "West of England: The Irish Specter in *Tamburlaine*," in *The Blackwell Companion to Tudor Literature*, ed. Kent Cartwright (Oxford: Wiley-Blackwell, 2010), 459–74.

———, "Moral Constitution: Elizabeth Cary's *Tragedy of Mariam* and the Color of Blood," in *Rethinking Feminism in Early Modern Studies: Gender, Race, and Sexuality*, ed. Loomba and Sanchez (Abingdon, Oxon, UK: Routledge, 2016), 149–64.

Kimberly Anne Coles, Ralph Bauer, Zita Nunes, and Carla L. Peterson, eds., *The Cultural Politics of Blood, 1500-1900* (Basingstoke, Hampshire: Palgrave Macmillan, 2015).

Kimberly Anne Coles, Kim F. Hall, and Ayanna Thompson, "BlacKKKShakespearean: A Call to Action for Medieval and Early Modern Studies," *Profession* (November 2019).

Kimberly Anne Coles and Eve Keller, eds., *The Routledge Companion to Women, Sex, and Gender in the Early British Colonial World* (New York: Routledge, 2019).

Hardin Craig, ed., *A Treatise of Melancholie by Timothy Bright* (New York: Columbia University Press, 1940).

Oliver Cromwell's Letters and Speeches, ed. Thomas Carlyle, 5 vols. (New York: John Wiley, 1845).

Brian Cummings, *The Literary Culture of the Reformation: Grammar and Grace* (Oxford: Oxford University Press, 2002).

Ambereen Dadabhoy, "The Moor of America: Approaching the Crisis of Race and Religion in the Renaissance and in the Twenty-First Century," in *Teaching Medieval and Early Modern Cross-Cultural Encounters*, ed. Lynn Shutters and Karina Attar (Hampshire: Palgrave, 2014), 123–40.

Drew Daniel, *The Melancholy Assemblage: Affect and Epistemology in the English Renaissance* (New York: Fordham University Press, 2013).
Peter Davidson and Thomas M. McCoog, "Father Robert's Convert: The Private Catholicism of Anne of Denmark," *Times Literary Supplement* 24 (November 2000), 16–17.
Jane Hwang Degenhardt, *Islamic Conversion and Christian Resistance on the Early Modern Stage* (Edinburgh: Edinburgh University Press, 2010).
Dennis Des Chene, *Physiologia: Natural Philosophy in Late Aristotelian and Cartesian Thought* (Ithaca, NY: Cornell University Press, 1996).
——, *Life's Form: Late Aristotelian Conceptions of the Soul* (Ithaca, NY: Cornell University Press, 2000).
——, *Spirits and Clocks: Machine and Organism in Descartes* (Ithaca, NY: Cornell University Press, 2001).
The Sermons of John Donne, ed. George R. Potter and Evelyn M. Simpson, 10 vols. (Berkeley: University of California Press, 1953–62).
Miriam Eliav-Feldon, Benjamin Isaac, and Joseph Ziegler, eds., *The Origins of Racism in the West* (Cambridge: Cambridge University Press, 2009).
Peter Erickson and Kim Hall, "'A New Scholarly Song': Rereading Early Modern Race," *Shakespeare Quarterly* 67:1 (2016), 1–3.
G. Blakemore Evans, "Donne's 'Subtile Knot,'" *Notes and Queries*, n.s., 34 (1987), 228–30.
Kasey Evans, "Temperate Revenge: Religion, Profit, and Retaliation in 1622 Jamestown," *Texas Studies in Literature and Language* 54 (2012), 155–88.
——, *Colonial Virtue: The Mobility of Temperance in Renaissance England* (Toronto: University of Toronto Press, 2012).
Jean E. Feerick, *Strangers in Blood: Relocating Race in the Renaissance* (Toronto: University of Toronto Press, 2010).
Margaret Ferguson, *Dido's Daughters: Literacy, Gender, and Empire in Early Modern England and France* (Chicago: University of Chicago Press, 2003).
Lori Anne Ferrell, "Transfiguring Theology: William Perkins and Calvinist Aesthetics," in *John Foxe and His World*, ed. Christopher Highley and John N. King (Aldershot, Hampshire: Ashgate, 2002), 160–79.
——, "Method as Knowledge: Scribal Theology, Protestantism, and the Reinvention of Shorthand in Sixteenth-Century England," in *Making Knowledge in Early Modern Europe: Practices, Objects and Texts, 1400–1800*, ed. Pamela H. Smith and Benjamin Schmidt (Chicago: University of Chicago Press, 2007), 163–76.
Karen E. Fields and Barbara J. Fields, *Racecraft: The Soul of Inequality in American Life* (New York: Verso, 2012).
Matthias Fischer, "A New Race of Christians: Slavery and the Cultural Politics of Conversion in the Atlantic World" (PhD diss., University of Maryland, 2020).
Mary Floyd-Wilson, *English Ethnicity and Race in Early Modern Drama* (Cambridge: Cambridge University Press, 2003).
Mary Floyd-Wilson, Gail Kern Paster, and Katherine Rowe, eds., *Reading the Early Modern Passions: Essays in the Cultural History of Emotion* (Philadelphia: University of Pennsylvania Press, 2004).
Mary Floyd-Wilson and Garrett A. Sullivan, eds., *Environment and Embodiment in Early Modern England* (Basingstoke, Hampshire: Palgrave Macmillan, 2007).

Valerie Forman, "Constructing White Privilege: Transatlantic slavery, reproduction and the segregation of the marriage plot in the late seventeenth century," in *The Routledge Companion to Women, Sex, and Gender in the Early British Colonial World*, ed. Coles and Keller, 304–21.

Michel Foucault, "Right of Death and Power over Life," in *The History of Sexuality, Volume I, An Introduction*, trans. Robert Hurley (New York: Vintage, 1980).

The Works of William Fowler: Secretary to Queen Anne, Wife of James VI, ed. Henry Meikle, James Craigie, and John Purves, 3 vols. (Edinburgh: Scottish Text Society, 1914–40).

Jerome Friedman, "Jewish Conversion, the Spanish Pure Blood Laws, and Reformation: A Revisionist View of Racial and Religious Anti-Semitism," *Sixteenth Century Journal* 18 (1987), 3–29.

Paul Friedman, *The Monstrous Races in Medieval Art and Thought* (Cambridge, MA: Harvard University Press, 1981).

Barbara Fuchs, "Spanish Lessons: Spenser and the Irish Moriscos," *Studies in English Literature, 1500–1900* 42:1 (2002), 43–62.

Ittzés Gábor, "'The Breath Returns to God Who Gave It': The Doctrine of the Soul's Immortality in Sixteenth-Century German Lutheran Theology" (PhD diss., Harvard Divinity School, 2009).

Rebecca Anne Goetz, *The Baptism of Early Virginia* (Baltimore: Johns Hopkins University Press, 2012).

Jonathan Goldberg, *The Seeds of Things: Theorizing Sexuality and Materiality in Renaissance Representations* (New York: Fordham University Press, 2009).

Angus Gowland, *The Worlds of Renaissance Melancholy: Robert Burton in Context* (Cambridge: Cambridge University Press, 2006).

———, "The Problem of Early Modern Melancholy," *Past and Present* 191 (2006), 77–120.

———, "Melancholy, Passion and Identity in the Renaissance," in *Passions and Subjectivity in Early Modern Culture*, ed. Brian Cummings and Freya Sierhuis (Farnham, Surrey: Ashgate, 2013), chap. 4.

———, "Religious Melancholy and the Afflicted Conscience," paper presented at the Warburg Institute, May 30, 2014.

Larry Gragg, *Englishmen Transplanted: The English Colonization of Barbados, 1627–1660* (Oxford: Oxford University Press, 2003).

Linda Gregerson, "Sexual Politics," in *The Cambridge Companion to Spenser*, ed. Hadfield, 180–99.

Eamon Grennan, "Language and Politics: A Note on Some Metaphors in Spenser's *A View of the Present State of Ireland*," *Spenser Studies* 3 (1982), 103–9.

Miles P. Grier, "Inkface: The Slave Stigma in England's Early Imperial Imagination," in *Scripturalizing the Human: The Written as Political*, ed. Vincent L. Wimbush (New York: Routledge, 2015), 194–220.

Eric Griffin, *English Renaissance Drama and the Specter of Spain: Ethnopoetics and Empire* (Philadelphia: University of Pennsylvania Press, 2009).

———, "Nationalism, the Black Legend, and the Revised *Spanish Tragedy*," *ELR* 39 (2009), 336–70.

Valentin Groebner, "*Complexio*/Complexion: Categorizing Individual Natures, 1250–1600," in *The Moral Authority of Nature*, ed. Lorraine Daston and Fernando Vidal (Chicago: University of Chicago Press, 2003), 357–83.

Michael Guasco, *Slaves and Englishmen: Human Bondage in the Early Modern Atlantic World* (Philadelphia: University of Pennsylvania Press, 2014).
Alexander Gunkel and Jerome S. Handler, eds. and trans., "A German Indentured Servant in Barbados in 1652: The Account of Heinrich Von Uchteritz," *Journal of the Barbados Museum and Historical Society* 33 (1970), 91–100.
Andrew Hadfield, ed., *The Cambridge Companion to Spenser* (Cambridge: Cambridge University Press, 2001).
Kim F. Hall, *Things of Darkness: Economies of Race and Gender in Early Modern England* (Ithaca, NY: Cornell University Press, 1995).
———, "'These bastard signs of fair': Literary whiteness in Shakespeare's sonnets," in *Post-Colonial Shakespeares*, ed. Ania Loomba and Martin Orkin (New York: Routledge, 1998), 64–83.
David M. Halperin, "Is There a History of Sexuality?" *History and Theory* 28 (1989), 257–74.
Jerome Handler and Matthew C. Reilly, "Father Antoine Beit's Account Revisited: Irish Catholics in Mid-Seventeenth Century Barbados," in *Caribbean Irish Connections*, ed. Alison Donnell, Maria McGarrity, and Evelyn O'Callaghan (Kingston: University of the West Indies Press, 2015), 33–46.
James Hankins, "Monstrous Melancholy: Ficino and the Physiological Causes of Atheism," in *Laus Platonici philosophi: Marsilio Ficino and His Influence*, ed. Stephen Clucas, Peter J. Forshaw, and Valery Rees (Leiden: Brill, 2011), 25–43.
———, "Cultural Revolution in the Renaissance?" *Quillette* (July 29, 2020), https://quillette.com/2020/07/29/cultural-revolution-in-the-renaissance (accessed August 19, 2020).
Cheryl I. Harris, "Whiteness as Property," *Harvard Law Review* 106:8 (1993), 1707–91.
Dag Nikolaus Hasse, *Avicenna's* De Anima *in the Latin West: The Formation of a Peripatetic Philosophy of the Soul, 1160–1300* (London: Warburg Institute, 2000).
Margo Hendricks and Patricia Parker, eds., *Women, "Race," and Writing in the Early Modern Period* (New York: Routledge, 1994).
Geraldine Heng, *Empire of Magic: Medieval Romance and the Politics of Cultural Fantasy* (New York: Columbia University Press, 2003).
———, *The Invention of Race in the European Middle Ages* (Cambridge: Cambridge University Press, 2018).
———, *England and the Jews* (Cambridge: Cambridge University Press, 2019).
William Walter Hening, ed., *The Statutes at Large, being a Collection of all the laws of Virginia*, 13 vols. (New York: R & W & G Barstow, 1819–23).
M. Thomas Hester, ed., *Letters to Severall Persons of Honour Written by John Donne* (New York: Georg Olms Verlag, 1977).
Ruth Hill, "The Blood of Others: Breeding Plants, Animals, and White People in the Spanish Atlantic," in *The Cultural Politics of Blood, 1500–1900*, ed. Coles et al., 45–64.
Sharon Patricia Holland, *The Erotic Life of Racism* (Durham, NC: Duke University Press, 2012).
Atiya Husain, "Retrieving the Religion in Racialization: A Critical Review," *Sociology Compass* 11:9 (September 2017), https://doi.org./10.1111/soc4.12507.
Sujata Iyengar, *Shades of Difference: Mythologies of Skin Color in Early Modern England* (Philadelphia: University of Pennsylvania Press, 2005).
Willis Johnson, "The Myth of Jewish Male Menses," *Journal of Medieval History* 24:3 (1998), 273–95.
Ben Jonson, ed. C. H. Hereford Percy and Evelyn Simpson, 11 vols. (Oxford: Clarendon Press, 1925–52).

———, *The Complete Masques*, ed. Stephen Orgel (New Haven, CT: Yale University Press, 1969).

M. Lindsay Kaplan, "Jessica's Mother: Medieval Constructions of Jewish Race and Gender in *The Merchant of Venice*," *Shakespeare Quarterly* 58 (2007), 1–30.

———, "'His blood be on us and on our children': Medieval Theology and the Demise of Jewish Somatic Inferiority in Early Modern England," in *The Cultural Politics of Blood, 1500–1900*, ed. Coles et al., 107–26.

———, "The Jewish Body in Black and White in Medieval and Early Modern England," *Philological Quarterly* 92 (2013), 41–65.

———, *Figuring Racism in Medieval Christianity* (Oxford: Oxford University Press, 2018).

Terence Keel, *Divine Variations: How Christian Thought Became Racial Science* (Stanford, CA: Stanford University Press, 2018).

Ibram X. Kendi, *Stamped from the Beginning: The Definitive History of Racist Ideas in America* (New York: Bold Type Books, 2016).

Eckhard Kessler, "The Intellective Soul," in *The Cambridge History of Renaissance Philosophy*, ed. Charles B. Schmitt, Quentin Skinner, and Eckhard Kessler (Cambridge: Cambridge University Press, 1988), 485–534.

Dorothy Kim, "Reframing Race and Jewish/Christian Relations in the Middle Ages," *Transversal* 13 (2015), 52–64.

———, "Introduction to Literature Compass Special Cluster: Critical Race and the Middle Ages," *Literature Compass* 16 (2019), 1–16, https://doi.org/10.1111/lic3.12549.

Gregory Kneidel, *Rethinking the Turn to Religion in Early Modern English Literature: The Poetics of All Believers* (Basingstoke, Hampshire: Palgrave Macmillan, 2008).

Steven F. Kruger, *The Spectral Jew: Conversion and Embodiment in Medieval Europe* (Minneapolis: University of Minnesota Press, 2006).

Sachiko Kusukawa, *The Transformation of Natural Philosophy: The Case of Philip Melanchthon* (Oxford: Oxford University Press, 1995).

Peter Lake, *Moderate Puritans and the Elizabethan Church* (Cambridge: Cambridge University Press, 1982).

Lisa Lampert [-Weissig], *Gender and Jewish Difference from Paul to Shakespeare* (Philadelphia: University of Pennsylvania Press, 2004).

———, *Medieval Literature and Post-Colonial Studies* (Edinburgh: Edinburgh University Press, 2010).

C. S. Lewis, *Spenser's Images of Life*, ed. Alastair Fowler (Cambridge: Cambridge University Press, 1967).

Daniel T. Lochman, "*Energeia* in Melanchthon's *Liber de Anima* and Philip Sidney's *Apology*," paper presented at the Sixteenth Century Society Conference, New Orleans, October 2014.

Sierra Lomuto, "The Mongol Princess of Tars: Global Relations and Racial Formation in *The King of Tars* (c. 1330)," *Exemplaria* 31 (2019), 171–92.

Ania Loomba, "The Color of Patriarchy: Critical Difference, Cultural Difference, and Renaissance Drama," in *Women, "Race," and Writing in the Early Modern Period*, ed. Hendricks and Parker, 17–34.

———, "Periodization, Race, and Global Contact," *Journal of Medieval and Early Modern Studies* 37 (2007), 595–620.

———, "Race and the Possibilities of Comparative Critique," *New Literary History* 40 (2009), 501–22.

———, "Identities and Bodies in Early Modern Studies," in *The Oxford Handbook of Shakespeare and Embodiment: Gender, Sexuality and Race*, ed. Valerie Traub (Oxford: Oxford University Press, 2016), 228–45.

Ania Loomba and Jonathan Burton, eds., *Race in Early Modern England: A Documentary Companion* (Hampshire: Palgrave Macmillan, 2007).

Ania Loomba and Melissa Sanchez, eds., *Rethinking Feminism in Early Modern Studies: Gender, Race, and Sexuality* (Abingdon, Oxon, UK: Routledge, 2016).

Dana Luciano, "Unrealized: The Queer Time of *The Hermaphrodite*," in *Philosophies of Sex: Critical Essays on* The Hermaphrodite, ed. Renée Bergland and Gary Williams (Columbus: Ohio State University Press, 2012), 215–41.

Julia Reinhard Lupton, *Citizen-Saints: Shakespeare and Political Theology* (Chicago: University of Chicago Press, 2005).

Martin Luther: Selections from His Writings, trans. John Dillenberger (New York: Anchor, 1962).

Joyce Green MacDonald, ed., *Race, Ethnicity, and Power in the Renaissance* (Madison, NJ: Fairleigh Dickinson Press, 1997).

———, "Race, Women, and the Sentimental in Thomas Southerne's *Oroonoko*," *Criticism* 40 (1998), 555–70.

Willy Maley, ed., "The Supplication of the Blood of the English Most Lamentably Murdered in Ireland . . . etc. (1598)," *Analecta Hibernica* 36 (1995), 1–77.

George Mariscal, "The Role of Spain in Contemporary Race Theory," *Arizona Journal of Hispanic Cultural Studies* 2 (1998), 7–23.

María Elena Martínez, *Genealogical Fictions: Limpieza de Sangre, Religion, and Gender in Colonial Mexico* (Stanford, CA: Stanford University Press, 2008).

Carla Mazzio and David Hillman, eds., *The Body in Parts: Fantasies of Corporality in Early Modern Europe* (New York: Routledge, 1997).

Carla Mazzio and Douglas Trevor, eds., *Historicism, Psychoanalysis, and Early Modern Culture* (New York: Routledge, 2000).

Sean McDowell, "The View from the Interior: The New Body Scholarship in Renaissance/Early Modern Studies," *Literature Compass* 3:4 (2006), 778–91.

Michael McGiffert, ed., "Constructing Race: Differentiating Peoples in the Early Modern World," *William and Mary Quarterly*, special edition, 54:1 (1997).

Clare McManus, *Women on the Renaissance Stage: Anna of Denmark and Female Masquing in the Stuart Court (1590-1619)* (Manchester: Manchester University Press, 2002).

Leerom Medovoi, "Dogma-Line Racism: Islamophobia and the Second Axis of Race," *Social Text* 30:2 (2012), 43–74.

Philip Melanchthon, *Liber de anima* in *Opera quae supersunt omnia* [*Corpus Reformatorum*], ed. Carol Gottlieb Bretschneider and H. E. Bindeil, 28 vols. (Braunschweig: C. A. Schwetschke and Son, 1834–60), 13:1–178.

Emily Michael, "Renaissance Theories of Body, Soul, and Mind," in *Psyche and Soma: Physicians and Metaphysicians on the Mind-Body Problem from Antiquity to Enlightenment*, ed. John P. Wright and Paul Potter (Oxford: Oxford University Press, 2000), 147–72.

Walter D. Mignolo, "What Does the Black Legend Have to Do with Race?" in *Rereading the Black Legend: The Discourses of Religious and Racial Difference in the Renaissance Empires*, ed. Margaret R. Greer, Walter D. Mignolo, and Maureen Quilligan (Chicago: University of Chicago Press, 2007), 312–24.

Charles de Miramon, "Noble Dogs, noble blood: the invention of the concept of race in the late Middle Ages," in *The Origins of Racism in the West*, ed. Eliav-Feldon, Isaac, and Ziegler, 200–216.
Gwenda Morgan, *Banishment in the Early Atlantic World: Convicts, Rebels and Slaves* (London: Bloomsbury, 2013).
Jennifer L. Morgan, *Laboring Women: Reproduction and Gender in New World Slavery* (Philadelphia: University of Pennsylvania Press, 2004).
Toni Morrison, *Playing in the Dark: Whiteness and the Literary Imagination* (New York: Vintage, 1993).
Molly Murray, "Performing Devotion in *The Masque of Blacknesse*," *Studies in English Literature* 47 (2007), 427–49.
———, *The Poetics of Conversion in Early Modern English Literature* (Cambridge: Cambridge University Press, 2009).
Noémie Ndiaye, "The African Ambassador's Travels: Playing Black in Late Seventeenth-Century France and Spain," in *Transnational Connections in Early Modern Theatre*, ed. M. A. Katritzky and Pavel Drábek (Manchester: Manchester University Press, 2019), 73–85.
Karen Newman, *Fashioning Femininity and English Renaissance Drama* (Chicago: University of Chicago Press, 1991).
Simon P. Newman, *A New World of Labor: The Development of Plantation Slavery in the British Atlantic* (Philadelphia: University of Pennsylvania Press, 2013).
Michelle O'Callaghan, "Christopher Brooke (c. 1570–1628)," *Oxford Dictionary of National Biography*.
P. M. Oliver, ed., *John Donne: Selected Letters* (New York: Carcanet Press, 2002).
William Oram, "Elizabethan Fact and Spenserian Fiction," *Spenser Studies* 4 (1984), 33–47.
Gail Kern Paster, *The Body Embarrassed: Drama and the Disciplines of Shame in Early Modern England* (Ithaca, NY: Cornell University Press, 1993).
———, *Humoring the Body: Emotions and the Shakespearean Stage* (Chicago: University of Chicago Press, 2004).
Carla Gardina Pestana, *The English Atlantic World in the Age of Revolution, 1640–61* (Cambridge, MA: Harvard University Press, 2004).
Samuel Purchas, *Hakluytus Posthumus, or, Purchas his Pilgrimes*, 20 vols. (Glasgow: Glasgow University Press, 1905–7; rpt., Cambridge: Cambridge University Press, 2014).
David Beers Quinn, "'A Discourse of Ireland (*Circa* 1599)': A Sidelight on English Colonial Policy," *Proceedings of the Royal Irish Academy* 47 (1942), 151–66.
———, "Edward Walshes's 'Conjectures' Concerning the State of Ireland (1552)," *Irish Historical Studies* 5 (1947), 303–22.
———, *The Elizabethans and the Irish* (Ithaca, NY: Cornell University Press, 1966).
Beth Quitslund, "Despair and the Composition of the Self," *Spenser Studies* 17 (2003), 91–106.
Shokoofeh Rajabzadeh, "The Depoliticized Saracen and Muslim Erasure," *Literature Compass* 16 (2019), https://doi.org/10.1111/lic3.12548 (accessed August 15, 2020).
Margaret Reeves, "From Manuscript to Printed Text: Telling and Retelling the *History of Edward II*," in *The Literary Career and Legacy of Elizabeth Cary, 1613–1680*, ed. Wolfe, 125–44.
Robert L. Reid, "Spenserian Psychology and the Structure of Allegory in Books 1 and 2 of *The Faerie Queene*," *Modern Philology* 79 (1982), 359–75.
Irven M. Resnick, *Marks of Distinction: Christian Perceptions of Jews in the High Middle Ages* (Washington, DC: Catholic University of America Press, 2012).

Barnabe Riche, "Rych's *Anothomy of Ireland*, with an Account of the Author," ed. Edward M. Hinton, *Proceedings of the Modern Language Association* 55 (1940), 73–101.

Thomas P. Roche, *The Kindly Flame* (Princeton, NJ: Princeton University Press, 1964).

Benedict Robinson, *Islam and Early Modern English Literature: The Politics of Romance from Spenser to Milton* (Basingstoke, Hampshire: Palgrave Macmillan, 2007).

——, "Returning to Egypt: 'The Jew,' 'the Turk,' and the English Republic," in *Milton and the Jews*, ed. Douglas A. Brooks (Cambridge: Cambridge University Press, 2008), 178–99.

——, "'Swarth' Phantastes: Race and Representation in *The Faerie Queene*," "Spenser and Race," *Spenser Studies* 35 (forthcoming), 133–52.

Robin Robbins, ed., *The Complete Poems of John Donne* (Harlow: Pearson Education Limited, 2008).

Edward B. Rugemer, "The Development of Mastery and Race in the Comprehensive Slave Codes of the Greater Caribbean During the Seventeenth Century," *William and Mary Quarterly* 70 (2013), 429–58.

W. N. Sainsbury, ed., *Calendar of State Papers, Colonial Series, 1574–1715*, 10 vols. (London: Longman, 1860–1928).

Melissa E. Sanchez, "The Politics of Masochism in Mary Wroth's 'Urania,'" *ELH* 74 (2007), 449–78.

——, "'What Hath Night to Do with Sleep?' Biopolitics in Milton's *Mask*," *Early Modern Culture: An Electronic Seminar* 10 (2014).

——, "Sex and Eroticism in the Renaissance," in *Edmund Spenser in Context*, ed. Andrew Escobado (Cambridge: Cambridge University Press, 2016), 342–51.

Elaine Scarry, "Donne: But Yet the Body Is His Booke," in *Literature and the Body: Essays on Populations and Persons*, ed. Elaine Scarry (Baltimore: Johns Hopkins University Press, 1988), 70–105.

Jeremy Schmidt, *Melancholy and the Care of the Soul: Religion, Moral Philosophy and Madness in Early Modern England* (Aldershot, Hampshire: Ashgate, 2007).

Michael Schoenfeldt, *Bodies and Selves in Early Modern England: Physiology and Inwardness in Spenser, Shakespeare, Herbert, and Milton* (Cambridge: Cambridge University Press, 1999).

——, "Eloquent Blood and Deliberative Bodies: The Physiology of Metaphysical Poetry," in *Renaissance Transformations: The Making of English Writing, 1500–1650*, ed. Thomas Healy and Margaret Healy (Edinburgh: Edinburgh University Press, 2009), 145–60.

William Shakespeare, *A Midsummer Night's Dream*, ed. Harold F. Brooks (New York: Routledge, 1996).

——, *Othello*, revised edition, with editorial matter by E. A. J. Honigmann and introduction by Ayanna Thompson (London: Bloomsbury, 1997, 2016).

——, *II Henry IV*, ed. A. R. Humphreys, The Arden Shakespeare (London: Bloomsbury, 1967).

——, *The Tempest*, ed. Frank Kermode (New York: Routledge, 1989).

Jenny Shaw, *Everyday Life in the Early English Caribbean: Irish, Africans, and the Construction of Difference* (Athens: University of Georgia Press, 2013).

Alison Shell, "Elizabeth Cary's Historical Conscience: *The Tragedy of Mariam* and Thomas Lodge's Josephus," in *The Literary Career and Legacy of Elizabeth Cary, 1613–1680*, ed. Wolfe, 53–67.

Ian Smith, "The Textile Black Body: Race and 'Shadowed Livery,' in *The Merchant of Venice*," in *The Oxford Handbook of Shakespeare and Embodiment: Gender, Sexuality, and Race*, ed. Valerie Traub (Oxford: Oxford University Press, 2016), 170–85.

Justin E. H. Smith, *Nature, Human Nature, and Human Difference: Race in Early Modern Philosophy* (Princeton, NJ: Princeton University Press, 2015).

Thomas Southerne, *Oroonoko: Adaptations and Offshoots*, ed. Susan B. Iwanisziw, Early Modern Englishwoman series (Aldershot, Hampshire: Ashgate, 2006).

Edmund Spenser, *Spenser's Prose Works*, ed. Rudolf Gottfried, in *The Works of Edmund Spenser: A Variorum Edition*, ed. Edwin Greenlaw, Ray Heffner, Charles Grosvenor Osgood, and Frederick Morgan Padelford, 11 vols. (Baltimore: Johns Hopkins University Press, 1932–58), vol. 10 (1949).

———, *The Faerie Queene*, ed. A. C. Hamilton (New York: Longman Group, 1977; revised, 1980).

———, *Edmund Spenser: The Shorter Poems*, ed. Richard McCabe (London: Penguin, 1999).

Elizabeth Spiller, "From Imagination to Miscegenation: Race and Romance in Shakespeare's 'The Merchant of Venice,'" *Renaissance Drama*, n.s., 29 (1998), 137–64.

———, *Reading and the History of Race in the Renaissance* (Cambridge: Cambridge University Press, 2011).

John Stachniewski, "John Donne: The Despair of the 'Holy Sonnets,'" *ELH* 48 (1981), 677–705.

———, *The Persecutory Imagination: English Puritanism and the Literature of Religious Despair* (Oxford: Oxford University Press, 1991).

Heinrich von Stadan, "Body, Soul, and Nerves: Epicurus, Herophilus, Erasistratus, the Stoics, and Galen," in *Psyche and Soma: Physicians and Metaphysicians on the Mind-Body Problem from Antiquity to Enlightenment*, ed. John P. Wright and Paul Potter (Oxford: Oxford University Press, 2000), 79–116.

Donald A. Stauffer, "A Deep and Sad Passion," in *Essays in Dramatic Literature*, ed. Hardin Craig (Princeton, NJ: Princeton University Press, 1935), 289–314.

Hamish Maxwell Stewart, "Convict Transportation from Britain and Ireland, 1615–1870," *History Compass* 8 (2010), 1221–42.

Will Stockton, "Chasing Chastity: The Case of Desdemona," in *Rethinking Feminism in Early Modern Studies*, ed. Loomba and Sanchez, 195–212.

Richard Strier, "John Donne, Awry and Squint: The 'Holy Sonnets,' 1608–1610," *Modern Philology* 86 (1989), 357–84.

Garrett Sullivan, *Sleep, Romance and Human Embodiment: Vitality from Spenser to Milton* (Cambridge: Cambridge University Press, 2012).

Ramie Targoff, *John Donne: Body and Soul* (Chicago: University of Chicago Press, 2008).

Ayanna Thompson, *Performing Race and Torture on the Early Modern Stage* (Abingdon, Oxon, UK: Routledge, 2008).

———, "Me, *The Faerie Queene*, and Critical Race Theory," "Spenser and Race," *Spenser Studies* 35 (2021), 285–90.

Christopher Tomlins, "Reconsidering Indentured Servitude: European Migration and the Early American Labor Force, 1600–1775," *Labor History* 42 (2001), 5–43.

Douglas Trevor, *The Poetics of Melancholy in Early Modern England* (Cambridge: Cambridge University Press, 2004).

Matthew Vernon, "Unkynde Monstrous Races and 'Curled Darlings of Our Nation,'" in *A Cultural History of Race in the Renaissance and Early Modern Age (1350–1550)*, ed. Kimberly Anne Coles and Dorothy Kim (London: Bloomsbury, forthcoming).

Mara R. Wade, "The Coronation of King Christian IV 1596," in *Europa Triumphans: Court and Civic Festivals in Early Modern Europe*, ed. J. R. Mulryne, Helen Watanabe-O'Kelly, and Margaret Shewring, 2 vols. (Basingstoke: Palgrave Macmillan, 2004), 2:245–67.

———, "Duke Ulrik (1578–1624) as Agent, Patron, Artist: Reframing Danish Court Culture in the International Perspective c. 1600," in *Reframing the Danish Renaissance: Problems and Prospects in a European Perspective*, ed. Michael Andersen, Birgitte B. Johannsen, and Hugo Johannsen (Copenhagen: National Museum, 2011), 243–61.

Roxann Wheeler, *The Complexion of Race: Categories of Difference in Eighteenth-Century British Culture* (Philadelphia: University of Pennsylvania Press, 2000).

"Extracts from Henry Whistler's Journal of the West Indian Expedition," in *The Narrative of General Venebles with an appendix of papers relating to the expedition to the West Indies and the conquest of Jamaica, 1654–1655*, ed. C. H. Firth (London: Longmans, Green, 1900).

Cord J. Whitaker, *Black Metaphors: How Modern Racism Emerged from Medieval Race-Thinking* (Philadelphia: University of Pennsylvania Press, 2019).

Heather Wolfe, ed., *The Literary Career and Legacy of Elizabeth Cary, 1613–1680* (Basingstoke, Hampshire: Palgrave Macmillan, 2007).

A. S. P. Woodhouse, "Nature and Grace in the *Faerie Queene*," *ELH* 16 (1949), 194–228.

Mary Wroth's Poetry: An Electronic Edition, ed. Paul Salzman, wroth.latrobe.edu.au.

Joseph Ziegler, "Physiognomy, science, and proto-racism, 1200–1500," in *The Origins of Racism in the West*, ed. Eliav-Feldon, Isaac, and Ziegler, 181–99.

INDEX

African(s), 45, 133–34, 161n27
  enslavement of, 47, 117, 118, 131, 135
  racialization of, 1, 52, 112, 122, 129, 130, 132–33
    legal implications, 136, 137, 139, 140–41
Akhimie, Patricia, xii, 9, 10–11, 11–12, 70
Algonquin (Indigenous group), 43
Anne of Denmark, Queen of England, 15, 49, 50–52, 57–58, 59
Aquinas, St. Thomas, 7, 8, 27, 53, 54, 153n13, 156n54
Aristotle, 8, 27, 64, 65
Augustine, Saint, 16, 64–65, 108, 153n13
Averroes, 7, 153n14
Avicenna, 55, 64, 97, 153n14

Barbados, 132, 133–35, 138, 175n48
Behn, Aphra, 118, 128, 129, 133
  Oroonoko; or The Royal Slave (novella), 118, 128, 129, 132
Blackness, 2, 15, 37, 55, 61, 65, 68, 117, 121, 138
  appropriation onstage, 51, 58–59 (*see also* Jonson, Ben)
  marker of Catholicism, 51–53, 55, 58, 66
  marker of Irishness, 84–85 (*see also* Spenser, Edmund)
  marker of paganism, 4, 6, 16, 66, 122, 133
blood (humor), xii, 15, 23, 28, 38, 43, 55, 65, 95, 107, 111, 131, 141
  hereditary x–xi, xii, xiii, 3, 9–10, 82, 85
  heathenism, 6, 18
  nobility, 74, 75, 83, 87, 119
  mixing, anxieties about, 72–73, 79, 135, 139
  in Ireland, 83, 84 (*see also* Ireland)
  in *Othello*, 120–21, 122, 123
  moral difference in, 17, 19, 71, 78, 118
  religion written in, 5, 6, 16, 64
  pagan, 45, 46, 47, 55,
  transmission through, 70, 117
  See also bloodline(s); heredity; humoral theory
bloodline(s), 72, 122
  legal implications of, 136
  moral superiority in, 9, 10, 83, 87
  in *Oroonoko*, 18, 128 (*see also* Southerne, Thomas)
  See also heredity
Bright, Timothy, 91, 114
  Treatise of melancholie, 3, 22, 29–31, 41, 55
  spirit separating body and soul, 27–28, 90, 91, 96
Britton, Dennis, 5, 50, 66, 89, 113, 123
Brooke, Christopher, 15, 21, 41–47, 113, 126, 158–59n107
Bryskett, Ludowic
  Discourse of Civill Life, A (treatise), 91, 94, 96–97, 171n69
Burton, Robert, 3, 42, 48, 68
  Anatomy of Melancholy, 16, 26, 50, 54
  atheism, defined, 95
  cognition and somatic operation, 56
  humoral nature of religious difference, 64–65, 113–14

Calvin, John, xii, 9, 26–27, 64, 97
Calvinism, xii, 30, 35, 41, 92
  materiality of the soul, 22, 25–26, 28–29, 31, 90–91, 92
Cary, Elizabeth, 81, 164n8
  Edward II, History of (prose), 78–79, 165n32
  Tragedy of Mariam, The (play), 16, 71, 73–82
Catholic(ism), xi, 4, 13, 36, 37, 42, 115, 126, 131
  as humoral temperament, 21, 27, 33, 67, 87
  as inherited trait, 16, 62

Catholic(ism) (*continued*)
  racialization of, 1, 3, 51, 52, 55, 66, 69, 88–89, 113
    converts, 15, 49, 50, 57
    Irish, 14, 17, 53, 70, 85, 116, 123
    in Barbados, 133–35
    Spanish, 52–53
  representation of, 101, 105, 106, 112, 127
Chakravarty, Urvashi, xi, xii, 9, 123, 141, 174nn31–32
Charron, Pierre, 28, 156n53–54
chastity, 102, 104, 108, 111, 112, 115
choler (humor), 23, 79, 106
colonial(ism), 1, 2, 6, 12, 13, 14, 69, 71, 88, 89
  Americas, 18, 43–45, 117, 119, 134, 140
  Ireland, 17, 70, 85, 87
color-codes, 13, 14, 19
  See also bloodlines; slave codes
complexion, 18, 65, 67
  change in definition of, 4, 117, 151n53
  conflation of external with internal, 3, 65–66, 77, 128, 142
  in *The Masque of Blacknesse*, 55–56
  external, 15, 16, 49, 55–56, 65–66, 121
  humoral, 30, 31, 72, 73, 83–84, 113
  as inherited trait, 10, 11
  as moral indicator, 3, 10
  See also humoral theory
  of the soul, 31, 37, 49, 55–56, 68
  atheists as "depraved," xii, 108, 110, 145n14
conversion, 9, 11, 76, 141
  to/from Catholicism, 14, 15
    Anne of Denmark, 51
    in Donne's poetry, 24, 32, 34, 37
    Ireland, 86
  to/from Christianity, 38, 47, 69, 118, 131, 139
  representation, 4–5, 119, 123, 133
  Masque of Blacknesse, 15, 49, 58
convict labor, 134, 177n59 (*see also* Barbados; Ireland)

Defoe, Daniel
  "The True-Born Englishman," 118, 119
degeneracy, 19, 70, 71, 78–79, 83, 87
  racialization of, 19, 71, 122
Donne, John, 2, 15, 41, 89, 90
  Holy Sonnets, 14, 23–24, 31–41

letters, 14, 21–23, 24–25, 33
material nature of the soul, 22–25, 26, 27–28, 34, 36–39, 91, 153n7
sermons, 38–39, 154n17, 157n87, 158n96, 158–59n107
somatic nature of religious conversion, 14, 24, 25–26, 32, 34–35, 45
theory of cognition, 24–25, 30–31

Elyot, Thomas, 11, 79, 83, 123
  The boke named the governour, 9, 72–73
embodiment, 19, 24, 71, 111, 114, 119
England (nation), 5, 6, 26, 42, 49, 57
  allegorized in Spenser's *Faerie Queene*, 106, 114–16
  lineage, system of, xiv, 78, 131
  slave trade
    codification of, 134, 136–38
    religious justification for, xiii, 46, 132
    treatment of non-Protestants, 13–14, 42, 66, 115
  racialization, 52, 70, 71, 113, 114, 141
    Ireland, 86–87, 116
England, Church of, 5, 105, 107, 123
Ethiopians, 50, 56, 66
  representation of, 16, 66
  Masque of Blacknesse, 15, 49, 50, 55–57, 68 (*see also* Jonson, Ben)

Faerie Queene. *See* Spenser, Edmund
Feerick, Jean, 9, 69, 166n52
Ficino, Marsilio, xii, 3, 11, 48, 64, 67, 108
  Platonic Theology, xii, 11, 65, 67, 145n14, 163nn66–68, 163n71, 164n72
  atheism as disease, xii, 16, 67, 108, 110, 151n60
Florio, John, 52
Forman, Valerie, 130, 133, 137, 175n42

Galen, xii, 7, 31, 56, 107
  early modern interpretations of, xii, 23, 47, 72, 90, 94
  Melanchthon, Philip, 8, 25, 54–55, 65, 149n34
  interaction of body and soul, 24–25, 54
  materialism, 22, 28, 29, 36, 92, 117
  See also humoral theory; materialism
Goodyer, Henry, 14, 21, 24–26, 30, 33–34, 41
Gowland, Angus, 3, 9, 42, 54, 64, 90, 114

Hall, Kim F., 4, 11, 52, 77
Hendricks, Margo, 143n5, 164–65n12
Heng, Geraldine, 1, 4, 12
heredity, 3, 122, 131
hermaphrodite, figure of. *See* Spenser, Edmund
Herod Antipater (character), 16, 71, 73–77, 79, 81, 124
   in *Antiquities of the Jews*, 74, 75–76, 80
   See also Cary, Elizabeth
humoral theory, 10, 41, 58, 63, 82, 112, 140
   complexion (*see* complexion; disposition under humoral theory)
   external, 11, 49, 52, 56, 73
   inheritance of, xiv, 10, 11, 73, 83
   concerns about mixing 72
   moral implications of, 3, 54, 73
      in *The Tragdy of Mariam*, 77, 82
   disposition, inheritance of, 9, 16–17, 119
   superiority, 69–70, 81
   emotional implications, 18
      in *Othello*, 125–26
   melancholy, dangers of, xiii, 50
   blackness as effect of, 9, 56
      in Spenser's *Faerie Queene*, 90, 92
   materiality of the soul, 14, 24, 25, 30, 38, 53
   political implications of, 11, 79
   psychosomatic relations, 6, 9, 23, 31
   religious belief as imbalance of, 3, 15, 26–27, 33, 34, 55
   racialization, 42, 45, 52, 67, 113, 141
      Ireland, 84, 86–87
   reformation of, 123
   temperance, 90, 94, 107, 110
   See also blood; bloodline(s); Galen; melancholy

identity, 11, 33, 61, 63, 82, 106
   cultural, 13,
   gender, 98–99
   racial, 19, 50, 63, 121–25, 127
   religious, 4, 12, 57, 89, 107, 116, 123, 132
      Catholic, 14, 16, 52, 53
      materiality of, 33–34, 40–41 (*see also* Donne, John)
      pagan, 42, 124, 133, 141
   social, 70, 82, 100–101, 120, 125
Indigenous peoples
   appropriation on stage, 16

   legal status of, 118, 151n44, 178n72
   racialization of, 1, 15, 42–47, 126, 136 (*see also* Brooke, Christopher)
   See also Algonquin; Powhatan
Ireland, 17, 115
   colonial occupation of, 70, 86
   transportation to Barbados, 134–35 (*see also* convict labor)
   racialization of Catholics, 83–86, 116, 135 (*see also* Catholicism)
   (hu)moral degeneracy, 85, 86–87, 118

James I, King of England, 51, 52
   in Jonson's *Masque of Blacknesse*, 49, 55, 57–58, 126–27
Jamestown, 15, 41, 43
Jonson, Ben, 16, 58–59, 64, 69, 85, 127
   Masque of Blacknesse (play), 15, 48–52, 65
   daughters of Niger, 65–66, 68, 123, 124, 126 (*see also* Ethiopians, representation of)
   humoral discourse in, 53, 55–58, 66, 67
Josephus, Flavius, 79
   Antiquities of the Jews, 74–76, 80, 81
   See also Lodge, Thomas; Cary, Elizabeth

Kaplan, Lindsay M., xi, 4, 71, 147n11

Lanyer, Aemilia, 69
Lemnie, Levine (Lemnius), 10, 11, 31, 150n51, 151n53
Lodge, Thomas, 164n8
   Antiquities of the Jews (translation), 74, 75
   See also Josephus; Cary, Elizabeth
Luther, Martin, 30, 64
   racialization of non-Lutherans, 62, 113
   spiritual melancholy, 9, 26, 91

Macdonald, Joyce Green, 133, 176n54
Maleger (character). *See* Spenser, Edmund
Mariam (character), 16, 71, 73–78, 79–82
   in *Antiquities of the Jews*, 74, 75, 76
   See also Cary, Elizabeth
Masque of Blacknesse, The (play). *See* Jonson, Ben
materialism
   Galenic, 22, 28, 29, 36, 92, 117 (*see also* Galen)
   Pauline, 99, 101 (*see also* Paul, Saint)

medicine, 92, 126
melancholy (humor), xii, 24, 25, 30, 33, 35,
    35, 69, 105
  Anatomy of Melancholy, 16, 26, 64–65,
    113–14 (*see also* Burton, Robert)
  bile, excess of, 9, 25
  black, 9, 117
    religious difference, x, xiii, xiv, 12, 14, 48,
      54–55, 66, 141
    Catholics, 84
    Jews, 71
    representation onstage, 15, 18, 50
      in Jonson's *Masque of Blacknesse,*
        55, 68
      in Shakespeare's *Othello,* 119, 127
      in Spenser's *Faerie Queene,* 17, 90,
        91–92, 93–94, 95, 106, 115
    wrong belief, 2, 84, 138
  body and soul, 3, 7, 90, 91
    connection between, 22
    distinction between, 29
    early modern definition of, 49–50
    external manifestation of, 13, 56, 67
    racialization of, 42
    physiological aspects, 31
    impact on materiality of soul, 53–54
Melanchthon, Philip, 9, 25, 26, 45, 64
  Liber de anima, 7–8, 29, 54, 65, 97,
    149nn31,34
Montaigne, Michel de, 24, 28

natural philosophy, 3, 5, 7–9, 22, 25, 29, 30,
    45, 117
Neoplatonism, 16, 65, 66, 67, 93
  in Shakespeare's *Othello,* 125
  in Spenser's *Faerie Queene,* 103

Oroonoko: A Tragedy (play). *See* Southerne,
    Thomas
Oroonoko; or The Royal Slave (novella). *See*
    Behn, Aphra
Othello (character), 18, 119
  inherited paganism, 124, 125–26, 127
  social rank, 120–21
    effect of racial logic, 121, 122–23, 124,
      126–27
  See also Shakespeare, William
Ovid
  Metamorphoses (poem), 56

paganism, 113
  as inherited trait, 47, 69, 123, 124
  racialization of, xi, 2, 16, 58, 122
Pamphilia to Amphilanthus (sonnet collection). *See* Wroth, Mary
Parker, Patricia, 143n5, 164–65n12
Paul, Saint, 89, 97, 102,
  conversion of, 38
  doctrine of universalism, xi, 89, 97, 100
  law, 101
  separation of flesh and spirit, 62, 67, 89, 97
    Spenser's hermaphrodite, 99–101
  See also materialism
phlegm (humor), xii, 55, 171n66
  water, association with, 105–6
Plato, 65, 92, 93, 95,
  separation of body and soul, 26, 27, 31, 106
  in Spenser's *Faerie Queene,* 105–6
Platonists (early modern philosophical school), 8, 28, 92 (*see also*
    Neoplatonists)
Pomponazzi, Pietro, 2–3, 7, 8, 22, 146n5,
    149n33,35
Portugal, 113
Powhatan (Indigenous group), 15, 41, 45
  See also Indigenous peoples

race, 2, 5, 9, 58, 61, 128
  chromatic, 88, 130, 137–38,
  construction of, 4, 10, 41–42, 46, 82, 141
  critical race studies, 11
  humoral explanation, 3, 19, 45
    materiality of the soul, 21
  lineage, 16, 70–71, 73–75, 80
  nation, 71, 74, 118–19, 121
    Antiquities of the Jews, 75–76
    Ireland, 83, 85, 86, 87 (*see also* Ireland;
      Spenser, Edmund)
  religion, 12–13, 52, 130, 131, 132
    colonial ideology, 14, 44, 89, 114
    representation, 49, 58–59, 62, 123 (*see
      also* Jonson, Ben; Shakespeare, William; Wroth, Mary)
racialization, 1, 5, 13, 69
  religion, 10, 14, 88, 114
rank. *See* social class

Salome (character), 74, 75, 82,
  in *Antiquities of the Jews,* 76–77

racialization of, 16, 71, 73, 77–78, 79, 80
See also Cary, Elizabeth
Shakespeare, William, 73
  Othello, 18, 118, 119–28
  Tempest, The, 44
slave(ry); enslavement, 6, 12, 44, 46, 61, 81, 129, 135
  African, 120, 122, 123, 128, 130, 131
  codification of, 19, 118, 136, 137, 138–39, 140–41
  Indigenous, 43, 47
  religious justification for, 18, 47, 132–33, 134
  slave codes, 6, 12, 18, 19, 130, 134, 136–38, 140, 141
  transatlantic, 119, 131, 132
Southern, Thomas, 18, 118
  Oroonoko: A Tragedy (play), 129–33
Spain, 52–53, 89, 113, 85
  Catholics from, 1, 3, 49
  racialization of, 52–53
Spenser, Edmund
  Epithalamion (poem), 98
  Faerie Queene, The (poem)
    hermaphrodite, figure of, 98–100, 102, 104, 108, 111
    Maleger (character), 17, 90–95, 110

    baptism, treatment by, 92, 95
    consequence of neglecting humoral regulation, 94
    melancholy, figure of, 90, 91
  An Hymne in Honour of Beautie (poem), 92
  View of the Present State of Ireland, 91, 116
Surinam, 128, 129, 133

temperance, 93, 94, 96, 101–2, 105–6
Tempest, The (play). *See* Shakespeare, William
Tragedy of Mariam (play). *See* Cary, Elizabeth
Turks, 113, 132
  stage representation of, 50, 51, 55, 127

Virginia, colony of, 43, 46, 138
  laws governing slavery, xiii, 47, 118, 131
  inheritance of enslaved status, 136, 137
  (*see also* slave codes)
Virginia Company, 43

Whiteness, 57, 59, 117, 124, 151n65
  Cary's *Mariam*, 16, 71, 78
  Christian salvation and, 4–5, 13, 37–38
Wroth, Mary
  Pamphilia to Amphilanthus (sonnet collection), 16, 58–64, 65, 66–67, 68

ACKNOWLEDGMENTS

These projects come from love: anything requiring so much care, attention, patience, and time can only come from there. I began this one—thinking about it, working on it—with the birth of my son. Every parent wants and works for a world in which their child can thrive in confidence and safety. That is surely not the world a Black boy in the United States inherits—and for the parents of Black sons the work feels urgent and uncertain. But I have always been aware of the fierce *desire* to remake his world, even if it is my corner of it, as a chief driver of my research in general and of this book in particular. It has given new meaning to the words of E. E. Cummings that I would recite to him as a boy: "whatever is done / by only me is your doing." Because this project is for, about, and, in many ways written by him, it makes sense that it is as old as he is—and that I can measure my time working on it by his height.

These projects are also fostered by love. My son's father and I spent many long hours talking about this one: about race, about race in America, about him and race in America. Mark McMorris has been the most constant and inspiring of friends and audiences, and this book would have never been written without him. The other most persistent interlocutor to this project has been Ayanna Thompson. In our conversations about it—walking, running, over the phone, and over the years—she has made this a much better book than I could have written on my own. I also have the best intellectual community in the University of Maryland: Amanda Bailey, Ralph Bauer, Tita Chico, Zita Nunes, Jerry Passannante, Carla Peterson, Kellie Robertson, and Christina Walter all bear particular mention as colleagues who have been profligate with their time, energy, attention, and affection. All have listened to—and most have read—parts or all of this project. Valerie Traub, Patricia Akhimie, and Jerry Singerman came to campus to workshop the project and help me rethink the book. I could not have had their help, or important intervention, were it not for the generosity of my department and my college. An

Arcan Research Award from my department also gave me a semester to work on the book exclusively at a crucial stage.

Such financial support is necessary to any major research project, and this one has required travel over continents in order to visit libraries and acquire languages. A year in Spain was made possible by a Research and Scholarship Award Semester Grant from the University of Maryland and a lectureship at the University of Barcelona; the generosity of the institution and the faculty at the University of Barcelona—to afford office space and library access in exchange for visiting lectures—was both remarkable and necessary, and John Stone bears particular mention in making this possible. Another semester in London was permitted by the University of London and the Warburg Institute through a School of Advanced Study Visiting Fellowship. My time at the Warburg was essential to advancing this project—not just in providing access to the Warburg, the Wellcome, the Dr. William's, and the British Libraries but in the colleagues who so generously advised and helped me shape it: John Carey, Guido Giglioni, Angus Gowland, Peter Mack, and Sue Wiseman bear particular mention among this group. The Folger Shakespeare Library has always been a home away from home, and support from the Folger—both financial and personal—has been crucial to my work. I owe particular thanks to Owen Williams, Mike Witmore, and the Folger librarians: Caroline Duroselle-Melish, Rosalind Larry, Camille Seerattan, Abby Weinberg, and Heather Wolfe.

While all research is collaborative in nature, this has been a genuine collaboration. The mistakes of this book are mine, but its credits must be shared. Besides those already mentioned, other readers of the book include: David Scott Kastan, Eve Keller, Ania Loomba, Noémie Ndiaye, Melissa Sanchez, and Jessica Wolfe. Dennis Britton and Urvashi Chakravarty stand apart as two collaborators who read almost every word, often more than once, and who own a share in this book (whether they want to or not). Sharon Achinstein, Liza Blake, Joe Campana, Susan Dwyer, Tobias Gregory, Musa Gurnis, Jennifer James, Mira Kafantaris, Leighla Khansari, Dorothy Kim, Carol Mejia LaPerle, Carole Levine, Dana Luciano, Elisa Oh, Kathryn Santos, and Nigel Smith are among the many friends who often did no more, but certainly no less, than to believe in this project with me.

Every parent wants and works for a world in which their child can thrive in confidence and safety. That is surely not the world a Black boy in the United States inherits. But I know that I am part of a community invested in the same work that I do. And that the world that my son will inherit is also the one in which we work and build.

*   *   *

Portions of Chapter 1 first appeared in *Renaissance Quarterly* 68 (2015) as "The Matter of Belief in John Donne's *Holy Sonnets*," 899–931. Much of the first section of Chapter 3 was published as "Moral Constitution: Elizabeth Cary's *Tragedy of Mariam* and the Color of Blood," in *Rethinking Feminism in Early Modern Studies: Gender, Race, and Sexuality*, ed. Ania Loomba and Melissa Sanchez (Abingdon, Oxon UK: Routledge, 2016), 149–64. Part of Chapter 4 appears in *Edmund Spenser in Context*, ed. Andrew Escobedo (Cambridge: Cambridge University Press, 2017) under the title "Gender in the 1590 *Faerie Queene*," 352–62. All of these are reproduced with permission, and I am grateful to the editors of these volumes for their invaluable feedback.

Zita Nunes, who has made my life more beautiful in many ways, helped me (as usual) to choose the cover art.

Lightning Source UK Ltd.
Milton Keynes UK
UKHW010058170322
400170UK00002B/13